The War On Poverty

A Short History - Kennedy to Reagan

George R. Mead

E-Cat Worlds Press

Comments and questions? –> gmead01@gmail.com

The War On Poverty.

LCCN 2018903736

Mead, George R.
The War On Poverty. A Short History 1960-1989 /
George R. Mead.
p. cm. – The War On Poverty
ISBN-13 978-0-9890927-1-5
                    1. Fantasy. I. Title. II. Series.

E-Cat Worlds established its publishing program as a reaction to the large commercial publishing houses currently dominating the book industry and the smaller intellectual clones. It is interested in publishing works of fiction and non-fiction that are often deemed insufficiently profitable or commercial or that are not necessarily reflective of current literary trends and fads.

E-Cat Worlds, 57744 Foothill Road, La Grande OR 97850
www.ecatworldspress.com
SAN 255-6383

In the middle of nowhere - Creativity.

First Edition:
Printed in the United States of America

Fiction

From Grandeville.
Portal
Lair
Search
Not Again
And Again.
Magiwitch
Rebirth
Offspring
Holiday
Treasure
E'Nilt
Braidna
Seemna and Chyndra

A Tale of The Feyra
Jonathon and Dee
Dee Of The Fontala
Dee and The People
Dee and The Golden Cartouche

The Seven Lands
Seventeen Siblings (assisted by Zakke L. Zacog)

Stream
Special Investigator
Dark Souls

Non-fiction

A History of Union County
The Ethnobotany of the California Indians, 2nd Edition
A History of The Chinese in The West: 1848-1880
Yachats. The Town Called "Dark Water at the Foot of the Mountains."
The War On Poverty. A Short History - Kennedy to Reagan

Table of Contents

PROLOGUE

In October, 1973, President John Kennedy stated that "a basic attack on the problems of poverty and waste of human resources" would be a central feature of his 1964 legislative program. He asked Walter H. Heller to draw up such a program. This process was given the greatest priority in the immediate aftermath of Kennedy's assassination by Vice President Johnson, now sworn in as President.

The Department of Labor felt that the way to combat poverty was through a more or less massive employment program. The Council of Economic Advisors and the Bureau of the Budget felt that the entire anti-poverty program should be set under a set of "Community Action Programs."

President Johnson, in December 1963, asked R. Sargent Shriver to end the stalemate and to impose some order in order to solve this problem.

The Labor Department's suggestion became Title I of a proposed bill. The Budget Bureau's approach became Title II. This became the Human Resources Development Act of 1964. Later, James L. Sunquist, Deputy under Secretary of Agriculture that suggested new title, the Economic Opportunity Act of 1974.

Assistant Attorney General Norbert A. Schlei wrote the first draft after a task force meeting on 23 February.

This draft proposed that there would be a Community Action Organization "which is developed and conducted with the maximum feasible participation of the residents of the areas" that were involved. The wording was virtually unchanged in the final act.

Richard Wolf Boone joined the White House Special Project Staff in 1963-1964, then served a Director of the Community Action Program in the Office of Economic Opportunity in 1964-1965. He was key in the concept and development of Head Start, Upward Bound, the Foster Grandparents, Community Health Centers, and Legal Services. He insisted that the war on poverty involved "maximum feasible participation" of the people in the programs. "I was very skeptical of 'top down' approaches to social action" (unpublished memoir).

James N. Adler, working with the Shiver task force stated:

> I would never conceived that it (participation) would really mean control by the poor of the community action represented on the community action organization . . . I expected that the poor . . . representation would be something in the order of 15 to 25% of the board . . . Moreover, I don't think it ever occurred to me, or may others that three representatives of the poor must necessarily be poor themselves (Moynihan 1969).

The war on poverty was initially about poverty. Then it became one about political strength and political control. The terminology "maximum feasible participation" meant to the individuals working in the field that it was to be community action with citizen participation. Citizen participation was to be by those who had been, for the most part, outside of the "normal" political system or political participation.

Neither the originators of the concept of "maximum feasible participation" nor the individuals who tried to put this concept into action understood what the impact of this phrase would be.

Maximum feasible participation began to create problems for the Office of Economic Opportunity almost from the first day of its existence. It meant a new concept in the existing political process, one which upset traditional political systems and networks. Whenever individuals in these systems began to be upset, or began to feel threatened, they started to engage in the "normal" political processes of attempting, via political pressures, to alter the situation. Somehow the people "on the ground," those individuals working in the Community Action Agencies, either forgot this basic fact of the political process inside the United States, or they were unaware of what such systems were all about.

Maximum feasible participation was seen, in many ways, as one more "minority" group attempting to move into the political system and then finding the usual resistence.

The problem was compounded, from the beginning of the anti-poverty program(s), by the fact of the polarization of the two major political parties that had developed around there programs.

In the main, the Democrats were for the program(s), the Republicans against.

The "war on poverty" became a battle between deeply held political belief systems as encapsulated within the Republican and Democrat parties.

The initial skirmishes began during the first hearings for the Economic Opportunity Act which gradually built up to a full-fledged assault on the Office of Economic Opportunity and its later incarnations through the careers of a number of Presidents.

There are strong indications that this war about poverty might have been avoided except for some exceptionally short-sighted behaviors during the initial Economic Opportunity Act hearings.

In many ways, the history about to unfold is, in itself, a powerful political lesson on how attempting to help citizens in need hinges on short-term political whims and belief systems as well as the ever-ongoing jockeying for political position and power.

A report from the Office of Economic Opportunity stated:

> Never before had a major nation attempted such a feat. To put an end to the poverty of the minority, at a time when the majority were enjoying their greatest prosperity. To enlist the services of a million volunteers at a time when they had earned the right to untroubled leisure. To change direction and alter the scope of established institutions which were serving adequately the needs of the vast majority. And to bring into sight and into mind, a segment of our society which could well have remained hidden and ignored (CSA 1969).

Sundquist (1969) saw the program this way:
> "America's War on Poverty is a story of superlatives.

It was the boldest national objective ever declared by the Congress – to do what no people have ever done . . .

It was reviewed by the Congress with the minimum of care, in the shortest of time, and with the least understanding of what was about to happen. It granted the broadest of power and discretion to a single administrator – Sargent Shriver – to upset and remake, if he could, the institutional structure of community to community across the land. It became – and remains – the most controversial of all the domestic programs of the Kennedy-Johnson era.
No, nothing about the War on Poverty is commonplace. In the zeal of its administrators, in the freshness of their ideas, in the innovations of organization and policy approach, it stands alone . ."

As you will see as you read the following pages, there are many, many quotes. This was done so the reader could "hear" the voices from all sides of what was an on-going argument. It could have been just an endless listing of events and dates. But I felt that it would be better to actually have as much of the actual "conversation" as possible. So, that is the way it is, or was, in the case of this subject.

Directors

Office of Economic Opportunity (OEO) /Community Services Administration (CSA)

R. Sargent Shriver   Director   1964 (August) - 1968 (March)

Bertrand Harding   Director   1968 (March) - 1969 (May)

Donald Rumsfeld   Director   1969)May) - 1970 (December)

Frank Carlucci   Director   1970 (December) - 1971 (September)

Phillip Sanchez   Director   1971 (September) - 1972 (December)

Howard Phillips   Acting Director   1973 (February) - 1973 (June)

Alvin Arnett   Director   1973 (June) - 1974 (July)

Bert Gallegos   Director   1974 (July) - 1976 (April)

Samuel Martinez   Director   1976 (April) - 1977 (January)

Robert Chase	Interim Director	1977 (February) - 1977 (April)
Graciela Olivarez	Director	1977 (April) - 1980 (March)
Dwight Albert Ink	Director	1981

Kennedy Begins The Renaissance

The 1930's, a period of social dislocation, social despair, and universal hardship saw the development of the New Deal with programs that felt that the national interest was best served when these programs worked to ensure the well-being and the security of all Americans. The focus was primarily on the unemployed skilled workers with an emphasis on proving jobs not creating new skills. This focus tended to bypass the hard-core poverty-stricken without job skills, looked at as the "unworthy poor" (CSA 1969).

The problem of poverty was largely ignored during the post World War II years. Widespread fear that the end of the war would bring mass unemployment led to the passage of the Employment Act in 1946, (ch. 33, section 2, 60 Stat. 23, codified as 15 U.S.C. § 1021), which committed the government to maintaining high employment and high purchasing power. Its main purpose was to lay the responsibility of economic stability of inflation and unemployment on the federal government. The Act stated that it was the "continuing policy and responsibility" of the federal government to coordinate and utilize all its plans, functions, and resources . . . to foster and promote free competitive enterprise and the general welfare; conditions under which there will be afforded useful employment for those able, willing, and seeking to work; and to promote maximum employment, production, and purchasing power. A Conservative Coalition of Northern Republicans and Southern Democrats controlled Congress. The bill was pressured to take on a number of amendments that forced the removal of the guarantee of full employment and the order to engage in compensatory spending.

Some of the reasoning behind this was that the Southern economic leaders feared what the "full employment" statement might have on their black labor force. Powerful Southern legislators insisted that they have legislation that allowed each state to create an employment office in order to protect their segregated labor system, to guarantee the availability of low-paid field workers. The law, as modified, listed many "unfair labor practices" but did not include racial discrimination (Harward 2016). The final law became mostly a set of suggestions.

Social welfare legislation held low priority during the years following World War II and no important laws were enacted during this period, the exceptions being a modification in minimum wages, the extension of coverage under unemployment insurance, and Old-Age Survivors, and Disability Insurance. The eight years of Eisenhower's Great Crusade put the stamp of respectability upon the New Deal programs but produced very few innovations of their own.

Wright (2007) writes in a footnote:

> "The discovery of poverty is generally attributed to journalists and social scientists writing during the early 1960s, but poverty historian Jennifer Mittelstadt demonstrates that the initial rediscovery of poverty occurred during the mid-1950s

within the ranks of a small group affiliated with the less exalted fields of social work and welfare administration. Mittlestadt argues that Wilbur Cohen, "one of the most influential social policy experts in postwar America," spearheaded the rediscovery of poverty. Former Social Security Administration analyst, professor of public administration at University of Michigan's School of Social Work, and later secretary of HEW under LBJ, Cohen initiated several poverty studies during the mid-1950s and shared his ideas with countless policy makers, relief workers, and academics. Several other developments furthered the rediscovery of poverty. In 1957 an elite Washington economic policy think thank [sp.], the Committee for Economic Development, produced a comprehensive study on poverty, and during the same year the Russell Sage Foundation provided a large, multiyear grant to University of Michigan for poverty studies. Yet none of these studies had much of an effect on the nation as a whole."

In 1950 and again in 1955, Senator John J. Sparkman, (D), Alabama, documented the persistence of rural poverty during extensive hearing of the Joint Economic Committee from the data buried rather deeply in their reports (Joint Committee on the Economic Report 1950, 1955). Beginning in 1955, Senator Paul Douglas, (D), Illinois, continuously pointed to the anomaly of depressed areas and pockets of deprivation in an economy of abundance. An attempt by Governor Averell Harriman, (D), New York, and his deputy, Daniel Patrick Moynihan, (D), in 1957 conducted a study to focus upon problems of poverty in the Empire State but it did not advance beyond the research state. When Harriman was defeated for re-reelection in the next year, the effort was dropped by his successor. In 1959 a Special Senate Committee on Unemployment, headed by Senator Eugene J. MacCarthy, (D), Minnesota, disclosed serious economic deprivation in many areas of the country. Systematic statistical analyses of the incidence of poverty were developed by Robert J. Lampman of the University of Wisconsin in a 1959 study made for the Joint Economic Committee of Congress. The paper was a study of employment, growth, and price levels (ASPE 2000). These findings were supplemented by a group of University of Michigan economists and the Conference on Economic Progress which prepared a popularized version of the data three years later (Levitan 1969). Cordes (1989) provided data on the rural poor as the percentage of residents classified as rural "farm population decreased *both* in absolute numbers and as a proportion of total population" [emphasis in original document] (Levitan 1969).

Coontz (1997) wrote:

> We now know that 1950s family culture was not only nontraditional; it was also not idyllic. In important ways, the stability of family and community life in the 1950s rested on pervasive discrimination against women, gays,

political dissidents, non-Christians, and racial or ethnic minorities, as well as on a systematic cover-up of the underside of many families. Families that were harmonious and fair of their own free will may have been able to function more easily in the fifties, but few alternatives existed for members of discordant or oppressive families. Victims of child abuse, incest, alcoholism, spousal rape, and wife battering had no recourse, no place to go, until well into the 1960s.

At the end of the 1950s, despite ten years of economic growth, 27.3 percent of the nation's children were poor, including those in white "underclass" communities such as Appalachia. Almost 50 percent of married-couple African-American families were impoverished – a figure higher than today [1997].

In the 1950s it was not really respectable to talk about poverty. When Hubert H. Humphrey announced his initial candidacy for the Democratic presidential nomination in 1959, he declared that he would be a "poor man's candidate." The press simply regarded this as an unsubtle reminder that Humphrey's three major rivals for the nomination were all multimillionaires. Even Kennedy's call for a "war against poverty" during the 1960 campaign went largely unnoticed (Levitan 1969).

It was a time when the country seemed to be on the verge of leaving behind a decade of directionless, a passive complacency about domestic problems. Theodore Schultz a University of Chicago economist felt: "We have long been complacent about American poverty, saying to each other, we have an affluent society. Unfortunately, we are ill prepared to act because we have been out of touch. Our ideas of poverty are mostly of the New Deal vintage which are very obsolete" (Weeks 1967).

Bill Moyers, who had been a summer intern for Congressman Johnson received a call, in 1959, from LBJ to leave the job he was preparing for, teaching Christian ethics at Baylor University, and become Johnson's Personal Assistant, In 1960 Moyers was running LBJ's pre-presidential campaign (Goldstein 2001).

Early in 1960, John F. Kennedy declared himself a candidate of the office of President of the United States.

On 14 August of that year, in a speech marking the anniversary of the signing of the Social Security Act, at Hyde Park, New York, he used the phrase, *war on poverty*. The opening battle, he remarked, against the suffering and deprivation had been won in the 1930's, but the war against poverty and degradation had not been won yet.

Daniel P. Moynihan served in the Kennedy administration as Special (1961–1962) and Executive (1962–1963) Assistant to Labor Secretaries Arthur J. Goldberg and W. Willard Wirtz. He was appointed as Assistant Secretary of Labor, in charge of the Office of Policy Planning and Research. He had a Ph.D., Political Science from the Fletcher School of Law and Diplomacy (1961) and had attended the London School of Economics on a Fulbright fellowship (Rainwater and Yancey 1967). He served from 1963 to 1965 under Kennedy and Lyndon B. Johnson, devoting much of his time to the War on Poverty. He had a small staff which included Paul Barton, Ellen Broderick, and Ralph Nader.

Moynihan wrote (1965):

> "Kennedy had ventured into West Virginia searching for Protestant votes, not for poverty. There he encountered the incredible pauperization of the mountain people, an industrial work force whose numbers had been reduced by nearly two-thirds in the course of a decade, but with hardly a sound of protest. The miners were desperately poor, shockingly unemployed, but neither radical nor in any [way] restive. . . . The Appalachian experience gave the Kennedy administration an early sensitivity to the issue of poverty and deprivation, but it was a self-imposed concern and politically an optional one. . . . The war on poverty was not declared at the behest of the poor: it was declared in their interest by persons confident of their own judgement in such matters."

Kennedy felt that the Eisenhower Administration had been indifference to the plight of the one hundred thousand unemployed people in West Virginia (Clark 2002).

During the campaign Hubert Humphrey introduced Walter Heller to Kennedy (Clark 2000).

Then in February of the same year the southern sit-in movement in Greensboro, North Carolina directed attention to the realities of the linkage between racism and poverty. The

Democrat platform singled out the problem of poverty as an issue to focus on.

In Kennedy's acceptance speech to run as the candidate for the President at the Democratic Convention, he stated, in part:

> "But I tell you the New Frontier is here, whether we seek it or not. Beyond that frontier are the uncharted areas of science and space, unsolved problems of peace and war, unconquered pockets of ignorance and prejudice, unanswered questions of poverty and surplus. It would be easier to shrink back from that frontier, to look to the safe mediocrity of the past, to be lulled by good intentions and high rhetoric – and those who prefer that course should not cast their votes for me, regardless of party.
>
> But I believe the times demand new invention, innovation, imagination, decision. I am asking each of you to be pioneers on that New Frontier. My call is to the young in heart, regardless of age – to all who respond to the Scriptural call: 'Be strong and of a good courage; be not afraid, neither be thou dismayed.' "

Shortly after the 1960 election, President-elect Kennedy and his brother Robert asked David Hackett, an old friend and campaign associate, a former Olympic hockey player, to organize an effort looking at juvenile delinquency. On March 16 Hackett arranged a conference of experts on that matter and came to the conclusion "that you can't get consensus among professionals, so I had to pick one of the best and rely on his judgement" (Sundquist 1969). Two participants in Heller's task force, David Hackett and Richard Boone, had begun circulating a new and potentially unifying theme for a campaign. Their idea was labeled "community action." It was based on the concept of "opportunity theory," developed Richard Cloward and Lloyd Ohlin, both from Columbia University. Heller's selection was Lloyd Ohlin. Ohlin, with his collaborator, Richard Cloward, had come to the conclusion that juvenile delinquency was not an individual pathology but one of a community pathology, the delinquent was not a deviant but one who conformed inside the patterns of a subculture that was itself deviant. Their concept was that the "social setting gives rise to delinquency" (Sundquist 1969).

A series of activities set forth to deal with behavioral problems linked with poverty, especially in terms of delinquency, led analysts to discover that beneath the symptoms of delinquency lay deeper problems of teenage unemployment, slum schools, ghetto living, and broken families. The studies felt that juvenile delinquency was not some sort of special disease that could be affected independently of the social environment (Weeks 1967). Gangs, the authors believed, weren't the product of teenage psychosis or problematic parenting. Gangs were a logical reaction to a system that provided urban youth with absolutely no opportunities for success (Stubbendeck 2013). From these studies came the 1961 Area Redevelopment Act (ARA) which emphasized the "elimination of poverty rather than the amelioration of some of its effects."

The concept of opportunity theory started as a strategy

for addressing the problem of youth gangs in low-income urban neighborhoods. The core idea was that members of such gangs did not entirely reject the norms and aspirations of mainstream society, they sought social status, personal security, material comfort, even wealth, but they lacked access to the normal range of opportunities for achieving such goals. Young people turned to the gang as an alternative social structure that would meet their goals. The solution to gangs and juvenile delinquency thus lay in opening the blocked avenues of opportunity in such communities, thereby reducing the allure of the gang.

During the 1960 Presidential race, Humphrey promoted the idea of an American version of what later became called the Peace Corps. When he withdrew from the race he sent his ideas to Kennedy (Aksamit 2014).

Kennedy asked Sargent Shriver to analyze whether a volunteer corps could work on projects in other countries. Shriver, with Kennedy, Walt Rostow, and Max Millikan, produced the plan that was signed as an executive order establishing the Peace Corps (Aksamit 2014). Vice-President Johnson recommended Moyers to Shriver as one of the key members of the Peace Corps team (Weeks 1967). Shriver, Director, Peace Corps (1961-1966) saw the Corps mission was to promote world peace and friendship by helping people of the interested countries, at the grassroots level, meet their needs for trained men and women. The unspoken rational was that it was also created as a means to prevent the expansion of communism in many of the undeveloped countries (Aksamit 2014). Later, under Johnson, Shriver felt that the Community Action program closely resembled the "community development program practiced for a number of years by the Peace Corps in certain countries." (Joseph 2015, Goldstein 2001). Bill Moyers, later an American journalist and political commentator, was appointed

(1961) Associate Director of Public Affairs, Peace Corps, then as Deputy Director (1962-1963).

After winning the nomination, and the election, in Kennedy's *Inaugural Address*, 20 January 1961, he stated, in part:

> "If the free society cannot help the many who are poor, it cannot save the few who are rich." He asked the nations of the world to join together to fight what he called the "common enemies of man: tyranny, poverty, disease, and war itself. .. The hand of hope must be extended to the poor and the depressed."

From his office, Kennedy directed that studies be made on poverty, authorizing the formation and funding of a special study group to investigate the related problems of the poor.

Secretary of Labor, Willard Wirtz had urged for a national program to eliminate poverty and ignorance. He described the job of retraining the poorly educated as "one of the most intractable problems of unemployment" (Sundquist 1969). The 1961 Juvenile Delinquency and Youth Offences Control Act provided 15-million dollars to finance experiments in "community action projects."

Orshansky wrote: "Year after year the same kinds of people continually appear at the bottom of the income pyramid (1963); "Except to allow for rising prices, the poverty index has not been adjusted since 1959. Between 1959 and 1966, the average income of 4-person families had increased by 37 percent but the poverty line by only 9 percent" (1965).

She had joined the Social Security Administration in 1958 as a Social Science Research Analyst.

Congress passed the Juvenile Delinquency Act of 1961.

Kennedy had set up a special study group (Executive Order 10940) to investigate how poverty related to the problems of the poor, the President's Committee on Juvenile Delinquency and Youth Crime (PCJD). This committee established a small, program staff inside the Justice Department under the direction of Attorney Robert Kennedy and his Special Assistant, David Hackett (Weeks 1967).

The language of The Area Development Act of 1961 (ARA) came from the President's Committee on Juvenile Delinquency and Youth Crime, a tripartite organization of the White House, the Department of Labor, and the Justice Department (Clark 2000), with a specific focus on the social antecedents of juvenile crime, youth-unemployment, poor housing and health, and the alienation of lower-class communities and neighborhoods. The President's Committee on Juvenile Delinquency tapped Lloyd Ohlin to serve as its lead expert (Stubbendeck 2013).The program they proposed emphasized through its intellectual and theoretical underpinning a requirement for innovation and a general anti-bureaucratic stance (Kravitz and Kolodner 1969).

Stubbendeck (2013) stated: The committee fell under the joint control of the Department of Justice (DOJ), the Department of Labor, and HEW. This structure reflected the traditional belief that youth crime was an issue best solved by a joint approach of the criminal justice system and of social service providers, a decision seconded by Robert F. Kennedy, the committee's head. The executive order establishing the committee also declared that the group's primary purpose would be to ensure that "the resources of the Federal Government be promptly mobilized to provide leadership and direction in a national effort to strengthen our social structure and to correlate, at all levels of government, juvenile and youth services." A new bill, introduced by Edith Green in the House of Representatives, the Juvenile Delinquency and Youth Offenses Control Act of 1961, was specifically targeted at gang violence by creating employment initiatives (Cazenave 2007).

> "The program ran into trouble with Congress, notably with the redoubtable Edith Green who very much took lead in educational matters in the merged House Committee on Education and Labor, repeatedly she made clear that the legislative mandate of the PCJD was not to reform urban society, nor yet to try out the sociological theories of Emile Durkheim on American youth: the legislative mandate was to reduce juvenile delinquency. To essay more was to trifle with Congressional intent" (Moynihan 1969a).

The second woman to represent Oregon in the House of Representatives, Edith Green was appointed during her freshman term (1955) to the Committee on Education and Labor as she was recognized as an expert on educational policy. Fearful that federal programs had done little to alleviate the plight of the poor or to improve the quality of American education, she advocated shifting responsibilities to state and local governments (US House of Representatives n.d.).

Green, the leading expert on juvenile delinquency in Congress, felt that Hackett was running the program in a political fashion. She chaired the Special Subcommittee on

Education which provided approval for appropriations for PCJD and its projects. Hackett felt that effective efforts to combat the problem was coordination by all relevant agencies in the planning process of a comprehensive program strategy. Green stated "Your first criterion is that it must be comprehensive in scope. As one who rather strongly believes in person to person program, both in the domestic level and at the international level, I am hard pressed to find the reason for this requirement that every program for which any federal funds will be given will be comprehensive." She asked whether the comprehensive criterion meant that worthwhile single-agency programs might not be funded. Hackett said yes. Green later asked Bernard Russell, Director of the Office of Juvenile Delinquency and Youth Development if "Mr. Hackett is the one who is really in charge of the overall program." Russell responded, "No, Madam Chairman. This is a rather complex thing." However, Hackett did run the program. When he left, it ended and the program became part of HEW (Cazenave 2007).

In January 1945, Congressman Adam Clayton Powell was appointed to the House Education and Labor Committee. On January 22,1960, Congressman Graham A. Barden, (D), North Carolina, Chairman of the House Committee on Education and Labor, announced his retirement. Powell was the highest-ranking Democrat on the committee and was sworn in as the new chairman. On April 14,1961, Powell took the same stance as Kennedy that he would abstain from introducing his anti-segregation amendment into the school aid legislation. Powell now possessed the influence and the status that he desired in Congress (Brisbon 2015).

This act, ARA was signed into law on 1 May 1961 and became the first major legislative achievement of Kennedy's "New Frontier."

ARA became law in 1961 mainly due to the fact that it had won the support of a large bipartisan congressional coalition which saw the need for public policy aimed at alleviating long-term unemployment. The first proposal of this type had been introduced during the summer of 1955 by Senator Paul Douglass, (D), Illinois. Twice the bill passed both houses of Congress only to be vetoed twice by Eisenhower. Kennedy had been a co-sponsor of the bills during his senatorial career.

The Conference On Economic Progress released a report (1962) which stated, in part:

> The most obvious unmet needs in the United States are concentrated among the more than two-fifths of a nation who still live in poverty or deprivation. They need better education, health services, and housing; vastly liberalized social security; further improvements in minimum wage standards; and release from the burden of unemployment which hits them with special force.
>
> The Common Market is not just a "trade" effort. It is the start of a much larger planning effort under freedom. It is but one manifestation of as growing popular consciousness, everywhere in the world, that the new technology makes persistent poverty intolerable by making it available. We cannot meet this challenge by saying that the lowest tenth of our population lives better than nine-tenths of

the people of India. When large portions of our most competent youth cannot afford to go to college, it is no answer to say that higher percentages of our youth are in college than in other countries. When we tolerate large and chronically rising unemployment, consequently freezing millions in poverty or deprivation when we have the technology to prevent it, it is no answer to say that unemployment is even higher in some underdeveloped countries which do not yet have the technology to prevent it.

Because people are poor, they save little; and because their saving are so meager, they are able to spend less for the adequate medical care and housing which would fit them to earn more – and for the education which would make it easier for their children to rise above poverty. Besides, if a breadwinner's saving are negligible, it is harder for him to leave a low-paying job and look for a better one in some other locality – even if a better job is available.

. . . a large amount of the progress among the higher income people, especially the affluent and wealthy, has been achieved only by trends which relatively have held down those at the bottom.

The region comprising the Rocky Mountains and the Great Lakes came closest to the national average [per capita income], with New England and the Midwest above these two regions, and the regions including the Plains and the Southwest below them.

Examined by States, the ten States with the lowest per capita incomes, all in the south except three border states . . . The ten with the highest per capita incomes (including the District of Columbia) were six along the eastern seaboard, and Illinois, Alaska, California, and Nevada. . .

The prime reason for the disparate amount of poverty on the farm is that farmers, unlike most others, sell their labor and their product for prices determined to a large extent by the so-called laws of supply and demand, which others to a considerable degree administer their prices and their wages. National farm policy, originated to counteract this disadvantage, has done so only to a very deficient extent.

More than 60 percent of nonwhite families were living in poverty in 1960, contrasted with 28½ percent of white families.

Looking at unattached individuals in 1960, about 66 percent of the nonwhites were in poverty, contrasted with 52 percent of the whites. . . More than 80 percent of the [all of the] nonwhites were living in poverty or deprivation, compared with less than 65 percent of the whites.

A bipartisan agreement wrote and enacted the Manpower Development and Training Act (MDTA) in the years 1961-1962. However it soon was criticized as failing with its major purpose – not reaching long-term chronic unemployment. In testimony to a House Subcommittee, a professor from Michigan stated: "A substantial portion of the 'hard core' unemployed are functionally illiterate and in the position where they cannot qualify for training." Forty-four percent of unemployed Negro workers had completed fewer than eight years of education but only 4 percent of Negro trainees in the MDTA program had the same level of education.

Raymond M. Hilliard, Director of the Department of Public Aid of Cook County, Illinois, urged a "massive attack" on illiteracy as the solution.

Amendments to the MDTA Act were passed in 1963 which lowered the minimum age requirement for the payment of training allowances to induce more unemployed youth to take MDTA training. The Youth Conservation Corps (YCC), modeled after the Civilian Conservation Corps of the 1930s became the vehicle for the purpose. When Kennedy took office the Bureau of the Budget submitted a staff paper that suggested that the CCC approach from the depression era was not suitable for 1960s problems. The problem of the YCC was never resolved inside the political process

The notion of "community action" was developed from the concept of social action and social psychology that had been discussed in a few universities. Community action was based, in the main, on the view that the principle hope for the poor was for them to develop sufficient strength and skill to maneuver themselves, largely by their own efforts, out of where they were and into something better. In addition to this belief was that if any reforms are feasible in the existing social system they will have to be accomplished through the best of poor people with the political and administrative power necessary to force those changes they considered important upon the power structure (Moynihan 1965, Cazenave 2007).

Kennedy's Council of Economic Advisors in 1962 included: Walter Heller, Chairman of the Council of Economic Advisors; Kermit Gordon; James Tobin; Kenneth J. Arrow; Richard E. Attiyeh, Barbara R. Berman; Charles A. Cooper; Richard N. Cooper; Rashi Fein; Catherine H. Furlong; Frances M. James; Edward D. Kalachek; David W. Lusher; Richard R. Nelson; Arthur M. Okun; George L. Perry; Lee E. Preston, Jr.; Vernon W. Ruttan; Walter F. Stettner; Robert Solomon; Warren Smith; Charles A. Taff; Nancy H. Teeters; Lloyd Ulman.

Kennedy, during his year end review of economic conditions (December 1962) told Walter Heller, chairman of the Council of Economic Advisors to gather statistics on poverty, and said: "Now look! I want to go beyond the things that have already been accomplished. Give me facts and figures on the things we still have to do. For example, what about the poverty problem in the United States?" (Sundquist 1969).

Heller spend a great deal of time looking at the special problems of the people passed over, left out, somehow remaining in Depression-like conditions even though there had been a long period of prosperity after World War II (Aksamit 2014).

In early 1963, Heller gave Kennedy a copy of a review written By Dwight MacDonald. After reading it, Kennedy charged Heller with launching a massive legislative assault on poverty.

In 1977 Michael Harrington's book, *The Other America: Poverty in the United States* was published. Michael Harrington, had worked for the *Catholic Worker*, and, the Fund for the Republic. He wrote the book as a statement of outrage of what he had seen the ghettos and slums and flophouses and tarpaper shacks (Weeks 1967). He was a contributing editor of *Dissent*, and chief editor of the Socialist Party biweekly, *New America*. Harrington did not expect that the book would have much effect. But the book burst into the nation's consciousness in an unexpected way (Rose 2008).

Harrington's book was reviewed, along with others treating the same topic of poverty in the United States, by Dwight MacDonald in a *New Yorker* (19 January 1963) article titled "Our Invisible Poor." It was a 13,000 word book review, the longest book review the magazine had ever produced.

Harrington's book sold 7,000 copies in the year after the article was produced. The *New Yorker* reprinted over 20,000 of the article, copies going to sociologists, economists, social workers, trade unions, and private citizens. Some inquiries came from Washington, D.C., one from Theodore Sorensen, Special Assistant to the President. The paperback of Harrington's book was reprinted, released in the fall of 1963, and sold several hundred thousand more copies (Levitan 1969).

The following comments (below) from the essay are treated in type font this way: MacDonald comments, *Harrington comments* quoted by MacDonald. The reason for the lengthily quotes from this article is because the essay brought a large focus of what poverty in the United States was really like to a very large audience.

> For a long time now, almost everybody has assumed that, because of the New Deal's social legislation and – more important – the prosperity we have enjoyed since 1940, mass poverty no longer exists in this county.

> Last April the newspapers reported some exhilarating statistics in a Department of Commerce Study . . . Only the specialists and the statisticians read the fine print, which is why illusions continue to exist about American poverty.

> In the last year we seem to have suddenly awakened, rubbing our eyes like Rip van Winkle, to the fact that mass poverty persists, and that it is one of our two gravest social problems. (The other is related: While only eleven per cent of our population is non-white, twenty-five percent of our poor are).

> The rich are almost as rich as ever and the poor are even poorer, in the percentage of the national income they receive.

The late French philosopher Charles Pguy remarks, in his classic essay on poverty, "The duty of tearing the destitute from their destitution and the duty of distributing goods equitably are not of the same order. The first is an urgent duty, the second is a duty of convenience . . . When all men are provided with the necessities what do we care about the distribution of luxury?" What indeed? Envy and emulation are the motives – and not very good ones – for the equalization of wealth. The problem of poverty goes much deeper.

What is "poverty"? It is a historically relative concept, first of all. *There are new definitions [in America] of what man can achieve, of what a human standard of life should be," Mr. Harrington write. "Those who suffer levels of life well below those that are possible, even though they live better than medieval knight or Asian peasants, are poor . . . Poverty should be defined in terms of those who are denied the minimal levels of health, housing, food, and education that our present stage of scientific knowledge specifics as necessary for life as it is now lived in the United States".*

These two minorities, sizable enough to feel they *are* the nation, have been unaware of the continued existence of mass poverty, as this reviewer was until he read Mr. Harrington's book. They are businessmen, congressman, judges, government officials, politicians, lawyers, doctors, engineers, scientists, editors, journalists, and administrators in colleges, churches, and foundations. Since their education, income, and social status are superior, they, if anybody, might be expected to accept responsibility for what the Constitution calls "the general welfare." They have not done so in the case of the poor. And they have a good excuse. It is becoming harder and harder simply to *see* the one-fourth of our fellow-citizens who live below the poverty level.

Now the American city has been transformed. The poor still inhabit housing in the central area, but they are increasingly isolated from contact with, or sigh of, anybody else . . . . Living out in the suburbs, it is easy to assumes that ours is, indeed, an affluent society . . . .Clothes make the poor invisible too: American has the best-dressed poverty the world has ever known . . . It is much easier in the United States to be decently dressed than it is to be decently housed, fed, or doctored . . . . Many of the poor are the wrong age to be seen. A good number of them are sixty-five years of age or between, an even larger number are under eighteen . . . Finally, the poor are politically invisible . . . They are without lobbies of their own; they put forward no legislative program. As a group, they are atomized. They have no face, they have no voice . . Only the social agencies have a really direct involvement with the other America, and they were without any great political power . . . Forty to fifty millions people are becoming increasingly invisible.

The problem of the aged poor is aggravated by the fact that, unlike the Italians or the English, we seem to have little respect for or interest in our "senior citizens," beyond given them that horrific title, and we don't include them in family life.

Emotional upset is one of the main forms of the vicious circle of impoverishment. The structure of society is hostile to these people. The poor tend to be pessimistic and depressed; they seek immediate gratification instead of saving; they act out. Once this mood, this unarticulated philosophy becomes a fact, society can change, the recession can end, and yet there is no motive for movement. The depression has become internalized. The middle class looks upon this process and sees "lazy' people who "just don't want to get ahead." People who are much too sensitive to demand of cripples that they run races ask of the poor that they get up and act just like everyone else in the society. The poor are not like everyone else . . . They think and feel differently; they look upon a different America than the middle class looks upon.

The poor are also different in a physical sense: they are much less healthy.

An obvious cause, among others, for the very poor being four times as much disabled by "chronic ill health" as the well-to-do is they have much less money to spend for medical care – in fact, almost nothing. This weighs with special heaviness on the aged poor. During the fifties, Mr. Harrington notes, *"all costs on the Consumer Price Index went up by 12 per cent. But medical costs, that terrible staple of the aged, went up by 36 per cent, hospitalization rose by 65 per cent, and group hospitalization (Blue Cross premiums) were up by 83 per cent."*

Mental health as physical illness is much greater among the poor, even though our complacent cliché is that nervous breakdowns are prerogative of the rich because the poor "can't afford" them. (They can't, but they have them anyway). This bit of middle class folklore should be laid to rest by a study made in New Haven; "Social Class and Mental Illness," by August B. Hollngshead and Frederick C. Redlich (Wiley).

Of those in the top four income groups who had undergone psychiatric treatment, 65 per cent had been treated for neurotic problems and 35 per cent for psychotic disturbances. In the bottom fifth, the treated illnesses were almost all psychotic (90 per cent). This shows there is something to the notion that the poor "can't afford" nervous breakdowns – the milder kind, that is – since the reason the proportion of *treated* neuroses among the poor is only 10 per cent is that a neurotic can keep going after a fashion. But the argument cuts deeper the other way. The poor go to a psychiatrist (or, more commonly, are committed to a mental institution) only when they are completely unable to function because of psychotic symptoms.

One reason our society is a comparatively violent one is that the French and Italian and British poor have a communal life and culture that the American poor lack. As one reads "The Other America," one wonders why there is not even more violence than there is.

But today the poor are a minority, and minorities can be ignored if they are so heterogeneous that they cannot be organized. When the poor were a majority, they simply could not be overlooked. Poverty is also hard to see today because the middle class . . . has vastly increased – from 13 per cent of all families in 1936 to a near-majority (47 per cent) today. That mass poverty can persist despite this rise to affluence is hard to believe, or see, especially if one is among those who have risen.

But in the last decade . . . laborers and service workers have gained 36% while professional-managerial workers have gained 68%. [MacDonald is talking about increase in wages] This is because in the wartime forties the unskilled were in great demand, while now they are being replaced by machines. "Automation is today the same kind of menace to the unskilled – that is, the poor – that the enclosure movement was to the British agricultural population centuries ago," Mr. Miller [Bureau of the Census article in the New York Times, 11 November 1962] concludes, "yet important segments of the American public, many of them highly placed Government officials and prominent educators, think and act as though it [increasing wage rates] were a continuing process."

Thus in the last fifteen years the bottom dogs have remained on the bottom, sharing hardly at all in the advances that the income groups above them have made on an ascending scale that is exquisitely adjusted, by the automatic workings of capitalism, so that it is inversely proportionate to need.

Kennedy's efforts to "get the county moving again" have been unsuccessful, possibly because he has, despite the suggestions of many of his economic advisers, not yet advocated the one big step that might push the economy off dead center: a massive increase in government spending. This would be politically courageous, perhaps even dangerous, because of the superstitious fear of "deficit spending" and an "unbalanced" federal budget. American folklore insists that a government's budget must be arranged like a private family's.

It's not that Public Opinion doesn't become Aroused every now and then. But the arousement never leads to much. It was aroused twenty-four years ago when John Steinbeck published "The Grapes of

Wrath," but Mr. Harrington reports that things in the Imperial Valley are still much the same: low wages, bad housing, no effective union. Public Opinion is too public – that is, too general; of its very nature, it can have no sustained interest in California agriculture. The only groups with a continuing interest are the workers and the farmers who hire them. Once Public Opinion ceased to be aroused, the battle was again between two antagonists with a real, personal stake in the outcome, and there was no questions about which was stronger. So with the rural poor in general In the late fifties, the average annual wage for white male American farm workers was slightly over $1,000; women, children, Negroes, and Mexicans got less.

Several years ago, Charles Abrams, whom was New York Rent Administrator under Harriman and who is now the president of the National Committee Against Discrimination in Housing, summed up what he had learned in two decades in public housing: "Once social reforms have won tonal appeal in the public mind, their slogans and goal-symbols may degenerate into tools of the dominant class for beleaguering the minority and often defeating the very aims which the original sponsors had intended for their reforms."

And this is not the end of tribulation. The poor, who can least afford to lose pay because of ill health, lose the most. A National Health survey, made a few years ago, found that workers earning under $2,000 a year had twice as many "restricted-activity days" as those earning over $4,0000.

The poor are even fatter than the rich. (The cartoonists will have to revise their clichés). "Obesity is seven times more frequent among women of the lowest socio-economic level than it is among those of the higher level," state Drs. Moore, Stunkard, and Srole in a recent issue of the *Journal of the American Medical Association*. (The proportion is almost as high for men).

Although they are the most in need of hospital insurance, the poor have the least, since they can't afford the premiums; only 40 per cent of poor families have it, as against 63 per cent of all families.

The poor actually pay more taxes, in proportion to their income, than the rich.

Sales and other excise taxes are largely responsible for this curious statistic.

Of the Welfare State, Mr. Harrington says, *"Its creation has been stimulated by mass impoverishment and misery, yet it helped the poor least of all. Laws like unemployment compensation, the Wagner Act, the various farm programs, all these were designed for the middle third in the cities, for the organized workers, and for the . . . big market farms."*

The big farmers put enough pressure on Henry Wallace, Roosevelt's first Secretary of Agriculture – who talked a good fight for liberal principals but was a Hamlet when it came to action – to establish the two basic propositions of Welfare State agricultural: subsidies that now cost $3 billion a year and that chiefly benefit the big farmers; and the exclusion of sharecroppers, tenant farmers, and migratory workers from the protection of minimum-wage and Social Security laws.

No doubt the Kennedy administration would like to do more for the poor than it has, but it is hampered by the cabal of Republicans and Southern Democrats in Congress.

It seems likely that mass poverty will

continue in this country for a long time. The more it is reduced, the harder it is to keep on reducing it. The poor, having dwindled from two-thirds of the population in 1936 to one-quarter today, no longer are a significant political force, as is shown by the Senate's rejection of Medicare and by the Democrats' dropping it as an issue in the elections last year.

For most families, however, the problem of chronic poverty is serious. One such family is headed by a thirty-two-year-old man who is employed as a dishwasher. Though he works steadily and more than full time, he earned slightly over $2,000 in 1959. His wife earned $3,000 more, but their combined incomes are not high enough to support themselves and their three children. Although the head of the family is only thirty-two, he feels that he has no chance of advancement partly because he finished only seven grades of school . . . The possibility of such families leaving the ranks of the poor is not high.

Children born into poor families today have less chance of "improving themselves" than the children of the pre-1940 poor. Rags to riches is now more likely to be rags to rags. "Indeed," the Michigan surveys conclude, "it appears that a number of the heads of poor families have moved into less skilled jobs than their fathers had."

In an important study of poverty, made for a Congressional committee in 1959, Dr. Robert J. Lampman estimated that eleven million of the poor were under eighteen. "A considerable number of younger persons are starting life in a condition of inherited poverty," he observed. To which Mr. Harrington adds, *"The character of poverty has changed, and it has become more deadly for the young. It is no longer associated with immigrant groups with high aspirations; it is not identified with those whose social existence makes it more and more difficult to break out into the larger society."*

While the economy is changing in a way which makes the eventual liquidation of the slums at least conceivable, young people are not seizing the opportunities this change presents. Too many are dropping out of school before graduation (more than half in many slums); too few are going to college . . . As a result there are serious shortages of teachers, nurses, doctors, technicians, and scientifically trained executives, but 4,500,000 unemployables.

"Poverty is the parent of revolution and

crimes," Aristotle wrote. This is now a
half truth. Our poor are alienated; they
don't consider themselves part of society.
But precisely because they don't they are
not politically dangerous. It is people
with "a stake in the country" who make
revolutions.

The literature on poverty grew large. It became apparent
that beneath the layers of American affluence there was a strata
of deprivation which was not restricted to those that lived in
Harlem or the other black ghettos or the depressed regions of
the South, but that the poor were ubiquitous, found in all parts
of country, in all the population and in all age groups (Trattner
1994).

Otis Dudley Duncan stated (1968 et al, 1969b) that "I
would argue, in particular, that Negroes (that is,
disproportionate numbers of them) are poor mainly because
they are "Negroes" and are defined and treated as such by our
society and their poverty stems largely not from the legacy of
poverty but from the legacy of race."

Kennedy directed Heller to start a study of potential
poverty programs, one of which would be a national service
program designed after and from the experience of the Peace
Corps. The National Service Program became a special project
of a Cabinet level study group under the offices of the Attorney
General. In began in November 1962 with the Presidential
instruction: "we shall be judged more by what we do at home
than what we preach abroad."

In January 1963 the National Service Program study
group made their report. While Congress failed to pass the
legislation suggested, the report contained a clear recognition of

the problem of poverty along with a description of the hardships faced by one-sixth of the nations population. The report also contained a brief bibliography of poverty.

Kennedy's *State of the Union Message* and a *Special Message Relative to the Nation's Youth* both raised the issue and feasibility of a national youth corps. Congress wasn't interested.

On 9 April, Kennedy authorized a Presidential Appalachian Regional Commission which brought national attention to the region and its problem.

The Selective Service had reported that half of the young men taking the pre-induction tests had failed. The causes were one or both physical or intellectual deficiencies. Among the sample group the task force studied eight out of ten were school dropouts, half of those came from families of six or more children, and that the rate of unemployment was almost double the rate for all men in the same age group (Keyserling 1964).

In May, 1963, Walter Heller, Chairman of Kennedy's Council of Economic Advisors, invited Professor of Economics Robert Lampman (University of Wisconsin) and William M. Capron, Member, Council of Economic Advisers, to help the Council began a study of a potential poverty program. Lampman had studied the income distribution of the poor, and had been a colleague of Heller's while Heller had been in graduate school at the University of Wisconsin studying economics. Lampman had noted the slow down in the rate at which the economy was moving people out of poverty (Clark 2000, Gillette 2010).

Informal Saturday "brown bag" lunches met where academics and Heller, Lampman, James Sundquist, Deputy Undersecretary of Agriculture, and officials from the Bureau of the Budget, the Department of Health, Education and Welfare (HEW), and staff from the Council of Economic Advisors, discussed the definitions of poverty and possible solutions (Harward 2016).

In early June, Heller read an article in the New York *Herald Tribune* that stated the republicans were planning some sort of anti-poverty program. Heller asked Lampman and others to start work on developing outlines for an attack on poverty (Weeks 1967), what might be "a practical Kennedy anti-poverty program." After sending their responses to the President, Heller was encouraged to proceed (Sundquist1969). Lampman said:

> "We would get into discussions about poverty. . . . . Some people would say poverty obviously means lack of money income . . . But other people said that's really not what poverty means; poverty is more or sometimes even less than money. It's a spiritual concept; or it's a participation-in-government concept; or it's a lack of some kind of self-esteem, sort of a psychological or image problem that people had . . . Still others would say it really has to do with lack of opportunity (Aksamit 2104).

Lampman wrote a series of memoranda which stated that the New Frontier had failed to live up to its promise to aid the poor (CSA 1969). He pointed out that the investment tax credit and the pending massive income tax cut would be of little help to large groups of the poor. Even if the economy did swing back to full employment he felt that additional programs would be required before the aged poor, the disabled, and fatherless families could rise above the threshold of poverty (Levitan 1969,

Sundquist 1969).

Lampham in another paper showed that after 1956 a decline of poverty had happened. During the decade 1947-1956 the proportion of families living in poverty declined by about 1 percent a year, dropping from 33 percent to 23 percent, but in the following five years the decline was only 0.4 percent annually while the number of people living in poverty increased. He also stressed that even if the pending income tax cut was passed, additional programs would be required before the aged poor, the disabled, the fatherless families would be able to rise above the threshold of poverty. Heller commented in his memorandum, dated 1 May 1963, when passing this material on to Kennedy that he found the data "distressing." It started the discussion within the Administration that eventually led to the "war on poverty" (Levitan 1969).

A message sent from Kennedy to the Congress helped enact the Mental Retardation Facilities and Community Mental Health Centers Act. It provided federal funds for research, training, and construction and staffing for community health centers across the United States (Trattner 1994).

However, nearly 40 percent of Kennedy's proposals for legislation had not been acted upon, by either House of Congress, by late July 1963 (Zarefsky 1968).

By August, the Council of Economic Advisors had a draft chapter prepared for the 1964 Economic Report of the President. It was a detailed analysis of poverty which found that over one-fifth of the nation's population lived in poverty as defined by the annual guide-lines utilized to measure poverty. A bipartisan coalition which supported the Area Development Act supported the Manpower Development and Training Act of 1962. The act stressed skills preparation in order to meet the job training and retraining necessary to offset the impact of technological displacement and other related forces in the economy.

The civil rights *March on Washington* in August, 1963, brought to the public's and the political structure's an awareness of racial discrimination in which minorities lacked the vote and basic civil rights protections."

Wright (2007) stated that: The media has sanitized King's speech, as each year the optimistic and extemporaneous "I Have a Dream" portion is replayed rather than the more radical content of the speech in which he declares that "the Negro lives on a lonely island of poverty in the midst of a vast ocean of material prosperity . . . In late June of 1963, Kennedy met with thirty civil rights leaders in an attempt to call off the march, and when that proved unsuccessful, the president co-opted the march for his own purpose—to build support in Congress for his proposed Civil Rights Act.

Congress stifled Kennedy's social legislation: the National Service Corps, the Youth Employment Act, while others were raising questions about life in America: *Night Comes to the Cumberlands* by Harry Cauldill (1963) speaking of the shortcomings of the welfare system in eastern Kentucky; *The Wasted Americans* by Edgar May (1965) described what it meant to be in the ghetto; the Committee on Youth Employment reported youth unemployment had reached a crisis level; the March on Washington civil rights movements demonstrated the unrest of a disenchanted minority most affected by poverty (SCA 1969).

Concurrently the Bureau of the Budget became "dominant in the planning of the anti-poverty programs . . . because it believed that a community action program applied locally all over the country would offer new leverage power in coordinating resources primarily of the Federal Government.

By mid-summer, the Bureau of the Budget began to

prepare their 1964 budget which would include a section on poverty.

An observer in 1963 of the PCJD suggested "a $30 million test of Ohlin's 'opportunity theory' " was what the program was all about (Sundquist 1969).

In September, Theodore Sorensen, Kennedy's special council, speech writer and one of his closest advisers, asked Heller to develop a set of measures which might be woven into a basic attack on the problems of poverty and the waste of human resources for the 1964 legislative program (CSA 1969, Moynihan 1969a).

Parallel to these activities a small group: Dave Hackett from the Juvenile Delinquency program; Dick Boone temporarily assigned to the White House Special Project from the defunct National Service Corps Task Force; Bill Canon, Chief Analyst on social legislation, Budget Bureau, and; Bill Capron, Staff Director, the Council of Economic Advisors, began to plan what kind of programs related to poverty might be started (Weeks 1967).

On 30 September Kennedy appointed a Cabinet-level committee, the Task Force of Manpower Conservation, chaired by Secretary of Labor, William Wirtz. The other members were Secretary of Defense Robert McNamara; Secretary of Health, Education and Welfare Anthony J. Celebrezze; and, General Lewis Blaine W. Hersey, Chief of the Selective Service System.

Wirtz developed programs for the war on poverty advocating remedial education for school dropouts and for retraining programs for unemployed workers which Cannon felt was "a utopia, a $ 5 billion-a-year job program" (Gillette 2010).

The Task Force produced a report titled "One-third of a Nation." It documented the very high percentages of young black men who failed mental and physical tests for the military draft came from single-parent families. The principal editor of the Report was Daniel P. Moynihan, Assistant Secretary of Labor (Patterson 2015).

The title of the report appears to be a deliberate tie back to President Franklin Roosevelt's *Second Inaugural Address*, made in January 1937, wherein he made the following statements:

> "But here is the challenge: In this nation I see tens of millions of its citizens – a substantial part of its whole population – who at this very moment are denied the greater part of what the very lowest standards of today call the necessities of life.
>
> I see millions of families trying to live on incomes so meager that the pall of family disaster hangs over them day by day.
>
> I see millions whose daily lives in city and on farm continue under conditions labeled indecent by a so-called polite society half a century ago.
>
> I see millions denied education, recreation, and the opportunity to better their lot and the lot of their children.
>
> I see millions lacking the means to buy the products of farm and factory and by their poverty denying work and productiveness to many other millions.
>
> I see one-third of a nation ill-housed, ill-clad, ill nourished."

Homer Bigart, a reporter, wrote an article, " Kentucky Miners: A Grim Winter," for *The New York Times*, 20 October, (Weeks 1967) about eastern Kentucky, in the mountains of Appalachia: "If you were *President* and lived on this creek, you wouldn't make enough to have gravy for breakfast." He described the conditions of poverty, squalor, and joblessness . . . . families that were too poor to buy clothes, children attended one-room school and rarely went past third or fourth grade, communities were isolated from impassable roads, then concluded: "The massive doling out of Federal welfare money had financed, and now sustains, a dozen or more crafty, amoral, merciless and highly effective county-wide political machines. They thrive on the present economic malaise and are powerful because the people are helpless" [emphasis in original] (Weeks 1967, Clark 2002).

In October the President instructed Franklin D. Roosevelt, Jr., Undersecretary of Commerce, to put together a comprehensive program for Eastern Kentucky.

In November $16-million had been allocated for a number of projects.

Congress did pass the Vocational Education Act of 1963 providing vocational training for young people.

Heller, Chairman of the Council of Economic Advisors, sent a memorandum on 30 October to all the cabinet members telling them:

> "As you know, Ted Sorensen has asked me to pull together for the President's consideration a set of measures which might be woven into a basic attack on the problems of poverty and waste of human resources, as part of the 1964 legislative

program."

A small group was formed to organize it.

They saw the problem of poverty as a life cycle, which they described this way:

"Poverty"

Leads to

"Cultural and Environmental obstacles to *motivation*"

Which leads to

"Poor health, and inadequate education, and low mobility

limiting *Earning Potential*"

which lead to

"Limited income opportunities"

which lead to

"Poverty."

(Moynihan 1966) [organization and emphasis in original]

This conceptualization of the "cycle of poverty" was suggested by Rist, a sociologist, in 1972 (Ille 1976) with the following diagram:

```
Poverty - - - - - - - - - leads to - - - - - cultural and environmental
   I                                          obstacles to motivation
   I                                                   I
leads to                                           leads to
   I                                                   I
limited income                                poor health, and inadequate
opportunities - - - - - - leads to - - - - - education and low mobility
                                              limiting  earning potential
```

Heller stated:

"These millions are caught in the web of poverty through illiteracy, lack of skills, racial discrimination, broken homes, ill health. These are conditions that are hardly touched by prosperity and growth. These are conditions which call for a specially focused and specially designed program" (*Newsweek* 1965).

In their report, the Council of Economic Advisors stated that "a separate nation of American poor would constitute the fifteenth largest country in the world" (Clark 2000).

Heller felt that by October that "President Kennedy had given us a green light to pull together a set of proposals for a 1964 attack on poverty" (Sundquist 1969).

Heller and his staff continued the development of the anti-poverty program although Kennedy refrained from committing himself until his meeting with Heller, 19 November 1963. In that meeting he instructed his Chief Economic Advisor to formulate legislative proposals for the next session of Congress. For any program submitted to Congress in the first weeks of 1964, planning had to start well in advance (Moynihan 1966).

No formal organization emerged although agreement was reached on a community action program and a designation "Widening Participation in Prosperity" as a means to remove the stigma from the national effort, from negative connotations of the word "poverty." William Capron recalled "that the response was disappointing, resulting in the reincarnation of all obsolete programs and stale ideas of the past with very little imagination" (SCA 1969, Gillette 2010).

Additional experiments had been funded by the Ford Foundation and a presidential committee on juvenile delinquency headed by Attorney General Robert F. Kennedy. This approach expanded into a strategy for attacking the problem of poor communities.

Heller, in a informal task force, including: Budget Director, Kermit Gordon; Willam Capron, Staff Member, Council of Economic Advisors; and, Burt Weisbord, Staff Member, Council of Economic Advisers, became convinced that none of the existing agencies could be counted on to take full responsibility for coordinating the various programs. These proposals were warmed-over revisions of various proposals that had been around for a long time that were completely unintegrated and piecemeal (Aksamit 2014). Hackett; Boone; Bill Canon; and, Paul Ylvisaker, Ford Foundation, convinced Heller to promote a new concept, an overall approach: "community action" (Weeks 1967).

Heller asked the President on 19 November whether he wanted to go forward on the assumption that the anti-poverty measure would be part of the 1964 legislative program and was told that it was. Kennedy said: "Yes, Walter, I am definitely going to have something in the line of attack on poverty in my program. I don't know what yet. But yes, keep your boys at work, and come back to me in a couple of weeks" (Levitan 1969, Moynihan 1969a, McKee 2014, Jansson 1977, Gillette 2010).

On 22 November while on a political trip to Texas to smooth over frictions in the Democratic party, Kennedy was shot and killed.

LBJ Declares War on Poverty

Johnson was sworn in as President on *Air Force One* in Dallas on 22 November 1963.

He retained the senior Kennedy appointees, some for the full term of his presidency.

The stimulus for his poverty program apparently came from conversation between Johnson and Walter Heller. On 23 November 1963, Heller mentioned to Johnson that he had been assigned by John Kennedy to draw up the concept of an anti-poverty program. "I told him very early in our conversation that the very last substantive conversation that I had with Kennedy was about a poverty program" (Gillette 2010). Johnson responded: "That's my kind of program; I'll find money for it one way or another." He then instructed Heller to speed the planning for the new initiative (Levitan 1969, McKee 2014, Weeks 1967).

Bill Moyers had joined Johnson's White House and became his most trusted Special Assistant (1963-1967). Moyers acted as the President's informal Chief of Staff (October 1964 - 1965), then as White House Press Secretary (July 1965-February1966).

Interagency meetings were held between 24 November 1963 and 1 February 1964 on the subject of poverty programs (CSA 1969).

David Hackett, President's Committee on Juvenile Delinquency and Youth Crime, and Richard Boone thought that some kind of cautious experimentation with comprehensive studies in a limited number of carefully chosen areas would be best before legislation was proposed. Budget Bureau staff member William Cannon, M.A., University of Chicago, suggested that a "development corporation" be formed for each chosen area. But by mid-December aid to communities shifted from selected areas into a large scale approach. Sam Hughes wrote a memorandum which he sent to Wilbur Cohen (Health, Education, and Welfare Department), William M. Capron (Council of Economic Advisers), Professor of Economics, mid-1950s, University of Illinois, Stanford, and Heller. The memorandum had the germ of the Community Action Program. One of the points said that what was needed was a very flexible program, because poverty was a flexible problem (Sundquist 1969, Gillette 2010).

Heller had sent a memorandum to Ted Sorenson, 20 December 1963, in which he proposed a way to break the cycle that had been described a few months ago by the Council of Economic Advisors. He suggested that the way to break this vicious cycle would be through Coordinated Community Action programs to attack the problem through three separate specifications:

> (1) "specific local areas of poverty;"
> (2) "well-organized local initiative, action, and self-help under Federally-approved plans and with Federal support;" and
> (3) "action programs to evaluate and coordinate existing Federal, State, local and private programs and to test and demonstrate new ones" (Moynihan 1966).

James L. Sundquist, Council of Economic Advisors, sent a list of about twenty proposals out of several hundred that had been collected, to Capron. This resulted in the Bureau of the Budget and the Council of Economic Advisers agreeing that community action was the solution to selecting a proposal from the many on hand (Gillette 2010).

Johnson's personal background was reflected in how he saw the proposed program. He had grown up in a region with high poverty and saw its effect on the young, and knew how the New Deal had brought relief and hope. He had grown up in the hardscrabble rural Texas Hill Country, taught the children of migrant workers as a schoolteacher in the Rio Grande Valley, Cotulla, Texas, in a small Mexican-American school where few of them could speak English, were poor and often came to class without breakfast, and in their youth felt the pain of prejudice. He had held a position as State Director of the National Youth Administration during the New Deal. Johnson's political prominence as a protégé of Franklin D. Roosevelt and as a New Deal loyalist were part of his enthusiasm for the poverty program (Zarefsky 1986, McKee 2010, Harward 2016).

President Johnson regarded Community Action not as a means for proletarian revolution but as an extension of the American political tradition of localism (Cannon 1985).

7 January 1964. A delegation of twenty-nine eastern Kentucky mine workers held a series of meetings with member of Congress and other officials of government to request federal aid for miners and their families left destitute by coal industry mechanization and dubious changes offered in union medical coverage. George Reedy, a Johnson Aid, suggested that they "go back home and organize so as to be in a better position to assist the government's efforts in the War on Poverty" (Goldstein 2012).

President Johnson (1964a) declared his "War on Poverty" in his *State of the Union* address in 8 January 1964, and later promised that their would be a dawning of a "Great Society" in which the poor and minorities would have "increased opportunity" in such fields as employment, education and housing.

In his speech he stated, in part:

> "This administration, today, here and now, declare unconditional war on Poverty in America, and I urge this congress and all Americans to join with me in this effort. It will not be a short or easy struggle – no single weapon or strategy will suffice – but we shall not rest until that war is won. The richest nation on earth can afford to win it. We can not afford to lose it. The program I shall propose will help that one-fifth of all American families with incomes too small to even meet their basic needs. Our chief weapon in a more pinpointed attack will be better schools and better health, better houses, better training and better job opportunities to help more Americans – especially young Americans – escape from squalor and misery and unemployment rolls where other citizens help to carry them. Very often a lack of jobs and money is not the cause of poverty, but the symptoms . . . our joint federal-local effort must pursue poverty – pursue it wherever it exists – in city slums and small towns, in sharecropper shacks,

or in migrant worker camps, on Indian reservations, among whites as well as Negroes, among the young as well as the aged, in the boom towns and in the depressed areas. Our aim is not only to relieve the symptoms of poverty, but to cure it, and above all to prevent it."

Until Johnson's speech on the plight of the poor, the poor were all but invisible (Humphrey 1964).

As it turned out, during his administration, the percentage of Americans living below the poverty line, dropped from 23 percent to 12 percent.

Keyserling (1964) felt that Johnson's actions "projected one of the most significant undertakings in the history of the American Presidency."

Goldstein (2012) wrote: "Only with the advent of the War on Poverty did research on poverty become an official component of investigation for the state, institutionalized and unified under a single administrative category and aligned with an overarching policy mandate."

Cohen (1965) stated it this way:

The war on poverty is providing am opportunity for us to reach democratic maturity, that is, a great fullness of economic and social as well as political democracy. To grasp the opportunity means giving up our *status quo* mentality and showing a willingness to approach the problem with a sense of innovation, creativity, and adventure. Our democracy, which was founded in freedom, can be destroyed by a state of mind which resists innovation and can be strangled by the closing of frontiers in the realm of ideas. *Status quo* was not the state of mind of our founding fathers. Theirs was a spirit of change in the cause of a society which would provide an orderly way to meet man's continuing quest to overcome economic, political, and social poverty."

The policy-makers assumed that the poor exhibited the same types of behavior in the same degree as similarly situated non-poor people (Cannon 1985).

However, the poor-whites differed from their Negro counterpart in only one aspect. The color of his skin saved them from the additional burden of discrimination (Humphrey 1964).

Moynihan wrote in 1965, (quoted in Cannon 1985):

"Nor did the War on Poverty come about because of any great surge of popular demand . . . The origins of this effort simply cannot be explained in deterministic terms. It was more rational than a political event. Men at the center of government perceived the fact . . . that ugliness, like poverty, is all around them and that the powers of government might eliminate it."

Budget Director Kermit Gordon; Walter Heller; Supreme

Court Justice-to-be Abe Fortes; some of Johnson's key advisors, argued that a new agency should be created with a separate director which would isolate the new agency from the existing bureaucracies and professional biases (Weeks 1967).

Johnson approved the Council Of Economic Advisors' *Report* calling for a "new federally-led effort" to combat poverty.

About two weeks after there meeting with George Reedy, the twenty-nine miners formed the Appalachian Committee for Full Employment (ACFE) with a mission to "organize the unemployed . . . without regard to color or creed . . . to bring union jobs with honest pay back into the area . . . to see to it that the 'War on Poverty' gets to the people who need it . . . [and] to obtain local government that works for us instead of against us." Unfortunately, as the organizations Secretary, Everett Tharp stated: "Our efforts to set up community actions to help the President's fight against poverty we were met with threats and coercion by local police." The local press attacked the organization as being Communists that had invaded Kentucky. The community action funding proposal was rejected by the Office of Economic Opportunity and no support arrived from Washington, D.C. (Goldstein 2012).

The *Economic Report of the President* (Johnson1964b), including the *Annual Report of the Council of Economic Advisors*, signed 20 January, stated, in part:

> "Americans today enjoy the highest standard of living in the history of mankind. But for nearly a fifth of our fellow citizens, this is a hollow achievement. They often live without hope, below minimum standards of decency."

"We cannot and need not wait for the gradual growth of the economy to lift this forgotten fifth of our Nation above the poverty line.

We know what must be done, and this Nation of abundance can surely afford to do it."
[emphasis in original]

"Poverty is costly not only to the poor but to the whole society. Its ugly by-products include ignorance, disease, delinquency, crime, irresponsibility, immorality, indifference. None of these social evils and hazards will, of course, wholly disappear with the elimination of poverty. But their severity will be markedly reduced. Poverty is no purely private or local concern. It is a social and national problem.
But the overriding objective is to improve the quality of life of individual human beings. For poverty deprives the individual not only of material comforts but of human dignity and fulfillment. Poverty is rarely a builder of character."

"Measurement of poverty is not simple, either conceptually or in practice. By the poor we mean those who are not now maintaining a decent standard of living – those whose basic needs exceed their means to satisfy them."

"By the standards of contemporary American society most of the population of the world is poor; and most Americans were poor a century ago."

"Some believe that most of the poor are found in the slums of the central city, while others believe that they are concentrated in areas of rural blight. Some have been impressed by poverty among the elderly, while others are convinced that it is primarily a problem of minority racial and ethnic groups. But objective evidence indicates that poverty is pervasive. To be sure, the inadequately educated, the aged, and the nonwhite make up substantial portions of the poor population. . . . The poor are found among all major groups in the population and in all parts of the country."

The following points were made:
- one-fifth of our families and nearly one-fifth of our total population were poor;
- of the poor, 44% were non-white and nearly one-half of all non-whites lived in poverty;
- the heads of over 60 percent of all poor families had only grade school educations;
- even for those denied opportunity by discrimination, education significantly

raised the chance of escape from poverty. Of all non-white families headed by a person with 8 years or less of schooling,

57 percent were poor. This percentage fell to 30 for high school graduates and to 18 percent for those with some college education;

• education did not remove the effects of discrimination;

• one-third of all poor families were headed by a person over 65, and almost one-half of the families headed by such a person were poor;

• when a family and its head had several characteristics frequently associated with poverty, the chances of impoverishment were particularly high; a family headed by a Negro young woman with less than an eighth grade education was poor in 94 out of 100 cases. Even if she was white, the chances were 85 out of 100 that she and her children would be poor."

"Poverty breeds poverty. A poor individual or family has a high probability of staying poor. Low incomes carry with them high risks of illness; limitations on mobility; limited access to education, information, and training."

"It is difficult for children to find and follow avenues leading out of poverty in environments where education is depreciated and hope is smothered. This is particularly true when discrimination appears as an insurmountable barrier. Education may be seen as a waste of time if even the well-trained are forced to accept menial labor because of their color or nationality."

"The Nation's attack on poverty must be based on a change in national attitude. We must open our eyes and mind to the poverty in our midst. Poverty is not the inevitable fate of any man. The condition can be eradicated; and since it can be, it must be done. It is time to renew our faith in the worth and capacity of all human beings; to recognize that, whatever their past history or current condition, all kinds of Americans can contribute to their county; and to allow Government to assume its responsibility for action and leadership in promoting the general welfare."

In 1910, the eleven states of the Old Confederacy contained over eighty-seven percent of all black Americans. By the 1960 census the percentage had been lowered to fifty-six and was declining. This had happened due the largest internal migration in American history, called The Great Migration, that of a population moving from the rural South to the Northern industrial cities, starting around 1900 (Adler1994). By the end of the Great Migration, 53 percent of the African-American population remained in the South, while 40 percent lived in the North, and 7 percent in the West. The bulk of the African-American population had become highly urbanized. The first wave moved from the 14 states of the South, especially Alabama, Mississippi, Louisiana, Texas, and Georgia. Initially, eight major cities attracted two-thirds of the migrants: New York and Chicago, Philadelphia, St. Louis, Detroit, Pittsburgh, and Indianapolis. Later migration increased the populations to these cities with others heading to Los Angeles, San Francisco, Oakland, Phoenix, Seattle, and Portland.

The President submitted a $97.9 billion budget request. In it he proposed a network of federal, state and local programs for the war on poverty to be backed by an initial federal authority of $500 million of new obligation funds. In all, more than $1 billion of federal money would be concentrated on the program.

On the same day (21 January), Lee White, Assistant Special Counsel sent to the Secretaries of Labor, Agriculture, HEW, Commerce, Interior, the Attorney General, and the Administration of the Housing and Home Finance Agency "the draft specifications for the poverty bill" whose title was: To authorize assistance for Community Action Programs to combat poverty (1969a).

R. Sargent Shriver, Chief, Peace Corps, while still on his trip to the Middle East and Asia on Peace Corps and other business heard that Johnson had declared a war on poverty and said "Pity the poor soul who gets charged with running this" (Joseph 2015).

29 January, 1964, Johnson said to John Kenneth Galbraith: "I saw your speech on this poverty thing. We're going to have quite a problem because its scattered all over the government . . . I sure would like for you to sit down and talk to me and talk

to Walter Heller and talk to Kermit Gordon, the director of the Budget, and get any ideas you might have as to just the best approach we could make to this thing because it means so much to the whole country. And it's got them all stimulated and inspired. We just can't afford to have it be a WPA flop" (Gillette 2010).

John Kenneth Galbraith was asked by Johnson to write a draft message for Congress urging support for the War on Poverty and Community Action. The staffs of the Bureau of the Budget and the Council of Economic Advisors wrote the document, to be sent to the White House for review. It stated:

> 1). Because existing categorical programs isolated elements in the complex structure of poverty, little progress was being made in the effort to dismantle the structure itself. The categorical programs currently operating out of a score of different federal agencies were useless; they did, however, need to be coordinated and focused before a comprehensive attack on poverty could be implemented.
> 2). In addition, new programs were needed to address the poverty problem. While these new programs would differ markedly from their categorical predecessors, it was still necessary to target for attention broad program areas such as housing and education. This would give substantive content to the War on Poverty without tying the government to ultra specific

commitments at this early stage.

3) A successful War on Poverty could only begin at the community level. Because poverty fundamentally affects the fabric of community life, any forceful effort to eradicate poverty would necessarily have an impact on the community. Because a community's relative autonomy is thereby implicated, the community should have a strong voice in developing and implementing programs intended to eliminate poverty at the local level. Therefore, the federal government's role should be limited to that of an energetic, facilitating and friendly overseer who would provide ongoing support for the community's efforts to combat poverty.

4) Poverty was a community phenomenon, not a macro-economic phenomenon. Hence poverty would not respond well to general fiscal measures initiated at the national level.

Shriver, just returned from his trip on an Executive mission for the Peace Corps met with Johnson, 31 January, to give him a personal report. When Shriver finished, as the pair walked toward the White House driveway, Johnson said, "You know we're getting this war against poverty started. I'd like you to think about that, because I'd like you to run the program for us" (Gillette 2010). Shriver felt that he didn't know anything about domestic poverty. Johnson suggested: "Well, you don't need to know much . . . You'll have an international Peace Corps – one abroad and one at home" (Aksamit 2014).

Johnson phoned (1 February) Shriver a number of times.

> (President Johnson and Sargent Shriver, 1:03 PM, February 1, 1964, telephone transcript).

> Johnson: You can write your ticket on anything you want to do there. I want to get rid of poverty, though.

> Shriver: Yes.

> President Johnson: And you can organize poverty right from the beginning. You'll have to get on the message Monday. But the Sunday papers are going to say that you're Mr. Poverty unless you've got real compelling reasons, which I haven't heard. And I'm going to say that you're going to maintain your identification with the Peace Corps and operate it to such an extent as you may think desirable.

> (President Johnson and Sargent Shriver, 1:20 PM, February 1, 1964, telephone transcript).

> Johnson: I'm going to announce your appointment at that press conference.

Shriver: What press conference?

Johnson: This afternoon.

Johnson: I want to say that you're going to be Special Assistant to the President and the executive in charge of the poverty program, and how that affects your Peace Corps relationship – you'll still maintain it, but you'll be glad to go into that at a later date. At present you're working up the organization for this. What's wrong with that?

Shriver: The problem is that it'll knock the crap out of the Peace Corps.

Johnson: Not if I tell them you're not severing your identification with the Peace Corps.

Shriver: Do you say that I'm going to continue as Director of the Peace Corps?

Johnson: Well, I'll just say you're going to continue your identification with the Peace Corps. Whatever identification you want, whatever you want to do with it.

(President Johnson and Sargent Shriver, 3:30 PM, February 1, 1964, telephone transcript).

Johnson: . . . It's done. The decision's made. The water's behind us. Now you do whatever you need to do with your Peace Corps and whatever you need to do with poverty, and let's get this advisory group together and then let's figure out how we're going to get this money through and get you the brains of this government. And I'll support you all the way to the hilt . . . This is the best thing this administration's done.

(President Johnson and Sargent Shriver, 6:28 PM, February 1, 1964, telephone transcript).

Johnson: Now, what you do is you've got to get together and see how in the hell you're going to administer this thing. Then you're going to have to get that bill and that message together. Then you're going to have to get up to that Congress and walk it through. And you've got to get on that television and start explaining it.

You'll have more influence in this administration than any man in it, because this will have to come if they want to get things. And you'll have a billion dollars to pass out.

So you just call up the Pope and tell him
you may not be at church every morning
on time, but you're going to be working
for the good of humanity.

They met and Shriver accepted.

As a brother-in-law of President Kennedy and a former Chicago businessman with a record of public service as Chairman of the Chicago Board of Education, Shriver had acquired an high reputation in his dealings with Congress as the Director of the Peace Corps from its inception in 1961. It was said that he was the only foreign-aid Administrator who was able to obtain "not just almost as much as he wants but almost as much as he asks for the Peace Corps." A reporter stated that Shriver could absorb a public attack by a Congressman "and then at night he will call up some power figure from [the Congressman's] district and the next morning [the Congressman] is unexpectedly slapped on the back of the head" (Levitan 1969).

Cynics who in the past had called the Peace Corps the "Kiddie Corps" now were praising it as Kennedy's greatest innovation (Weeks 1967).

Michael Harrington, Paul Jacobs, and Frank Mankiewicz sent (6 February) a memorandum to Shriver. "If there is any single dominant problem of poverty in the U.S., it is that of unemployment" (Moynihan 1969a).

Keyserling (1964) suggested that descriptions of the poor by color or race, age or sex, geographic location, type of employment or lack of job opportunity was a distraction from the one universal characteristic of the poor: they do not receive enough income in money or other forms to rise above poverty. To reduce poverty one most increase their incomes.

In a letter written 11 February that appointed Shriver to be his Special Assistant in the anti-poverty effort, Johnson outlined some of his duties.

> "As my representative you will direct the activities of all executive departments and agencies involved in the program against poverty. You will also be my representative in presenting to the Congress the Administration's views with respect to necessary legislation."

He empowered Shriver to attend Cabinet meetings. In addition he stated:

> "You will also undertake the coordination and integration of the federal program with the activities of state and local governments and of private persons, including Foundations, private business and industry, labor unions, and civic groups and organizations. I ask that you invite their close cooperation; that to the extent of the federal level; and that you encourage joint planning, joint programs and joint administration, wherever feasible."

Shriver accepted while remaining in charge of the Peace Corps. He later said that the poverty program was "the most discussed and most criticized domestic program in the United States" (Joseph 2015).

In 1980, during an interview Shriver said, "In fact, community action – which the people in community action thought was so revolutionary – was something that we had been running in the Peace Corps for four years before it ever got into the War on Poverty. So I thought community action was absolutely sort of normal. To me it was routine; to them it was a giant revolution" (Aksamit 2014).

Shriver held a luncheon meeting with Michael Harrington in Washington and asked, "Now you tell me how I abolish poverty?"

Harrington replied, "You've got to understand right away that you've been given nickels and dimes for this program You'll have less than a billion dollars to work with."

Shriver replied, "Well, I don't know about you Mr. Harrington, but this will be my first experience at spending a billion dollars, and I'm quite excited about it" (Raskin 1964, CSA 1969).

Shriver was now a Special Assistant to the President for the war on poverty and as such he was able to secure cooperation from various departments that had assigned representatives on his staff. Adam Yarmolinsky, Special Assistant to the Secretary of Defense and a civil rights expert, former law clerk for Supreme Court Justice Stanley F. Reed, Yale law degree, one of Kennedy's trusted idea men from the 1960 campaign, worked as unofficial Chief of Staff. Other members of Shriver's staff included: Harold Horowitz, a lawyer from HEW; Daniel P. Moynihan, Assistant Secretary of Labor; James L. Sundquist, Deputy Under Secretary of Agriculture. In addition, Hyman Bookbinder, a former member of the AFL-CIO, liaison with the labor movement, was Assistant Secretary to the Secretary of Commerce; and, Richard Boone, who had been with the Public Affairs Department of the Ford Foundation, now

White House staff working on planning the Community Action Program (Weeks 1967, Levitan 1969, Moynihan 1969a).

Three days later Shriver organized an all-day conference devoted to doing preliminary planning (*New York Times*, 8 February 1964). Those attending were: Heller and his aid William Capron; Adam Yarmolinsky, one of the top advisors to Secretary of Defense McNamara; John Kenneth Galbraith; Richard Boone; Secretary of Labor Willard Wirtz, Daniel Patrick Moynihan; Assistant Secretary of HEW, Wilber Cohen; Michael Harrington; Paul Ylvisaker; writer Paul Jacobs; John Baker and James Sundquist, two Agricultural specialists on rural problems; Minneapolis Mayor Arther Naftalin; Frank Mankiewicz (M.A. journalism - Columbia, law degree - University of California Berkeley) of the Peace Corps; Justice Department legal expert, Assistant Attorney General Norbert Schlei; Donald Petrie of Avis Rent-a-Car; Virgil Martin of Carson, Pirie & Scott; Lane Kirkland of the AFL-CIO; Richard Goodwin from the White House staff; and, James Dixon, President of Antioch College.

The Conference agreed to a three point attack: to emphasize the concept of individual economic independence; to build around the theory that poverty was cyclical; and to focus on the young. Labor was to handle jobs and training, HEW would deal with educational and health problems, and Agriculture would develop special rural programs.

In an unpublished document written by David Grossman, the community action concept was discussed by the team on the Urban Community Action study group headed by Frederick O'Reilly Hayes, who while still Assistant Commissioner of Urban Renewal was enlisted to work with the President's Task Force on the War on Poverty, and Sanford Kravitz, along with a number of federal employees loaned from various agencies as well as a small number of outside consultants. The concept was sketched out in detail with a strong feeling among the members that state governments were anti-urban (Kravitz 1969).

Conferences with members of the task force were set up to talk with people who had ideas, such as: Mayor Richard Lee, who had initiated much of New Haven's urban renewal efforts, and Mitchell Sviridoff, who had been the Executive Director, Community Progress, Inc., an antipoverty program set up by the Ford Foundation, of New Haven; Governor Terry Sanford of North Carolina, who in 1963 called for the end of job discrimination against blacks and created a biracial panel, the North Carolina Good Neighbor Council to work toward than end; Mayor John C. Houlihan of Oakland, a nationally renowned theorist on urban issues, researcher and administrator of major studies on inner-city problems, funded by the Fund for the Republic and the Center for the Study of Democratic Institutions; and Raymond Hilliard of Chicago, Director, Department of Public Aid, Cook County. Shriver listed 137 persons who had participated in the writing of the act (Zielbauer 2003, *New Haven Register* 2000, Stout 1998, Oakland Wiki 2013, Sundquist 1969).

The team read the books (total 15-20) and articles on poverty. If they looked useful they invited the author to come and discuss it. Shriver would then say: "The President has given me an assignment to eliminate poverty in this country. What would you do if you had to eliminate poverty in this country? Where would you start? Give me some ideas" (Aksamit 2014, Gillette 2010).

Edgar May, who had published *The Wasted American*, won Pulitzer Prize (1961) for a series of articles on poverty and welfare, received a phone call from Shriver, and held the following conversation:

Shriver: "My name is Sargent Shriver, and I'm down here

in Washington with the Peace Corps, and we're trying to put together a task force to do something about poverty. I read your book last night, and I just want to know, how long are you going to criticize this stuff, and when are you going to do something about it?"

May: "Well, Mr. Shriver, what do you want me to do about it?"

Shriver: "Well, for openers, can you come down here?"

May: "Sure, I'd be glad to do that. When would you like me to come?"

Shriver: "What are you doing tomorrow? No, no, no, wait a minute, tomorrow's out. I've too many things to do. But how about Sunday?"

May: "Sunday, I'm leaving for Texas, as a matter of fact – for Austin, to give a speech to the Texas Welfare Association."

Shriver: "What time is your plane?"

May thought three of four in the afternoon.

Shriver: "Well, that's plenty of time for you to come down here. We'll get you back to Kennedy Airport to get your plane."

They met at Shriver's house. When they were finished, Shriver asked, "Would you come back down a few weeks later again?"

May agree to come for thirty or sixty days, and spent ten years working in the poverty program (Gillette 2010).

Willard Wirtz, Secretary of Labor; Anthony Celebrezze, Secretary of HEW, and other government officials, wanted anti-poverty programs within their departments rather than see this activity turned over to a new agency. Wirtz also called for an employment project to create more jobs. Other members felt that doing this would mean that the money "would just get gobbled up in the usual bureaucratic crap." Idea men, Michael

Harrington and Paul Jacobs, researched poverty and provided information; legal and political experts, John Steadman, Department of Justice, and Christopher Weeks, Bureau of the Budget, drafted the actual legislation (Harward 2016).

A consensus emerged that agreed that community action programs would be only part of the war on poverty; that the design of the legislation should stress the breath of the approach (Levitan 1969). A great deal of the criticism of the concept of community action came from the Department of Labor who felt that the power of the concept threatened their operations (Cannon 1985).

Community action had been conceived as a method of combating poverty rather than a solution; it was difficult to predict immediate or long-term effects of that approach in a community (Cannon 1985).

The need for a special youth program was a reflection of a report that had circulated during the Kennedy Administration describing the high rejection rate of draftees by the arm forces due to causes associated with poverty, particularly among Negroes (Keyserling 1964, Levitan 1969).

One official present described the meeting as a "full, free discussion – I think we're on the way" (*New York Times*, 8 February 1964).

The President's Task Force on Poverty began to draft the President's special message on poverty and to put together the legislation.

The Task Force members were: Andrew Brimmer, Deputy Assistant Secretary of Commerce; William Capron, Staff Economist, Council of Economic Advisors; Ronald Goldfarb, Justice Department; Richard Goodwin, International Peace Corps Secretariat; David Hackett, Justice Department; Harold Horowitz, Associate General Counsel, HEW; Frank Mankiewics, analyst, Bureau of the Budget; Norman Shlei, Assistant Counsel, CFA, HHFA; James L. Sunquist, Deputy Undersecretary of Agriculture; Christopher Weeks, analyst, Bureau of the Budget; Stephen Polack, Office of the Solicitor General; Erich Tolmach, Labor Department; and Adam Yarmolinsky, Special Assistant to the Secretary of Defense (CSA 1969).

Hyman Bookbinder recalled these early days as "chaotic, hectic, unorganized, disorganized, but also historically productive . . . a constant traffic of people. Government people were in and out of the fifth floor of the Peace Corps building. At one point traffic got so heavy that Shriver said we have to find some more rooms, and we found some on the 12th floor." From there they moved to the Old Federal Court of Claims building, then to the basement of the unused Emergency Hospital, then to the New Colonial Hotel, finally to the newly constructed Brown Building (SCA 1969).

Shriver said, in 1980, that:

> The answer is nobody knows now or knew then *exactly* how to do that [abolish poverty]. The next reality was that everybody thought that some different way of dealing with poverty would be beneficial. Some people were devotees of giving people jobs; others of providing them with an education; others saying it was all a question of health; or another one saying it was all a question of whether they could speak English or not; another would say it was simply a question of "unleashing the free enterprise system. So the immediate

reality was if you asked ten people how to go about eliminating poverty, you'd get ten different answers [emphasis in original] (Aksamit 2014).

During the first meeting, 4 February 1964, of the task force, Richard Boone, who had served on the Ford Foundation's gray area program and the President's Juvenile Delinquency Committee, urged that the poor be assigned a more definitive responsibility in implementing community action programs. The final language in Section 202 (a)(3) was the result. The term "community action program" means a program which is developed, conducted, and administered with the maximum feasible participation of residents of the areas and members of the group served.

Whether anyone fully understood what the implications of this definition was or the stir that it might create is unknown (Jansson 1977).

To most of the task force "maximum feasible participation" was a nice sentiment and a means of giving the administrator of the program power to present segregation in the community action programs (Levitan 1969).

Sundquist stated:

"The clause . . . relating to participation of the poor was inserted with virtually no discussion in the task force and none at all on Capital Hill . . . I cannot say that I was aware of the implications of the clause. It just seemed to me like an idea that nobody could quarrel with . . . The phrase 'maximum feasible participation' entered our discussion largely at the insistence of Dick Boone . . ." (Rubin 1969).

There was some discussion as to what "maximum feasible participation" was, but no consensus: Harold Horowitz -- "that you made all good-faith efforts to have participation of the people involved in the programs, and that going further than just that wouldn't make much sense;" Norbert Schlei – simply meant that community action should include people in the community, the target population. Put in practice, this would mean that there would be advisory committees made up of poor people in the community who would alert the administrators to issues that needed to be addressed; John Baker, Assistant Secretary for Rural Development and Conservation– it meant "starting with the most downtrodden. It mean that women ought to have and equal say-so with men. It meant that poor black folks ought to have equal say-so with upwardly mobile, upper-class [people] . . . A the community level, everybody that perceived themselves to have a unique concern or contribution should be geared into the decision-making mechanism" (Aksamit 2014).

Stanford Kravitz, who worked on the Economic Opportunity bill, also felt that government programs planned by the agencies in Washington didn't make sense in matters that were going on in any particular neighborhood. It was characteristic of planning from the top down. He felt that there should be a process for planning from the bottom up (Gillette 2010).

Richard Boone had been the first president of the Juvenile Officers Association in Cook County, Illinois, the director of the Program for Detached Workers at the Young Men's Christian Association in Chicago. He had a background in sociology and criminology and had seen the importance of involving the local residents in programs (Clark 2000).

Moynihan (1969a) suggested:

> "In that sense, the community action programs of the war on poverty, with their singular emphasis on 'maximum feasible participation' of the poor themselves comprise far the most notable to date to mount a systematic social response to this problem. As the work of social scientists and professional reformers, it must stand as a perceptive and timely initiative."

Goldstein (2012) felt that "The qualifying language of feasibility insisted that the established order and relations of power were not to be disturbed, and existing limits were to be respected."

The hard nucleus of the Task Force met around the clock with representatives of business, labor, education, and government to sort out and design the program. The Task Force decided to set up a separate agency within the Executive Office to control major programs, while supervising others operating at federal, state and local levels. The problem was not with the Secretaries of Departments involved but with the hundreds of key officials who attended the dozens of meetings day after day and who resisted what they considered to be the beginnings of a gradual dissolution of the prerogatives of their departments (CSA 1969).

The President's Task Force on Manpower Conservation had issued a report that pointed out that one third of the eighteen-year-old men could not meet the basic mental or physical standards for entrance into the Armed Forces. It stated that "major proportion of these men are the products of poverty. They have inherited their situation from their parents, and unless the cycle is broken, they will almost surely transmit it to their children" (Weeks 1967).

The Task Force assigned various development projects to: the Department of Labor the jobs and job training programs; HEW, the educational and health problems; the Department of Agriculture, the special programs for rural areas; the Budget Bureau, the overall organizational plans for the poverty administration; and, to Richard Boone and Paul Ylvisaker, the work-study and volunteer programs with the Community Action concept. In addition, Shriver thought a boarding school concept for dropouts and draft rejectees would be something that would have wide impact across the nation.

The Task Force suggested several names: Youth Conservation Corps; American Youth Corps, Youth Opportunity Corps, National Youth Corps, Opportunities for Young Americans, National Training Corps, among others. Finally Shriver said"Nuts. Let's just call it the Job Corps. That's what these kids are really interested in – a job" (Weeks 1967).

Various attempts were made to have it designed by the Department of Defense, then Vernon Alden, President of the University of Ohio; Congresswoman Edith Green asked why girls and young women were excluded from the Job Corps; John Rubel, Vice-President of Litton Industries suggested that the Job Corps would seek bids from industry for designs to run the centers; staff members argued that making a profit out of poverty was appalling.

By mid-May the planning group had expanded and shifted through four different office locations. Agricultural and

Interior staffs forwarded 308 proposed locations for training centers. The one point that was felt to be the most important one was to assume that civilian personnel will be utilized exclusively in the educational aspects of the program and that it would be non-military in character and operation. Congresswoman Green had gotten an ironclad commitment to open Job Corps to women and that they would live in separate quarters from the young men.

The National Youth Administration and the Civilian Conservation Corps (CCC) of the New Deal approach were urged upon the construction of the bill by Hubert Humphrey in his discussion with Shriver and Wirtz, Secretary of Labor. The Job Corps and Neighborhood Youth Corps program became the new CCC incarnations (Cannon 1985).

In February, Dorothy Perez, a member of JOIN (Jobs or Income Now), one of the first "community unions" organized under the auspices of the Students for a Democratic Society's Economic Research and Action Project, said, at the Cleveland Community People's Conference, "We are not truly a democratic country now, for the wealthy and politicians make all the decisions for us (the poor). . . From community, to city, to state, to federal government[,] poverty can and must be abolished . . . We must act for ourselves, for the wealthy and the politicians have failed to [act]" (Goldstein 2012).

In Johnson's *State of the Union, Special Message to the Congress Proposing a Nationwide War on the Sources of Poverty to Congress*, 16 March 1964, discussing his anti-poverty bill, he stated, in part (Johnson 1964c):

> "The path forward has not been an easy
> one.
> But we have never lost sight of our goal:

an America in which every citizen shares all the opportunities of his society, in which every man has a chance to advance his welfare to the limit of his capacities.
We have come a long way toward this goal.
We still have a long way to go.
The distance that remains is the measure of the great unfinished work of our society.
To finish that work I have called for a national war on poverty. Our objective: total victory.
There are millions of Americans – one fifth of our people – who have not shared in the abundance which has been granted to most of us, and on whom the gates of opportunity have been closed.
What does poverty mean to those who endure it?
It means a daily struggle to secure the necessities for even a meager existence. It means that the abundance, the comforts, the opportunities they see all around them are beyond their grasp."

"The war on poverty is not a struggle simply to support people, to make them dependent on the generosity of others.
It is a struggle to give people a chance.
It is an effort to allow them to develop and use their capacities, as we have been

allowed to develop and use ours, so that they can share, as others share, in the promise of this nation.

We do this, first of all, because it is right that we should."

"Because it is right, because it is wise, and because, for the first time in our history, it is possible to conquer poverty. I submit, for the consideration of the Congress and the country, the Economic Opportunity Act of 1964.

The Act does not merely expand old programs or improve what is already being done.

It charts a new course."

"It will give the entire nation the opportunity for a concerted attack on poverty through the establishment, under my direction, of the Office of Economic Opportunity, a national headquarters for the war against poverty."

He called for an Office of Economic Opportunity and designated it to draw up the tactics necessary to wage the "war."

Douglass Cater, Johnson's resident education specialist who specialized in education and health matters, helped create the first legislation establishing a long-range federal aid to education, asked Johnson after the speech what possible advantage came from launching a war on poverty. The President replied, "I don't know if I'll pass a single law or get a single dollar appropriated, but before I'm through, no community in America will be able to ignore the poverty in its midst." Cater had been an original editor for *The Reporter* magazine in Washington, D.C., writing about government for 14 years before becoming Johnson's specialist (Clark 2000, *Los Angeles Times* 1995, Thomas 1995).

The Office of Economic Opportunity would have to coordinate and work out arrangements involving the established 21 governmental agencies dealing with the U.S. Welfare system in the 200 federal projects, many of which were already overlapped and interlocked. This is essentially what Johnson had instructed Shriver his job would be.

Shriver asked Adam Yarmolinsky to draft the bill, then he transferred it to the Justice Department feeling that a department of lawyers could do a better job (Cannon1985).

The poverty bill was generated and drawn up by the executive branch without congressional participation.

The Economic Opportunity Act, at least in its specifics, was very much a manifestation of the "professionalization of reform" which was proceeding apace at the time, having resulted from the convergence of such forces as Keynesian economics, Democratic politics, a certain thaw in the cold war, the civil-rights revolution, and the emergence of social sciences as an influence in government.

> ". . . the war on poverty–rather like the
> war in Vietnam–was pre-eminently the
> work of intellectuals–specifically those
> liberal, policy-oriented intellectuals who
> gathered in Washington, and in a
> significant sense came to power, in the
> early 1960's under the Presidency of John

F. Kennedy. Kennedy's Presidential campaign had propounded a fairly radical critique of American Society. The Eisenhower era had not been barren of governmental initiatives, but even when these were of massive dimensions, as in the case of the Interstate Defense and Highway Program, they intended to be most mindful of the needs and interests of the middle classes of America, with the concomitant inference that other, more pressing needs did not in fact exist" (Moynihan 1968).

Moynihan (1965, 1968) quotes Nathan Glazer:

"Without benefit of anything like the Beveridge report to spark and focus public discussion and concern, the United States is passing through a stage of enormous expansion in the size and scope of what we may loosely call the social services – the public programs designed to help people adapt to an increasingly complex and unmanageable society."

William Beveridge, the Liberal economist, published *Social Insurance and Allied Services* (November 1942) and *Full Employment In A Free Society* (1944) in Britain. His first document was influential in the founding of the welfare state in the United Kingdom in such reforms known as the Welfare State, which included National Insurance, and the creation of the National

Health Service. William Temple, the Archbishop of Canterbury said that it was "the first time anyone had set out to embody the whole spirit of the Christian ethic in an Act of Parliament."

Shriver, in 1961, had visited every single Congressman and Senator to tell them the Peace Corps story in order to gain support. He did the same thing about the proposed law for the war on poverty (SCA 1969).

Edgar S. Cahn and Jean C. Cahn wrote (1964) "The War on Poverty: A Civilian Perspective" in the *Yale Law Journal*, arguing that neighborhood law offices and neighborhood lawyers should be a part of an anti-poverty effort. Edgar Cahn worked as Shriver's Executive Assistant, and Jean S. Cahn joined the OEO staff as a consultant from the State Department. Her task was to establish national level legal services program for the poor (Clark 2002). The Legal Services Program became part of the Special Programs and Assistance section inside the Economic Opportunity Act of 1964. In September 1965, the American Bar Association recommended a Baltimore trial attorney, Clint Bamberger, who was selected to be the first Director of the Legal Services Program (Clark 12002).

Before the bill, the Economic Opportunity Act, went to Congress, the leadership agreed to assign it to the House Committee on Education and Labor, and the Senate Committee on Labor and Public Welfare. The chairmen of the other committees agreed. However, the relevant committees were unable to assess all parts of the bill thoroughly.

The Administration's draft bill was introduced in Congress, 16 March 1964, with hearings beginning on the next day by the House Education and Labor Subcommittee on Poverty. The legislation was sponsored by Senator McNamara, Michigan, and Congressman Phillip M. Landrum, Georgia, the two men were at opposite poles of the Democratic party when it came to domestic issues (Moynihan 1968).

Moynihan (1965) felt:

> "There are two aspects of the poverty program which distinguish it from earlier movements of its kind: The Initiative came largely from within. The case for action was based on essentially esoteric information about the past and probable future course of events."

> "The essential fact is that the main pressure for a massive government assault on poverty developed within the Kennedy-Johnson Administration, among officials whose responsibilities were to think about just such matters."

> "More importantly, they have at their command an increasing fund of information about social conditions in the United States."

> "Significantly, the war on poverty began in the same year of the great tax cut. The President was not forced to choose between measures; he was able to proceed with both. In that sense, the war on poverty began not because it was necessary (which it was), but because it was possible."

Nathan Glazer (1965) wrote:

" 'Poverty in the richest country in the world' – this is the first paradox with which we are confronted."

"We cannot easily resolve the question of why an income that would spell comfort in some countries is actually poverty in Americas, but there is not question that it is so."

"If the paupers of Edwardian England lived on tea and bread and margarine and scraps of meat, then the poor of our country are doing only a little better. If the poor fifty years ago lived in crowded and crumbling rooms, with inadequate plumbing and heating, then we find the same living conditions for a large part of our poor population today. There have been gains – the automobiles that have bemused some writers on poverty, the television sets that are almost universal, the clothing that is cheaper and better than that of fifty years ago, the public health service. But it is odd to note the extent to which the improvement of living conditions of the poor, which are undoubtably reflected in the higher income level we now draw to mark the line of poverty, have gone to peripheral improvements – televison sets replacing the stoop for conversation and the automobile replacing cheap public transportation."

"The chief reason why our impoverished population forms a major social problem, and England's does not, is because of who they are." [emphasis in original]

"One of the most characteristic enterprises we have seen proposed in the Community Action Programs to fight poverty consists of efforts to increase pressure on government bureaucracies."

"When local government protests that federal money is used to attack it and its services, the Federal administrator will have to explain: but that is the only way to get you to do your job."

The presentation made to Congress stated that poverty "is handed down from generation to generation in a cycle of inadequate education, inadequate homes, inadequate jobs and stunted ambitions"(Raab 1966).

Barry Goldwater felt that "Under the enterprise system, America was already winning the War on Poverty; federal welfare was leading to rates of fraud of 50 percent or more; the idea that people cannot find jobs because of insufficient education is "like saying that people have big feet because they wear big shoes. The fact is that most people have no skills, have no education for the same reason – low intelligence or low ambition" (Perlstein 2001).

Keyserling (1964) argued that "the many millions who are deprived" live in a situation that is ironic; "the vast majority of them have breadwinners who are hard-working and employed, and thus they have obtained 'respectability;' but their right to a respectable level of living has not been honored" and that "even when working, women in general receive less pay than men . . . The median pay of women working full-time the year round is about 60 percent that of men." He further pointed out that: "In 1963, more than 43 percent of all nonwhite families in the United States lived in poverty, contrasted with less than 16 percent of all white families." And "When the head of household families are grouped within the industrial classification by job type that 44 percent who are in agriculture, forestry, fisheries are in poverty; poverty rate of 38 percent for personal services, and 18 percent in entertainment or recreation services."

Humphrey (1964) wrote that three-fifths of the farms produced about one-fifth of market commodities. For the most part they are farms on thin soil. These farmers, farmers living in poverty, are scattered through: the Appalachian areas; the southern Piedmont and Coastal Plains; the Southeast hilly regions; the Ozarks; and, the Mississippi Delta.

Throughout the Congressional hearing by the House Education and Labor Subcommittee on Poverty, chaired by Adam Clayton Powell, (D), New York, it was stressed that local community action programs should be flexible in order to develop, oversee and coordinate the design and delivery of a series of programs specifically suited to the particular situation. A program for a rural area would be different than an urban one.

Shriver had testified before the House Committee and

stated that "it was an authority which the President wants because he wants to be at the focal point with respect to this aspect of our domestic effort." On 17 March he further stated: the bill was both "new in the sweep of its attack" as well as "prudently planned" as "it does not raise the national budget by a single dollar" (Sundquist 1969).

A precedent existed for this unique position.

By the terms of the Executive Reorganization Act of 1939 and the recommendations of the Committee on Administration Management, President Roosevelt had promoted the cause of scientific management and had established tools for a national governing body in initiating bureaucratic changes. A 1939 report provided guidelines for future executive reorganization, one of which was the need to install coordinating "managerial arms" for the President in the area of personnel, fiscal policy, and national planning. They were all to be at a level between the President and his Cabinet (SCA 1969).

Though the subcommittee was chaired by Adam Clayton Powell, (D), the Chairman of the parent committee, Phil Landrum of Georgia was asked to sponsor the legislation (H.R. 10440) in order to give the bill an aura of conservative support. In addition to the 1,741 pages of testimony, Chairman Powell commissioned an additional preparation of a volume of facts relating to poverty by the technicians in other appropriate executive departments (Levitan 1969).

Powell stated as part of his opening statement: "In far too many communities, giant fiestas of political patronage have been encouraged on both the local and the State levels of the war on poverty administrative mechanisms, having been seduced by politicians who have used the reservoir of poverty funds to feed their political hacks at the trough of mediocrity" (Zarefsky 1986).

Shriver, testified that the major thrust of the bill, the

Economic Opportunity Act, was contained in Title II, the community action program. Its purpose was to "change institutions as well as people." It challenged "hostile or uncaring or exploitive institutions," attempting to make them responsive to the peculiar needs of the "whole community." It departed from traditional federal welfare approaches by placing the main responsibility on local communities, the reason being that local leadership was more in touch with indigent problems, it would be more acceptable to the states, that it enabled communities to unify through widespread local participation (SCA 1969).

Historian Alice O'Connor felt that "the community action idea held considerable appeal: It kept program responsibility out of the hands of any single one of the 'old line' federal agencies, it offered a way to cut through bureaucratic inefficiencies, it had an attractive air of localism while asserting a strong federal role in community change, and it would not require major new spending. It also seemed innovative, a major selling point as the administration tried to construct its domestic program in the aftermath of President Kennedy's assassination – and to come up with something distinctive for President Johnson to propose" (Aksamit 2014).

Eighty-five witnesses appeared during the twenty days of hearing, seventy-six of them speaking in favor of the bill. Of those opposed, three represented the Chamber of Commerce, the National Association of Manufacturers, and the Farm Bureau Federation, while four Republican members of the Joint Economic Committee wrote the minority report, two were educators who felt that the bill was misdirected and the programs unnecessary. Of those in favor were twelve from technical advisors representing government statistical services; twenty-nine members of the administration or original members of the Task Force; the rest represented social-welfare, civic and religious organizations, state and local governments, and business (SCA 1969). Only Attorney General Robert Kennedy discussed the probable impact of Title II upon local communities (Davidson 1969). For two weeks the Administration's top brass appeared before the committee to push to bill forward: The Secretaries of Defense; Labor; Interior; Commerce; Agriculture; HEW; the Attorney General; and Jack Conway, United Auto Workers; Senator Pat McNamara, Michigan; and Warren Magnuson, Washington (Levitan 1969, Zarefsky 1968).

Robert Kennedy, Attorney General, discussed "maximum feasible participation" as a requirement:

> The institutions which affect the poor – education, welfare, recreation, business, labor – are huge, complex structures, operating far outside their control. They plan programs for the poor, not with them. Part of the sense of helplessness and futility comes from the feeling of powerlessness to affect the operation of these organizations.
>
> The community action programs must basically change these organizations by building into the program real representation for the poor. This bill calls for "maximum feasible participation of residents." This means the involvement of the poor in planning and implementing programs: giving them a real voice in their institutions (Adler 1994).

Congressman Pucinski, on the committee, remarked: "As far as I know, this is the first time in the history of this country that all of the Cabinet members, except the Secretary of State, have testified in support of an important measure. The President has assigned this as one of the most important measures of his administration" (Zarefsky 1968).

Arguments and voting tended to follow partisan lines in both the House and the Senate. In the House, Charles Goodell, (R), New York questioned the absence of a prohibition against aid to religious groups; Robert Taft, Jr., (R), Ohio felt community action programs ignored the proper federal-state relationships; Toman Pucinski, (D), Illinois compared farm development corporations scheme with "the type of farming we most often criticize behind the Iron Curtain;" Peter Frelinghuysen, (R), New Jersey, said that the bill charted "a new and unjustified course for governmental responsibility in general and for the Federal role in particular" . . . an influence that would "permeate every nook and cranny of civic responsibility – public and private." He further argued: "The label of 'anti-poverty' on this poisonous concoction does not alter its content. Every power-struck totalitarian regime in modern history has promised to eliminate poverty. Such nonsense has been the lowest common denominator of totalitarianism of both the right and of the left" (Zarefsky 1968).

In the Senate, Barry Goldwater and John Tower produced a minority report that stated that The Administration's technique in ram-rodding the bill through Congress recalled "Madison Avenue" and "The Wizard of Oz" practices. It was a "poverty grab bag" based on obsolete programs which treated the results and not the causes of poverty. Some of its program were totally alien to the best traditions of our country (SCA 1969).

In the House and the Senate more than twenty-five amendments were put forth by the Republicans varying from abolishing the Office of Economic Opportunity all together, to reducing the authorizations, the way funding would work for community actions, or to spin off the programs to existing federal bureaucracies (SCA 1969).

It should be noted here that it was apparently the behavior of Chairman Powell during these hearings that alienated a number of Republicans to such a degree that they never felt that they were part of the program. Powell had excluded Republicans from raising their objections in the hearings and from subsequent participation in amendments to the bill (Bailey and Duquette 2014). Republicans charged that the hearings were structured in the Administration's favor, that opposition was gagged. In one instance when Republicans on the committee tried to get additional information that they felt was needed before the legislation could be drafted, Powell stated: "I am the chairman. I will run this committee as I desire" (Levitan 1969). From those hearings to the present day the Republicans have worked to undo the overall program proposed by the Economic Act of 1964 and to replace it with one their own. There is also some indication that this also stemmed from Shriver who was not interested in Republican-sponsored amendments to a bill written by the Johnson administration.

A Republican alternative bill (H.R. 11050) was introduced by Peter H. Frelinghuysen, (R), New Jersey. He charged that the bill currently proposed would produce a confusion of purpose, create a "poverty czar," and usurp the authority of Cabinet officers. His bill required that states had to contribute one-third of the total funds for the first year and one-half the following two years. This bill was rejected by a vote of 295 to 117. No Democrat voted for it, 49 Republicans opposed the bill as well

(Levitan 1969).

Shriver, responding to all the criticism replied: "for six months we had our sign out like a lawyer's shingle, begging for constructive ideas on how to wage this war . . . Those who have challenged the substantive parts of our program have been asked by me to come up with something better. For half-year I've been saying, 'If you've got a better mousetrap, show us,' and they proposed nothing" (Raskin 1964, SCA 1959).

Raskin (1964) wrote: " . . . Shriver, accustomed to easy sailing on bills to expand the Peace Corps, learned how savage the men on Capitol Hill could be in dealing with a measure many of them did not like. Northern Republicans, convinced the poverty bill was a political hoax, and Southern Democrats, convinced it was another device for promoting "civil rights" fought against it.

Once all the hearings were completed, Powell caucused with the Democrats on the committee to reach a majority consensus and to presented it to the Republicans as a final take-it-or-leave bill.

From the hearings onward the Republicans worked to undo the overall program and replace it with one that had their input and approval.

At an April press conference, Richard Nixon called the war on poverty a "cruel hoax."

Johnson suggested that such statements were the sort "who would turn the American dream into a nightmare."

Dave Martin, (R), Nebraska, and M.G. Snyder, (R), Kentucky, stated that "The President's poverty program is nothing more than an election year gimmick."

William Hanes Ayres, (R), Ohio, felt that the poverty program had been "mired in politics ever since [1964], providing the richest lode of political patronage ever mined by political gold diggers . . . Now, this should come as no surprise to anyone, because it was planned that way." Glen Andrews, (R), Alabama, saw the war on poverty as "a political extravaganza, a political carnival – filled with barkers, shell game artists, cupie dolls, and cotton candy" (Zarefsky 1986).

Shriver in his testimony before the Senate Committee on Labor and Public Welfare said: "I think that if the national administration had failed to propose this bill, just because it was afraid that someone would say that it was an election year gimmick, as they have, then I would think the federal Government would be derelict in its responsibilities."

Fearful that some state governors were pushing for state's right in order to sidetrack the proposed activities, the drafters of the Administration bill bypassed the states and fashioned direct relationships between the federal government and the localities (Levitan 1969).

Senator Gaylord Nelson, (D) of Wisconsin, (2 April 1964) stated, in part, that:

> "But we do have a unique opportunity presented to us, and instead of dwelling on the crisis in conservation, I would like today to point out the dimensions of this new opportunity.
> The opportunity comes to us in President Johnson's "war on poverty," and the direct way in which that war is tied to the conservation of natural resources."
>
> "It is true that some of the worst poverty is in the cities of America, but about one-sixth of our poor people live on farms and

almost one-third more live in rural areas."

"Last October, there were 730,000 young men and women between the ages of 16 and 21 who were out of school and out of work. This was a 22% increase over the previous year. Many of them live in impoverished rural areas, isolated mountain communities or city slums. Many of them lack motivation, and life in America offers them little but a continuation of their life in grinding poverty" (Nelson 1964).

Walter Reuther, Leader of the United Automobile Workers (UAW) union, stated (8 April 1964) before the subcommittee of the House Committee on Education and Labor that:

"Poverty in America is more destructive of human values because (it) not only robs people of economic opportunity but spiritually. They are invisible citizens of America. When they are set aside they are denied the sense of belonging and the sense of participating as useful members of our society. They are denied their measure of human dignity" (CSA 1969).

On 5 May 1964, four months after Lyndon Johnson committed America to a "War on Poverty," Sargent Shriver addressed a meeting of the Advertising Council in Washington,

DC. At the time, Shriver was working two jobs: he was head of the Peace Corps and, as a Special Assistant to run Johnson's anti-poverty initiative.

He talked of a meeting that he'd had with an unnamed journalist the previous week. He said that the journalist had stated that "before you can do anything about poverty, you'll have to fumigate the closet in which Americans keep their ideas about the poor. You'll have to rid America of all its clichés about the poor, clichés like the one which says that only the lazy and worthless are poor, or that the poor are always with us." His response to that comment was: "I think she may be right. Our minds are so cluttered up with myths, slogans and clichés about the poor that it would be a great public service if you would help us clear the air."

He added: "It simply isn't true that the poor enjoy poverty. Quite the opposite. They resent it. Wherever local communities have started programs to help the poor help themselves, the response has exceeded all expectations ... It is gibberish to say that families enjoy living in rat-infested slums or that they want only a poor education" (Abramsky 2014).

Sometime in May, President Johnson instructed Robert McNamara, Secretary of Defense, to pare defense production cost, and called for a general federal job curb. Johnson called this reallocation of funds as a form of wealth redistribution, taking from "those who have it to those who don't have it." Shriver explained that this meant taking from the "have government programs," and not people (CSA 1969).

During the summer both major political parties held Presidential nominating conventions.

The Republican Party platform contained a plank condemning the poverty program as overlapping and contradicting "42 existing Federal poverty programs, and charged that the program "would dangerously centralize Federal controls." Goldwater was nominated on the first ballot (Weeks 1967).

The Democrats gave unqualified endorsement as they pledged to "carry the war on poverty as a total war against the causes of human want" (CSA 1969).

Shriver summarized for the delegates the meaning of poverty; he described the Democrats as the party which historically "cared and acted" for the poor and that the President's program was no hoax or gimmick, but a practical effort to enable the unfortunate to get back on their feet, turning "relief-receivers into taxpayers." The war on poverty was "the challenge to our generation – to build a world for our children in which relief is unknown and opportunities are unlimited."

The local community action program, the primary weapon in the War of Poverty, had been discussed as a conservative action, tested by experience, and was a reflection of the values of a grass-roots democracy. The Senate Labor and Public Welfare Committee felt that the community action program was based upon "the traditional and time-tested American methods of organizing local community action to help individuals, families, and whole communities to help themselves" (Zarefsky 1968).

The Office of Economic Opportunity was to be the President's managerial arm which could cut across Departmental lines to facilitate coordination.

In May, Eric Goldman, an on leave Princeton history professor serving as a Special Assistant to the White House, came up with a phrase that he felt was a vision of dignity, identity, and fulfillment in the affluent society – "Great Society" (Goldstein 2001).

President Johnson gave two speeches, one in May and

one in June, stating what he proposed.

He gave a *Commencement Speech* to the graduating class and the state's Congressional delegation at the University of Michigan on 22 May 1964 (Johnson 1964d). He said, in part:

> "For a century we labored to settle and subdue a continent. For half a century we called upon unbounded invention and untiring industry to create an order of plenty for all of our people. The challenge of the next half century is whether we have the wisdom to use that wealth to enrich and elevate our national life, and to advance the quality of our American civilization.
>
> Your imagination and your initiative and your indignation will determine whether we build a society where progress is the servant of our needs, or a society where old values and new vision are buried under unbridled growth. For in your time we have the opportunity to move not only toward the rich society and the powerful society, but upward to the Great Society.
>
> The Great Society rests on abundance and liberty for all. It demands an end to poverty and racial injustice, to which we are totally committed in our time. But that is just the beginning.
>
> The Great Society is a place where every child can find knowledge to enrich his

mind and to enlarge his talents. It is a place where leisure is a welcome chance to build and reflect, to enrich his mind and to enlarge his talents. It is a place where leisure is a welcome chance to build and reflect, not a feared cause of boredom and restlessness.

It is a place where the city of man serves not only the needs of the body and the demands of commerce but the desire for beauty and the hunger community. It is a place where man can renew contact with nature. It is a place which honors creation for its own sake and for what it adds to the understanding of the race. It is a place where men are more concerned with the quality of their goals than the quantity of their goods.

But most all, the Great Society is not a safe harbor, a resting place, a final destination, a finished work. It is a challenge renewed, beckoning us toward a destiny where the meaning of our lives matches the marvelous products of our labor"

Johnson gave a *Commencement Speech* (Johnson 1964e), from drafts, 3 and 4 June, by Moynihan, and presidential assistant speech writer Richard Goodwin, *"To Fulfill These Rights,"* at Howard University, 4 June 1964, a federally chartered, private, coeducational, nonsectarian, historically black university in Washington, D.C. as Johnson received an honorary degree of Doctor of Laws (Rainwater and Yancey 1967). He said, in part:

> "Freedom is not enough. You do not wipe away the scars of centuries by saying: Now you are free to go where you want, and do as you desire, and choose the leaders you please."

> "You do not take a person who, for years, has been hobbled by chains and liberate him, bring him up to the starting line of a race and then say, "You are free to compete with all the others," and still justly believe that you have been completely fair."

> "Thus it is not enough just to open the gate of opportunity. All our citizens must have the ability to walk through those gates."

> "In far too many ways American Negroes have been another nation: deprived of freedom, crippled by hatred, the doors of opportunity closed to hope."

> "Thirty-five years ago the rate of unemployment for Negroes and whites was about the same. Tonight the Negro rate is twice as high."

"First, Negroes are trapped – as many whites are trapped – in inherited, gateless poverty. They lack training and skills. They are shut in, in slums, without decent medical care. Private and public poverty combine to cripple their capacities."

"But there is a second cause – much more difficult to explain, more deeply grounded, more desperate in its force. It is the devastating heritage of long years of slavery; and a century of oppression, hatred, and injustice."

"These differences are not racial differences. They are solely and simply the consequences of ancient brutality, past injustice, and present prejudice. They are anguishing to observe. For the Negro they are a constant reminder of oppression. For the white they are a constant reminder of guilt. But they must be faced and they must be dealt with and they must be overcome, if we are ever to reach the time when the only difference between Negroes and whites is the color of their skin."

"What is Justice, for what is justice?"

"It is to fulfill the fair expectations of man."

"Thus, American justice is a very special thing. For, from the first, this has been a land of towering expectations. It was to be a nation where each man could be ruled by the common consent of all – enshrined in law, given life by institutions, guided by men themselves subject to its rule. And all – all of every station and origin – would be touched equally in obligation and in liberty."

"Beyond the law lay the land. It was a rich land, glowing with more abundant promise than man had ever seen. Here, unlike any place yet known, all were to share in the harvest."

"And beyond this was the dignity of man. Each could become whatever his qualities of mind and spirit would permit – to strive, to seek, and if he could, to find his happiness."

"This is American justice. We have pursued it faithfully to the edge of our imperfections, and we have failed to find it for the American Negro."

"So, it is the glorious opportunity of this generation to end the one huge wrong of the American Nation, in so doing, to find America for ourselves, with the same immense thrill of discovery which gripped those who first began to realize that here, at last, was a home for freedom."

"All it will take is for all of us to understand what this country is and what this country must become."

"The scripture promises: "I shall light a candle of understanding in thine heart, which shall not be put out."

"Together, with millions more, we can light that candle of understanding in the heart of all America."

"And, once lit, it will never again go out."

This speech utilized various facets of Moynihan's report, completed in March 1965, labeled "for official use only," *The Negro Family: The Case for National Action*, issued by the Office of Policy Planning and Research, Depart of Labor. It had been prepared by Moynihan, Assistant Secretary of Labor, assisted by Paul Barton and Ellen Broderick, members of the staff (Rainwater and Yancey 1967).

In reference to the Moynihan Report, Herbert Gans wrote to Richard Goodwin and stated (Rainwater and Yancey 1967):

I think the emphasis [on family difficulties] is all to the good, if not overdone. There is danger, however, that it may result in a wave of social work and psychiatric solutions intended to change the Negro female-based family to a middle class type. Such solutions could maintain the already overly paternalistic and manipulative way with which we have been dealing with the problems of the Negro, and more important, they could deflect attention away from the economic causes of the Negro problem. Whatever the ravages of slavery, the female-based Negro family today is the result of the current unemployment among Negro males, and secondarily, of the pattern of social welfare, especially ADC, which as you know encourages women to reject (or hide) their men, and in both cases, downgrades their familial role and power. These two causal factors ought to be emphasized in the forming of new programs.

President Johnson waged a campaign soliciting public support for the Economic Opportunity Act, enlisting organizations from the Daughters of the American Revolution to the Socialist Party; visiting poverty-stricken regions, highlighting their conditions and reminding Congressmen of their responsibilities to their constituents; in some cities and states he promised federal aid as soon as the bill was passed, and visited the AFL-CEO Communications Workers convention (SCA 1969).

W. Marvin Watson became, in 1965, the White House

Chief of Staff in-all-but-title as White House Appointments Secretary to help to coordinate the passage of much of the Great Society domestic agenda.

The House vote on the bill hinged on two blocks of undecided Congressmen.

One bloc was a dozen liberal to moderate Republicans, mainly from Pennsylvania in the Northeast, smarting from the Goldwater steamroller at the Republican Nominating Convention, who were sympathetic to the overall aims of the program but faced the problems that this was a Democratic bill backed by a Democratic President. In addition it appeared the bill was designed to force compliance with the Civil Rights Act. They got an agreement for their support that a percentage of Job Corps enrollees would be consigned to a Youth Conservation Corps.

The other bloc, marginal southern states Democrats, who tended to share the historic southern distrust of northern intellectuals and know-it-alls, illustrating the often quoted statement by many politicians "that politics is a blood sport," in their dislike of Adam Yarmolinsky, who they claimed as one "who had been even more instrumental than Shriver in designing the structure of the poverty bill." They wanted him out of the picture. William Ayres, (R), Ohio, quoted an internal memo that implied that the Defense Department was using funds to build and equip Job Corps centers before the bill was actually passed. Shriver said, "We were meeting in John McCormack's office. Cooley, chairman of the North Carolina delegation and chairman of the [House] Agriculture Committee, was there, and some other congressmen, and all the whips. The Speaker had all the whips in. These people, led by Cooley, said that if Adam Yarmolinsky was in the program, they would not vote for it to pass the Congress (Gillette 2010).

Christopher Weeks, one of the task force members, noted (Weeks 1967) that "the southern Democrats had asked for and gotten their pound of flesh – assurance that the abrasive, intellectual Jew of Russian extraction who had roughed up the military rank and file in the Defense Department, and who was reputed to have been responsible for orders forcing base commanders in the South to declare segregated facilities in nearby town off-limits to servicemen, would thereafter be barred from any job in Johnson's poverty program."

The North Carolina group continued to press the question of Yarmolinsky's position (Clark 2000).

Among southern Congressmen, Yarmolinsky's image was that of a liberal Jewish intellectual, whose mother, the Poet Babette Deutsch, was a professed communist (Clark 2000).

Lewis (2000) wrote:

"Mr. Yarmolinsky also was Mr. McNamaras unofficial liaison to the nation's liberal, intellectual community, explaining and defending the Defense Department. He was an apostle of modernizing the government, and, after World War II, he advocated that military bases be located only near communities that were desegregated and once proposed using military bases to train poverty-stricken youths in job skills.

Mr. Yarmolinsky served first as a talent recruiter for the President-elect Kennedy and, inside the administration, as a special assistant to Mr. McNamara. In that role, he was a principal force in bringing modern management to the Pentagon.

Mary McGrory, the columnist, attributed the dislike of Mr. Yarmolinsky to his efforts at integration, jealousy over his brilliance and the fact that he was anathema to Southern Congressmen. 'He is an egghead, a New Yorker, and the son of liberal intellectual parents,' Ms. McGrory wrote. 'Barely concealed anti-Semitism contributed to his downfall as well.' "

To get their votes, Phil Landrum, (D),Georgia, announced that Yarmolinsky would be excluded from the operations of the Office of Economic Opportunity "on the highest authority" (Weeks 1967, CSA 1969).

Yarmolinsky returned to the Defense Department working for Secretary Robert McNamara, and later on special assignment to the White House. Shriver later said, "That was the most unpleasant experience I ever had in the Government of the United States. In fact, despite the fact that I didn't think I had any choice, I felt then as if I ought to just go out and vomit, it was such a despicable proceeding. And if fact, I didn't admire myself for the role I had to play in it" (Gillette 2010, Clark 2000).

Jack Conway, United Auto Workers, stepped into the position of chief of staff vacated by Yarmolinsky (Zarefsky 1968).

Herbert J. Gans in his review of *The Wasted American* by Edgar May (Gans 1964) wrote, in part:

Americans have often been described as impulsive consumers of material goods whose tastes change with frequent regularity. Much the same can be said about the growing group of Americans who consume social problems—or at least books, articles, and plays about them. Just a short time ago, the dominant problems were National Purpose, Conformity, and Suburbia but they have been abruptly replaced by the Negro Problem, and, more recently, by Poverty.

Almost every society has persecuted its poor, and the Calvinist strain in American culture has further reinforced and justified the tendency here. But the more immediate reasons lie elsewhere. An important one is that the business community remains opposed to taxation for welfare purposes. Another is that the working-class and lower-middle-class population which forms the bulk of the taxpayers has little sympathy for the poor. Not far removed from poverty themselves, many of them are fearful of backsliding and exaggerate the moral failings of the poor. Others vote down public expenditures for welfare because they cannot do anything about the rising prices at the supermarket. Still others need a group that they can feel superior to.

. . . the poor cannot expect substantial or

rapid help from either the social welfare profession or the poverty warriors. Since poverty is preserved by our politics, it will have to be attacked through political means that will become available only through direct action by the poor themselves. Such action requires greater political strength and skill than they can now muster, and must probably await the time when automation has further enlarged the ranks of the unemployed. Even then, effective political action will depend upon whether the newly unemployed will join ranks with the present victims of poverty and discrimination in an organized coalition that can formulate and press demands for economic and social change.

Meanwhile, the upper middle class will write, read—and review—books like The Wasted Americans, and leave the rest of the society free to keep the poor in their place.

On 19 June 1964, the Capital Building office of Hubert Humphrey saw reporters, Senators, and staff shouting, cheering as The Civil Rights Bill of 1964 passed (Weeks 1967).

July 2, 1964, the Civil Rights Act of 1964 was signed by President Johnson who said to his staff: "I think we have just gave the South to the Republicans for your lifetime and mine" (Goldstein 2001). The Civil Rights Act of 1964 (Pub.L. 88–352, 78

Stat. 241), outlawed discrimination based on race, color, religion, sex, or national origin. It prohibited unequal application of voter registration requirements, racial segregation in schools, employment, and public accommodations.

Goldwater felt that the bill would:

> "Require the creation of a federal police force of mammoth proportions. It also bids fair to result in the development of an 'informer' psychology in great areas of our national life – neighbors spying on neighbors, workers spying on workers, businessmen spying on businessmen, where those who would harass their fellow citizens for selfish and narrow purposes will have ample inducement to do so. These, the federal police force and an 'informer' psychology, are the hallmarks of the police state and landmarks in the destruction of a free society" (Goldstein 2001).

On 8 August 1964, the House passed the bill, the Economic Opportunity Act, by roll-call vote, 226-185. President Johnson had held 60 of the southern Democrats and an additional 22 Republicans along with his base of 144 northern and western Democrats. On 11 August the Senate passed it 61-34 with 10 of 32 Republicans in support (Sundquist 1969).

The Task Force members who had worked so hard, nearly a hundred, celebrated in Georgetown at a victory party although for many it was a time for tears and disillusionment over the Adam Yarmolinksy debacle (Weeks 1967).

The Economic Opportunity Act was the most experimental initiative for instituting social change since the New Deal of the early 1930s mainly because it required participation of the poor (Adler 1994).

All the programs within the bill functioned on the logic that cultural values created poverty (Aksamit 2014), mostly as an implicit understanding, but explicitly stated during much of the designing phases.

Donald Baker had been counsel to the Senate Select Committee on Poverty. He became general counsel of the Office of Economic Opportunity in November 1964 (Clerk 2000). Changes in the bill were few. Congress added a provision exempting the first $85 along with half the additional monthly income earned by the poor for purposes of determining basic needs under public assistance programs as most states deducted those earnings from the allowance a family was entitled to receive (Levitan 1969).

On 14 August 1964, the House Appropriations Committee subcommittee began hearings.

Shriver said, in part:

> "I can just say the objective of the community action program is to get action initiated against poverty at the point closest to where the poor people live by encouraging and inspiring local government units, and local private voluntary agencies to initiate programs at the local level."

> "The philosophy behind this is that poverty can be analyzed and combated

best by those who are closest to it; so, rather than putting the individual communities of the United States in a planning straightjacket originated here, or in a state capitol, we are trying to take this responsibility as close to the local government level as we can" (CSA 1969).

Subcommittee Chairman John F. Fogarty (D), Rhode Island, concluded the day's hearing by saying to Shriver, "I think you have done a good job today in justifying this appropriation. I wish you a lot of luck. You will need it."

"I will need it," came the reply.

Shriver was sworn in as Director, OEO, 20 August, 1964. Edgar May said, "The Bible used was stole from a warehouse belong to the Department of Commerce by Emedio Tini. We always felt that was appropriate, because where else would the Department of Commerce keep a Bible but in a warehouse. So that's where we copped the Bible from" (Gillette 2010).

On 22 September the House approved the appropriation's bill by a roll-call vote, 209-103.

The House-Senate Conference Committee appropriated $800 million for the program (CSA 1969).

The peak combat period in Vietnam cost $500 million a week.

During the signing (20 August 1964) of the Economic Opportunity Act of 1964 (P.L. 88-452), ceremonies in the White House Rose Gardens, Johnson signed the Act into law utilizing 72 give-away pens. He proclaimed: "The days of the dole in our country are numbered. We are not content to accept the endless growth of relief roles or welfare roles. We want to offer the forgotten fifth of our people opportunity and not dole."

Congress, before passing the act, added in a governor's veto of Job Corps centers and all contracts with non-governmental agencies including community-action agencies. Governors saw the veto as a weapon for coordinating poverty efforts by insuring that their political position would not be jeopardized by policies and "patronage" associated with the programs. However this veto was only a token power as the Director of the Office of Economic Opportunity (OEO) was permitted to reverse a veto after thirty days if he wished. A few governors used vetoes to gain political capital by fighting OEO's "waste and extravagance" (Levitan 1969). Thirty vetoes were invoked in ten states during OEO's first three years of which Governors Wallace of Alabama (George and Lurleen) and Governor Ronald Reagan of California accounted for three of every five vetoes (Davidson 1969).

In the bill the Office of Economic Opportunity was authorized and established in the Executive Office of the President.

In his assignment from Johnson, Shriver helped to develop and to get established anti-poverty programs as the first Director of the Office of Economic Opportunity, from 1964 (August) to 1968 (March).

The liberals of the time felt that they could make progress toward eliminating poverty and that times were better to so than it had been for many years. They had faith that the federal government "could solve big social problems" (Joseph 2015).

In the Economic Opportunity Act of 1964, As Amended, Findings and Declaration of Purpose it stated:

> Sec. 2. Although the economic well-being
> and prosperity of the United States have
> progressed to a level surpassing any

achieved in world history, and although these benefits are widely shared throughout the Nation, poverty continues to be the lot of a substantial number of our people. The United States can achieve its full economic and social potential as a nation only if every individual has the opportunity to contribute to the full extent of his capabilities and to participate in the workings of our society. It is therefore, the policy of the United States to eliminate the paradox of poverty in the midst of plenty in this Nation by opening to everyone the opportunity for education and training, the opportunity to work, and the opportunity to live in decency and dignity. It is the purpose of this Act to strengthen, supplement, and coordinate efforts in the furtherance of that policy.

The Economic Opportunity Act of 1964, as amended, established:

Title I – Youth Programs: The Job Corps, Work Training Programs, Work-Study Programs; (authored by Daniel P. Moynihan);

Shriver felt that the legislation must have a jobs component. The Youth Programs included Job Corps - basic education and training; Neighborhood Youth Corps - providing work and training for young men and women; Work Study - providing grants for college and university part-time employment for students from low-income families (Joseph 2015).

Title II – Urban and Rural Community Action Programs: General Community Action Programs, Adult Basic Education Programs, Voluntary Assistance Program for Needy Children; (authored by Richard W. Boone, Juvenile-Delinquency staff);

Title III – Special Programs to Combat Poverty in Rural Areas: Authority to Make Loans;

Title IV – Employment and Investment Incentives; (title III and IV written by James Sundquist, Agricultural Loans and Grants; Harold Gallaway, Small Business Administration, SBA loans);

Title V – Work Experience Programs; (written by James Alder, Health, Education, and Welfare);

Title VI – Administration and Coordination; (written by William Canon, The Budget Bureau);

Title VII – Treatment of Income for Certain Public Assistance Purposes (Zarefsky 1968)

Community Action Programs were defined in the act as a program. Title III (Sec. 202. (A) stated that "The term community action program" means a program--

1. Which mobilizes and utilizes resources, public or private, of any urban or rural, or combined urban and rural, geographical area (referred to in this part as a "community"), including but not limited to a state, metropolitan areas, county, city, town, multicity unit, or multi-county unit in an attack on poverty;

2.. Which provides services, assistance, and other activities of sufficient scope and size to give promise of progress toward elimination of poverty or a cause or causes of poverty through developing employment opportunities, improving human performance, motivation, and productivity, or bettering the conditions under which people live, learn and work;

3. Which is developed, conducted, and administered with maximum feasibly participation of residents of the areas and members of the groups served;

4. Which is conducted, administered, or coordinated by a public or private non-profit agency (other than a political party), or a combination thereof (Levitan 1969).

Shriver stated that the agency's task was "to serve the poor, to speak for the poor, to marshall America's resources on behalf of the poor" (Davidson 1969).

C. Robert Perrin, liaison between OEO and other federal agencies, local and state officials, said, "The flexibility of the OEO charter was such that you could do practically anything and justify it under the law. Now, whether you could justify it politically or through common sense was something else" (Gillette 2010).

Title II was probably the Act's most lasting contribution both to political theory and practice as it envisioned comprehensive community wide planning and implementation of programs aimed at combating poverty (Davidson 1969).

James Gaither (Economic Degree - Princeton, law degree - Stanford), Staff Assistant to President Johnson, said, about the program, "They launched that incredible mass of programs in a very short period of time, with almost no constraints on the money. If you read the original OEO act, it is an unbelievable piece of federal legislation, because it basically said, 'Here is a big pot of money, and you can spend it to alleviate the problems of the poor." They just launched these programs without worrying too much about being able to account for every last penny, feeling it was more important to start addressing the program, start training people; to start getting kids in school, starting giving them their first dental checkup, their first health exam; getting parents involved in early childhood education. All of those things they first got started, and the controls came later" (Gillette 2010).

The problem quickly arose as to how to contact individuals, groups, and communities, about the community-action grants. An early attempt was one of the pamphlets produced, "A Hometown Fight." It described the role that local action could have on the War Against Poverty. It stated (Wofford 1969; Adler 1994):

> Local community action programs are central to the war on poverty. These programs are designed to fight poverty in the community through local initiative. The individual community decides how best to attack poverty in its midst. Initiative and direction must come from the community itself. The decision to participate in the War on Poverty becomes a local responsibility.
>
> The Community Action Program reflects confidence in the ability of individual communities to organize and carry out anti-poverty programs tailored to local needs and priorities. In developing its program the local community is asked to:

1. Mobilize its own public and private resources for this attack.

2. Develop programs of sufficient scope and size to give promise of eliminating cause of poverty.

3. Involve the poor themselves in developing and operating the anti-poverty programs.

4. Administer and coordinate programs through public or private nonprofit agencies, or a combination of these.

Local community action programs should be broadly based, involving representatives of the chief elected officials of the community, key public and private agencies and representatives of the poor themselves.

Community action programs should see that existing local, state and federal programs are linked in a concentrated drive against poverty. They should fuse older programs which have proved effective with new attacks against the varied problems confronting the poor.

In a community with limited resources, local leaders can begin a community action program in stages. For example, with the "building block" approach a community might start with a child development program including health services. This should be followed by other specific programs all linked to each other in a coordinated campaign.

The major goal of community action programs is to help individuals help themselves. Inherent in this approach is the conviction that the poor should play an active part in helping to develop, manage and work in community action programs.

OEO established seven regional offices: Western-San Francisco, California; North Central-Kansas City, Missouri; Southwestern-Austin, Texas; Great Lakes-Chicago, Illinois; Southeast-Atlanta, Georgia; Mid-Atlantic-Washington, D.C.; and, Northeast-New York City, New York (Rose 2008)

Robert Perrin, Liaison OEO said, "Our management procedures were pretty good, really. We've established a lot of procedures that I don't think many federal agencies even today [speaking in 1969] have. Ours haven't always worked precisely right, but on the other hand, no one has ever had to deal with these kinds of programs before and these kind of grantees, Our audit procedures, our inspection, the management training are all quite unique in the federal establishment. I think we've taught other agencies quite a bit about it" (Rose 2008, Gillette 2010).

By September Shriver, in responding to heavy criticism of the "war on poverty" ticked off the allegations and made the following replies:

Charge – The Office of Economic Opportunity hasn't really done anything to fight poverty.

Response – In its first year of operation, the agency has made grants to about 750 American cities and counties to underwrite "community action programs" designed to eliminate such root causes of poverty as illiteracy, lack of job skills and the like. More than 3 million people are benefitting directly from these programs. In addition, 600,000 poor children, who have otherwise have begun school this fall under hopeless handicaps, have been given eight weeks of valuable preschool training under "Project Head Start." About 300,000 teen-age boys and girls, including many school dropouts, have enrolled in the Neighborhood Youth Corps, where they receive job training and paychecks while living at home. More than 10,000 youths have bent sent to Job Corps camps for basic literacy and vocational training. Nearly 90,000 unemployed parents are participating in "work experience" projects designed to make them employable, and to give them an income while they're learning marketable skills.

Charge – an exodus of top Office of Economic Opportunity executives show there's serious trouble behind the scenes in the administration of the program.

Response – the resignation of Office of Economic Opportunity's Deputy Director, Job Corps Chief, Public Relations Officer, Head Inspector and other top officials mean nothing more than a lot of busy men agreed to leave their regular careers temporarily to help get the agency going. Most of them already have stayed longer than they agreed to, and their departure does not imply any dissatisfaction with Office of Economic Opportunity policy.

Charge – Job Corps camps are failing to maintain discipline or impart any useful training.

Response – Out of 76 Job Corps camps and training centers now in operation, only about 6 have had any serious disciplinary problems, and even in those cases, the disorders have been exaggerated and overpublicized by the press. Despite the fact that they're dealing with some of the nation's toughest, most disillusioned and rebellious youngsters, more Job Corps centers are doing a good training job without fanfare or disorder.

Otis A. Singletary, Jr., the first Director, Job Corps, speaking about the problems of recruiting trained personnel, said, "We begged, borrowed, and stole. Part of the problem we had was that you couldn't get anybody on the payroll, even thought you had the money. The Washington problem of dealing with the Civil Service Commission and the Bureau of the Budget almost was a great, in my opinion, as the problem of trying to create and operate the program" (Gillette 2010).

Also in September, Dr. Joseph A. Kershaw, the former Provost of Williams College and an Economist for the Rand Corporation, began to set up a computerized cost analysis system at the Office of Economic Opportunity to help figure out how the war on poverty could get the best possible return for money spent. With Leon Gilgoff, he compiled a book three inches thick that listed, for the first time in the Government's history, the names of all Federal aid programs for the poor. This was an entire library for programs affected by legislation (*Newsweek* 1965). This national compendium eventually evolved into the Catalog of Federal Domestic Assistance, now maintained by the U.S. General Services Administration (Clark 2000).

Kershaw had been recruited by Shriver.

"I was sitting on the veranda last September [1964] at Martha's Vineyard," he recalled, when the phone rang. 'My name is Sargent Shriver,' a voice said. 'We're going to spend a lot of money.' "(*Newsweek* 1965)

The Senate Committee on 29 September recommended an appropriation of $861.5 million, an increase of $111.5 million over the House figure, but still a reduction of $85.95 million below what the Administration had requested. On 1 October, the Senate passed its bill.

The House-Senate Conference Committee sent out a report appropriating $800 million for the program. The bill (H.R. 12633) was cleared 3 October, the last day of the session.

The President signed the measure, 7 October, with the Office of Economic Opportunity beginning operations on 8 October.

In November, the Office of Economic Opportunity send out a press release that stated that there were six fronts involving 119 separate anti-poverty project in two-thirds of the states of the nation.

The United States presidential election was held on Tuesday, November 3, 1964, between Democratic candidate and incumbent President Lyndon B. Johnson and the Republican candidate, Senator Barry Goldwater of Arizona, who had suffered from a lack party support and his deeply unpopular political positions. Lawrence F. O'Brien was appointed by Johnson to be the national director of his presidential campaign. He had, in 1959, built the foundation for Kennedy's 1960 presidential campaign by touring the United States and was appointed then to be the national director of Kennedy's campaign. During the run-up to the current Presidential election, William Moyers worked with the "Anti-Campaign" of Johnson's where he pioneered a unit for a campaign of full-time espionage, sabotage, and mudslinging. The Democratic election team included: Daniel P. Moynihan, Depart of Labor; Myer Feldman, White House counsel; Richard J. Murphy, Assistant Postmaster; the Assistant Secretary of Agriculture; Hyman Bookbinder, labor lobbyist; a number of top D.C. lawyers; Adam Yarmolinsky, the Pentagon; Clifton Cooper, CIA liaison to the White House (Perlstein 2001).

Johnson called upon W. Marvin Watson to help organize the 1964 Democratic Convention in Atlantic City, New Jersey.

Six Federal agencies simultaneously announced projects, 25 November, involving $35 million affecting impoverished Americans ranging from unemployed adults to school children.

Details of this initial programming were announced by Shriver following a meeting with President Johnson.

Thirty-one colleges and universities including in the Washington, D.C., Chicago, and Detroit areas agreed to conduct work-study programs to assist needy students by providing part-time jobs on and off campus.

VISTA reported the first 150 Volunteers would begin training before the year's end. The program had received requests for Volunteers from 78 communities in 34 states, the District of Columbia, Puerto Rico, and American Samoa.

Stephan J. Pollack, detailed from the Department of Justice, worked on the legislation to establish the VISTA program, said, "The major sponsor was Robert Kennedy. I'm confident that the inserting of the VISTA program into the antipoverty bill, which came late, was at the urging and insistence of Robert Kennedy. It wouldn't have been in there if he hadn't pushed for it." Glen Ferguson, first Director, VISTA, said, "The Peace Corps was highly decentralized. Each Peace Corps unit in the field worked virtually alone, with minimal policy guidance from headquarters. VISTA had no field organization and no regional offices. The small staff worked almost by sufferance with local officials. There was no chain of command." He recognized that they couldn't call the new program a "domestic Peace Corps" so "We went to the drawing boards and tried to come up with something creative. My effort produced 'VISA: Volunteers in Service to America.' Then, I think it was probably Steve Pollak who did a little research and found that there was an incipient VISA credit program. So we put the 'T' in the acronym, and from the first days we were calling it 'VISTA' " (Gillette 2010).

Edgar May, Deputy Director, VISTA, said in looking back at the program, "The older we got, the worse we were politically, because they began to understand what the hell we were really about, and what we were about was to make change. And the one thing that scares the living hell out of a politician, whether he's a state representative in little Vermont or in Texas or anyplace else, is a lot of unknowns . . . change" (Aksamit 2014).

Augenbraun (2009) wrote: "In the summer of 1964, Philadelphia became one of the first major cities to throw its hat into the ring for federal funding to create an anti-poverty program . . . Yet the program would never be used for its intended purpose, quickly being hijacked by the city's Democratic machine."

In November an avalanche of telegrams of protest began to arrive protesting the alleged failure of the "mayors committee" to consult the residents of the area (Wofford 1969).

Arnstein (1969) in looking back at the community action programs process, stated, in part:

> Because the question [citizen participation is citizen power] has been a bone of political contention, most of the answers have been purposely buried in innocuous euphemisms like "self-help" or "citizen involvement." Still others have been embellished with misleading rhetoric like "absolute control" which is something no one–including the President of the United States – has or can have.
>
> In the name of citizen participation, people are placed on rubberstamp advisory committees or advisory boards for the express purpose of "educating" them or engineering their support.
>
> This illusory form of "participation" initially came into vogue with urban renewal when the socially elite were invited by city housing officials to serve on Citizen Advisory Committees (CACs).
>
> At meetings of the Citizen *Advisory* Committees, it was the officials who educated, persuaded, and advised the

citizens, not the reverse.

This style of nonparticipation has since been applied to other programs encompassing the poor. Examples of this are seen in Community Action Agencies (CAAs) which have created structures called "neighborhood councils" or "neighborhood advisory groups." These bodies frequently have no legitimate function or power.

Among the arguments against community control are: it supports separatism; it creates balkanization of public services; it is more costly and less efficient; it enables minority group "hustlers" to be just as opportunistic and disdainful of the have-nots as their white predecessors; it is incompatible with merit systems and professionalism; and ironically enough, it can turn out to be a new Mickey Mouse game for the have-nots by allowing them to gain control but not allowing them sufficient dollar resources to succeed. These arguments are not to be taken lightly. But neither can we take lightly the arguments of embittered advocates of community control – that every other means of trying to end their victimization has failed!

Maximum Feasible Participation irritated all manner of people as expressed by Wofford (1969) and Arnstein (1969) in the above quotes. Over time, and in places this would occur over and over. In many ways, one might suggest, that the act that created OEO and defined Community Action Agencies with an emphasis on the need to include the poor into the boards of those agencies on the ground that the people being affect ought to have some way to speak to those programs directly affecting them, was based on the idea, in a sense, on a utopian concept. The people who wrote this into existence truly recognized a social need but what they failed to understand was the social and culture resistence to change which is quite normal in any population. This was coupled with nothing in the system that was responsible for insuring that this process, would in fact, operate the way that they wanted them to, that is, they did not build into the total system a bureaucratic oversight to insure that the poor actually would get their voice and that the overall program would react when these voices were denied.

There are few academic discussion of programs in detail which illustrates how things really worked, for good or ill. For the next number of pages or so, several well documented Community Action Agencies will be described.

One place where there is ample documentation to illustrate this discussion was Mingo County, West Virginia.

Mingo County was created 30 January 1895 as the youngest county In West Virginia. It is the southwest edge of the state sharing a boundary with Kentucky. The county has vast coal deposits whose commercial mining began, in 1890, before the county was created (Meter 2017).

Stone (1988) wrote:

Coal is still king in southern West

Virginia, but unemployment is its too-constant consort. Mingo County is so economically blighted, says a local mayor, "that this is where President Kennedy invented poverty." And though the mine owners no longer pay wages in scrip for the company store, much of Mingo continues to operate on the near-feudal model of a company town, where a few men and women control every aspect of local life.

Barry (2010) posted:

For *County Health Ranking 2010*, a collection of each state in the union, comparing the health status of every county in each state Robert Wood Johnson Foundation and the University of Wisconsin Population Health Institute.

Mingo County is one of the unhealthiest counties in West Virginia, which is one of the unhealthiest states in the nation.

For health behaviors (tobacco use, diet & exercise, alcohol use, unsafe sex) 55th out of 55 counties.

For clinical care (access to care, quality of care) 54th of 55.

For social and economic factors (education, employment, income, family and social support, community safety)

48th of 55.

For physical environment (environmental quality, built environment) 44th of 55.

While this gives a sense of place for the county today, we now need to look at the county as it interacted in the War on Poverty.

Biggers noted (Perry and Biggers 2010), speaking on the war on poverty in Mingo County: it is "a timeless cautionary tale of good intentions in a land of greed and political corruption." He quotes Perry: "Although I had lived in Appalachia all my life, I was stunned by the conditions I saw during my initial weeks of looking into the hollows of Mingo. The visible effects of poverty were everywhere–the shacks, the filth, the pale, pot-bellied babies, the outhouses, the dirt roads, and the one-room schools. Up and down the hollows, the front yards were strewn with junked cars and the seats of abandoned automobiles were used for beds and sofas... Fifty percent of the county's inhabitants were poor; 20 percent were welfare recipients; and the unemployment rate was 14 percent... infant mortality, usually as a result of pneumonia, was fantastically high compared to the national average . . . Adding to the problem was the fact that Mingo's middle class went to great lengths to hide the injustices inflicted on the poor. Many claimed that there was no poverty in the county." Even as one of the top coal-producing areas in central Appalachia, 50 percent of the population in Mingo County lived in poverty: one out of five was a welfare recipient. Half of the homes were substandard, and many were without plumbing. Infant mortality ranked higher than anywhere else in the country. He quotes a pamphlet written in 1969 by Don West, *Romantic Appalachia: Poverty Pays*

If You Ain't Poor, " . . . the southern mountains have been missionarized, researched and studied, surveyed, romanticized, dramatized, hillbillyized, Dogpatchized, and povertyized again. . . The 'missionaries' – religious or secular – had and have one thing in common: they didn't trust us hill folk to speak, plan, and act for ourselves. Bright, articulate, ambitious, well-intended, they become our spokesmen, our planners, our actors. And so they'll go again, leaving us and our poverty behind."

Huey Perry, in his narrative, (Perry and Biggers 2010), tells of how community action agencies began and engaged the poor and the political forces resisting their interests.

The Mingo County Court, a three-man governing body, hearing that the neighboring county, McDowell, had just applied for a million dollar federal grant, established a six-man commission to apply to the OEO for a federal grant. With their newly created Economic Community Commission (ECC), headed by Gerald Chafin, a mortician from the town of Delbarton, they advertized for a Director and hired Huey Perry. The eighteen-member board of the ECC was six representatives of the County Court, one representative of the county's four towns and the city of Williamson, representatives from civic groups and women's clubs. They had an $18,160 grant for development of the project. Margaret McQueen, ECC Secretary and representative of the Williamson Women's club, read a letter from OEO requesting that at least four poor people be on the board. Virgil Marcum, insurance salesman, appointed by the County Court to the board, stated "I really don't see anything wrong with that if that's what they want. But I think we ought to be careful and make sure we get four good ones. Does anyone know somebody that wouldn't cause us any trouble?"

Perry saw that it was obvious that the greatest resistance would eventually come from the entrenched Democratic machine, completely controlled by Noah Floyd, State Senator for Mingo and McDowell counties. Floyd discussed the poverty program with Perry and said: "Now you know we will have no trouble working together and if you need any help, of if I can do anything for you in Charleston, let me know. If we work together, we ought to be able to bring a lot of money into the county. And Johnson wants to give it away. Now I don't know whether you can do anything for these poor people or not. You know most of them are so lazy they won't work. Anyway, keep them happy; we'll need them on election day."

Huey Perry ended his five-year term with ECC and took a new job with a low-income housing program in Charleston. He had managed to create thirty community action programs. What he left behind was a county were crooked elections had been a way of life in which thousands of county residents had been involved, including the poor, schoolteachers, and attorneys, among others.

5 August 1970, a federal grant jury returned indictments against Noah Floyd (the State Senator from Mingo and McDowell Counties who controlled the entrenched Democratic machine in those counties), T.I. Verney (Mingo County's Probation and Parole Officer), Harry Artis (Member of the Mingo County Court), and Arnold Starr (Mingo County Assessor), for conspiring to influence the 1968 November general election. The jury deliberated for three hours and voted "not guilty" in all four cases.

Silberman in his book, *Crisis in Black and White*, argued that the search for "community-wide consensus" caused the system to not consider the "warring self-interests" of politics in which "We the people" become "Some of us people" and then become "Some of you people" instead of the system being in favor of politics that seek to promote the common good

(Cazenave 2007).

The Dallas City approach illustrates this problem.

The Dallas city elites amended, in 1930, the city charter from a commission to the council-manager form. This form of government moved slower than the previous from where the mayor could make quick decisions. The new form, a nine-member council, with three at-large seats, was approved by a two-to-one vote with only 26 percent of the voters actually casting votes. The Dallas County Community Action Committee (DCCAC) was formed as a community action agency within the Texas Office of Economic Opportunity. It was designated as the primary agency to receive grants and to disburse these funds to delegate agencies. John Connally, Texas Governor, vetoed a proposal what would have given jobs to migrant farm worker youth, as well as a $1.25 minimum hourly wage the enrollees in programs would receive, as he felt that his office ought to oversee any distribution of funds coming into the community action agencies. However the veto was overridden by the OEO Director's capability to do so. DCCAC was fully established by August 1965 and put out an information sheet which defined their process: "It is neither an extension of Welfare, nor a training ground for revolt. But it like a box of tools made available to communities to use where they will do the most good." They established neighborhood centers in five areas catered to the needs of the individual neighborhood. In the 1960s the Chicano Movement came into existence. It was argued the term "Chico" was not a derogatory term but one that meant "Pride and Cultural heritage" much as the shift from the term Negro to black had occurred. But African Americans were drawing critical response with some upset citizens over the hiring of controversial African Americans causing those employees to resign. In 1969 controversy arose over the hiring of a black community organizer at the West Dallas center. The *Dallas Morning News* reported: "A desire for self-destruction, along with a chronic disregard for public opinion, seems to have overtaken the Dallas Community Action board in the wake of the Ruth Jefferson incident, which has angered and disgusted a majority of county residents." Racial tension began to rise as more people became critical of the program. Mexican and African American youths threw bottles at the center. In September 1969 community houses were formed as neighborhood centers for the Mexican American areas. But there was upset over the argument that while the city council had an African American on the city council no one from the Mexican American community had been offered a seat. It was felt that the Mexican American community was "disgracefully neglected in Dallas." Growing frustrations of neglect and poverty were politicizing the community to push for equality. A law suit filed against the Equal Employment Opportunity Commission, February 1968, with the court recognizing that the tensions between the racial groups arose because of the limited resources within the poverty programs: "The Court believes that the Mexican-Americans' Concern over the amount of Control the Dallas Black population had over DAC [DCCAC] operations compounded the alleged legal reason for this suit." By 1970, it seemed that the program was unraveling as federal funds were diminishing and internal problems were leading to a stagnant organization. The major problem was the conservative approach adopted by the leaders with the result that, the poor, mostly minorities, reaped few of the anticipated benefits which resulted in pitting the African American and Mexican American communities against each other, compounded by mismanagement of funds and inner conflict within the agency. Given all this it was not surprising that the War on Poverty failed as it did (Rose 2008).

The Laredo-Webb County Economic Opportunity Development Corporation, one of the earliest programs, offered insight about a Community Action Agency can work, in spite of tensions between the poor and the successful operation of the program (Garza 1969).

In 1964, Loredo, Texas, population 65,000, was considered the city with the lowest per-capita income among cities in the United States. It was selected as a "model project." The Laredo-Webb County Economic Opportunity Development Corporation was established (1964) as a non-profit corporation to address the citiy's social and economic problems.

Poverty had almost become a way of life, with approximately 2,500 able-bodied individuals normally unemployed with the unemployment rate more than 13 percent in February-March, up to 11,000 people receiving surplus food in some months, more than 400 families collected aid-to-dependent children payments. The yearly family median income was $2,952; one-sixth of the population was illiterate; 8,000 of 17,000 houses were substandard; 20 percent of the city did not have a sanitary sewer system; of the 265 miles of streets, 165 were unpaved; almost 2,000 elementary students only had a half-day schedule due to a classroom shortage.

The Board of Directors of the agency had three groups: local public officials; public agencies conducting anti-poverty programs; and, representatives of the poor. The personnel of the Community Action Agency had been screened by the local political machine.

The Mayor had been in office for 17 years, with members of his family having been in that office for 35+ years.

The poor representatives on the board were young and eager to have a voice with some influence and meaning.

In 1967, Alfredo Cervera, Manpower Training Coordinator, said:

> One evening, 150 residents of the poverty-stricken Azteca neighborhood collected outside their run-down homes to complain that distribution of poverty jobs had been unfair. Bitterly they expressed their dissatisfaction at the way administrators had been treating them. "They never keep their promises," cried one.

The unrest forced a reorganization of the board with greater numbers of the poor being included.

Great debates arose as to the qualifications of individuals in paid positions with a great pressure to hire from the ranks of the poor as well as those working as Volunteer Aids. The poor wanted more and more ability to oversee the actions/performance of staff in the programs.

Many saw the war on poverty as a political machine of the Democratic party and feared that the election of Republicans would lead to the removal of those programs.

The program came under heavy criticism, 20 September, from regional officials of the poverty program directing the local agency to get its program reorganized by 1 December.

The Survey Team evaluating the Loredo agency felt efficiency and economy in the program were being lost not so much from the participation of the poor in the policy-making but because of a lack of well organized effort with the result that the taxpayers and the poor were not getting their money's worth. However, the poor had little to do with the inefficiency of the local programs as the board was controlled by the local public officials.

But streets did get paved and other aspects were addressed as well.

Johnson gave his *Annual Message to Congress on the State of The Union*, 4 January 1965, and stated, in part (Johnson 1965a):

"We built this Nation to serve its people."

"We want to grow and build and create, but we want progress to be the servant and not the master of man."

"We do not intend to live in the midst of abundance, isolated from neighbors and nature, confined by blighted cities and bleak suburbs, stunted by a poverty of learning and an emptiness of leisure."

"The Great Society asks not how much, but how good; not only how to create wealth but how to use it; not only how fast we are going, but where we are headed."

"It proposes as the first test for a nation: the quality of its people."

"This kind of society will not flower spontaneously from swelling riches and surging power."

"It will not be the gift of government or the creation of presidents. It will require of every American, for many generations, both faith in the destination and the fortitude to make the journey."

"And like freedom itself, it will always be challenge and not fulfillment."

"And tonight we accept that challenge."

". . .we must open opportunity to all our people."

"Most Americans enjoy a good life. But far too many are still trapped in poverty and idleness and fear."

"Let a just nation throw open to them the city of promise:
—to the elderly, by providing hospital care under social security and by raising benefit payments to those struggling to maintain the dignity of their later years;
—to the poor and the unfortunate, through doubling the war against poverty this year;
—to Negro Americans, through enforcement of the civil rights law and elimination of barriers to the right to vote;
—to those in other lands that are seeking the promise of America, through an

immigration law based on the work a man can do and not where he was born or how he spells his name."

18 January 1965, President Johnson announced $101,960,782 cluster of projects in 33 states and Puerto Rico.

David Gelman, Information Officer on loan from the Peace Corps to the Office of Economic Opportunity to write early presentations, stated: "The program was roundly denounced long before it got its first dime. The problem was that it was visible right from January as a task force."

The Republican National Committee released a pamphlet that stated:

> It has always been the Republican approach to assist the poor and disadvantage in their climb up the economic and social ladder; not to drag them forcibly by a green rope of dollar bills." It quoted the 1964 Annual Economic Report of the Joint Economic Committee of Congress, Minority opinion: "a war on poverty will not be won by slogans; nor by the defeatist relief concept of the 1930's; nor by cynical use of poverty for partisan political ends; nor by overstating the problems and thereby inexcusably lowering America's prestige in the eyes of the world.

The Office of Economic Opportunity adopted Orshansky's poverty level threshold as its official poverty indicator (Orshansky 1963, 1965). She felt, however, that it was not appropriate to adopt this as a nationwide application of her statistical calculations to define the poor (Goldstein 2012).

The Government established a poverty yardstick at $3,000 per year for a family of four. This broke down to about $600.00 a week. The Council of Economic Advisors had estimated typical expenditures to be: $5 per week per person would be spent for food; about $800 per year would go for housing, leaving only $1,200 – less than $25 per week – for clothing, transportation, school supplies, home furnishings and supplies, medical care, personal care, recreation, insurance and other basic needs. "Obviously," the Advisors declared, "it does not exaggerate the problem to regard $3,000 as the boundary."

The cutoff figure was $ 3,000 (Humphrey 1964).

Johnson stated, in part, in *The President's Inaugural Address*, 20 January 1965, (Johnson 1965b) that:

> "First, justice was the promise that all who made the journey would share in the fruits of the land."

> "In a land of great wealth, families must not live in hopeless poverty. In a land rich in harvest, children just must not go hungry. In a land of healing miracles, neighbors must not suffer and die untended. In a great land of learning and scholars, young people must be taught to read and write."

> "For more than 30 years that I have served this Nation I have believed that

this injustice to our people, this waste of our resources, was our real enemy. For 30 years or more, with the resources I have had, I have vigilantly fought against it. I have learned and I know that it will not surrender easily."

"But change has given us new weapons. Before this generation of Americans is finished, this enemy will not only retreat, it will be conquered."

"Justice requires us to remember: when any citizen denies his fellow, saying: 'His color is not mine or his beliefs are strange and different,' in that moment he betrays America, though his forebears created this Nation."

"I do not believe that the Great Society is the ordered, changeless, and sterile battalion of the ants. It is the excitement of becoming—always becoming, trying, probing, falling, resting, and trying again—but always trying and always gaining."

"In each generation, with toil and tears, we have had to earn our heritage again. If we fail now then we will have forgotten in abundance what we learned in hardship: that democracy rests on faith, that freedom asks more than it gives, and the judgment of God is harshest on those who are most favored."

"If we succeed it will not be because of what we have, but it will be because of what we are; not because of what we own, but rather because of what we believe."

"For we are a nation of believers. Underneath the clamor of building and the rush of our day's pursuits, we are believers in justice and liberty and in our own union. We believe that every man must some day be free. And we believe in ourselves."

In February, 1965, Bayard Rustin, an American leader in social movements for civil rights, socialism, nonviolence, and gay rights, wrote: "The decade spanned by the 1954 Supreme Court decision on school desegregation and the Civil Rights Act of 1964 will undoubtedly be recorded as the period in which the legal foundations of racism in America were destroyed. To be sure, pockets of resistance remain; but it would be hard to quarrel with the assertion that the elaborate legal structure of segregation and discrimination, particularly in relation to public accommodation, has virtually collapsed" (Rainwater and Yancey 1967).

The Office of Economic Opportunity gave its first *Congressional Presentation* in April 1965. It stated, in part:

"In its first six months the War on Poverty translated a Congressional mandate into a working program." It did not wait "until perfection could be guaranteed, or criticism avoided. Staff having determined at the outset that such an approach would condemn programs to committees or drafting boards for process.

In the first days many of the myths about poverty, and what would happen when OEO was established, were effectively destroyed, in including the charges:

-- that no Southern official would voluntarily cooperate with Negro leaders in local anti-poverty programs;

– that the poor were apathetic, inarticulate, incapable of working for their own welfare in organized systems;

–- that nobody would volunteer for VISTA without the exotic appeal of service in foreign countries;

– that Negroes would not live with whites in Job Corps Centers, or vice versa;

– that towns and cities wouldn't want Job Corps camps nearby."

But Shriver stated:

"We have a Job Corps. We have a Neighborhood Youth Corps. There are Community Action programs across the country. Work Study, Work Experience and Adult Basic Education are in operation as are the Small Business and Rural Loan programs. VISTA volunteers are at work. The beginning has not only shown the difficulty, but the possibility."

On *Face the Nation*, 18 April, Shriver felt that Powell's "fiesta of patronage" was an exaggeration. "I would suspect that there are 10 times as many private citizens, philanthropists, social workers, welfare workers, and so on, involved in this war already as anybody who would be identifiable as a politician" (Zarefsky 1986).

Johnson, during his news conference, 27 April, felt that activist critics were in the same category as those who initially opposed the Economic Opportunity Act. "I think there has been unjust criticisms and unfair criticism and uninformed criticism of the poverty program even before Congress passed it. Some people opposed it every step of the way. Some people oppose it now."

A May 1965 report stated that less than 2 years after the assault on poverty had begun, with a total cost, so far, of $2.3-billion, that the program had directly reached 3,000,000 of the poor, and generated a spectrum of social-welfare commitments unmatched by any previous administration in U.S. history. At the same time large amount of political pressure were beginning to flow into Washington, D.C., as scores of mayors became upset because the programs were insisting that the poor be given a voice in dispensing the manna that traditionally had been a city hall prerogative.

In the second fiscal year of the anti-poverty program, beginning 1 July 1965, community action received 45 percent of the total appropriation. However, by the Spring of that year protests from city governments about the tactics of the new community action agencies were already pouring in. The issue was policymaking.

William P. Kelly, Jr., became Assistant Director for Management, OEO, when OEO was created, said, in discussing early problems, "Traditionally, within the government, the best government grades had been reserved for those bureaucrats who stayed in Washington and who had little to do with what went on at the grass roots, out where the people were . . . So that by the summer of 1965 . . . Shriver couldn't get a decision out of the Civil Service Commission on how to conduct as least the regional part of the war. They talk about management inefficiency! That's really probably one of the most monumental bits of management inefficiency that ever was called to my attention in some eighteen years in the federal service" (Gillette 2010).

Mayors John Francis "Jack" Shelley, (D), San Francisco, and Samuel William Yorty, (D), Los Angeles, introduced a resolution at the U.S. Conference of Mayors, June, that accused the Economic Opportunity Office of "fostering class struggle" and "creating tensions" between the poor and the existing agencies. Vice President Hubert Humphrey stated: "It is absolutely essential that the mayors take the leadership in the anti-poverty program." This statement kept the resolution from passing in the Conference (Zarefsky 1986, Selover 1969).

Theodore McKeldin, Mayor of Baltimore, complained that the federal government was ignorant about local government needs (Rose 2008)

Mayor Richard Daley of Chicago, as an example, was known to be mightily upset. In the tradition of urban, Democratic, ethnic politics, the Chicago anti-poverty program was roaring ahead, and predictably, became a champion grabber and distributer of anti-poverty funds. What was not distributed was the power to make allocations of that funding. While Mayor Dailey wanted the poor to be employed by the program, he wanted the decisions to be made by his office. From the point of view of the usual working class politics it reflected the usual approach. In the view of the middle class liberals who ran the poverty program, it was seen as sinister, evil, hateful. The President, however, sided with the Mayor (Moynihan1969a).

In the spring, a group of mayors, led by Daley, met with Vice President Humphrey to voice their concerns and Humphrey decided that the mayors required greater ability over programs in their cities.

Daley set up, as reported by Lois Wille inthe *Chicago Daily News*, 5 April, 1965, what he called a blue-ribbon poverty committee, the local Community Action Agency (CAA), the Chicago Committee on Urban Opportunity. The committee included twenty-five chairmen or directors of governmental agencies, five aldermen, one judge, nine business leaders, four union executives, six private welfare agency leaders, three clergymen, and Edwin Berry of the Urban League, with Daley appointing Dr. Denton Brooks as executive director, a black civil servant and educator, with Daily as head of the committee. Daley and his political machine saw the CAA as a way to use federal dollars, that were intended to reform institutions and give greater power to poor, as a way to prevent either from happening (Adler 1994).

In 1965, OEO launched its Legal Services Program, supported by the American Bar Association, led by Lewis F. Powell Jr., who stated: "Everybody from Sargent Shriver down thought that it was extraordinarily important that the American Bar Association get behind the legal services program, that it would give it a credibility and an acceptance around the country that it wouldn't otherwise have . . . There isn't any question that while, I guess, the Cahns and Shriver can claim to be the parents of the federal legal services program, Lewis Powell has certainly got to be the godfather."

The OEO program provided a testing period to learn about funding legal services for the poor. As with many new federal initiatives, the OEO Legal Services Program weathered skepticism and encountered controversy. Within nine months, 130 OEO legal services programs were being funded and many had the support of state and local bar associations.

Almost at the outset, the Executive Office of the President began to exert pressure on the Office of Economic Opportunity to keep the community actions programs as quiet as possible, which in effect meant to keep the role of the poor in policymaking to a minimum.

Mayor Samuel W. Yorty refused to include the poor on the City of Los Angeles poverty board (Selover 1969).

From August 11th to the 16th The Watts Riots took place in Los Angeles. It started in the evening of Wednesday, August 11, when 21-year-old Marquette Frye, an African American man behind the wheel of his mother's 1955 Buick, was pulled over for reckless driving by California Highway Patrol motorcycle officer Lee Minikus. After administering a field sobriety test, Minikus placed Frye under arrest and radioed for his vehicle to be impounded. Marquette's brother, Ronald, a passenger in the vehicle, walked to their house nearby, bringing their mother, Rena Price, back with him to the scene of the arrest who then scolded Frye about drinking and driving. Then someone shoved Price, Frye was struck, Price jumped an officer, and another officer pulled out a shotgun. Backup police officers attempted to arrest Frye by using physical force to subdue him. As the situation intensified, growing crowds of local residents watching the exchange began yelling and throwing objects at the police officers. Frye's mother and brother fought with the officers and were eventually arrested along with Marquette Frye. Police came to the scene to break up the crowd several times that night, but were attacked with rocks and chunks of concrete. Eventually a 46 square mile piece of Los Angeles would be transformed into a combat zone

The 37th Mayor of Los Angeles, Samuel William Yorty, known at that time as Shoot-From-The-Lip Sam, The Maverick Mayor, Mad Sam Yorty, charged in a telegram (17 August) to Senator George Murphy, the first notable Republican actor elected to the Senate from California, that the Office of Economic Opportunity objections to the local anti-poverty program in Los Angeles constituted a "reckless effort to incite the poor for political reasons" and "was the factor in precipitating the Watts riot." He further stated that the delaying in approving funds results from "strong-arm tactics" and pressures from the Los Angeles Democratic delegation in the House of Representatives.

Shriver said at a news conference the following day that Yorty's allegations were "intemperate and unfortunate" and "untrue." He further stated that Los Angeles was the "only city in the United States" which had failed to organize an acceptable anti-poverty organization and that in Los Angeles "a few local officials have made it extremely difficult for private agencies, minority groups and the poor to join in the war on poverty."

Yorty then included seven representatives of the poor on the city board but they were hand-picked by the mayor (Selover 1969).

In a survey of urban historians and political scientists Yorty was rated the third worst big-city mayor since 1960.

Riots broke out in New York (1964), Chicago (1964),

Detroit (1967), and Newark (1967) as well as hundreds of black communities around the nation. They resulted from long-festering wounds: unemployment, poverty, poor housing, crowded living conditions, economic exploitation, widespread desperation, frustration, hopelessness, and a profound disillusionment with urban conditions (Trattner 1994).

In floor debate, 19 August, on the Senate floor, Everett McKinley Dirksen, (R), Illinois, saw the program as the "greatest boondoggle since bread and circuses in the days of the ancient Roam empire when the republic fell" . . . it was "the very acme of waste and extravagance, and unorganization and disorganization . . . a colossal disgrace, and, in some cases, an absolute fraud upon the taxpayer of this country. We are a binge, it can't last" (Selover 1969).

Less than a week later *U.S. News and World Report*, 23 August 1965, jumped into the criticism business. In an article they alleged that there was Presidential concern "about the swelling volume of criticism," complaints of "administrative chaos, bureaucratic bungling, waste, extravagance, costly duplication of existing services and internal squabbling," among other indictments.

The Office of Economic Opportunity issued a memorandum stating among other things that:

> "Of course the White House is concerned – just as it is over attacks on any key Administrative program. Only last week the President gave high praise to the entire program, and the OEO, before a meeting of Congressional leaders. There is no evidence whatsoever of his dissatisfaction."

"The article conveniently omits the preponderance of favorable reaction, the consensus that recently led to such overwhelming victories for the new anti-poverty bills in Congress. And it fails to question how, in the light of such 'bungling' the program managed to serve over three million poor people in 2,000 communities in its first nine months."

President Johnson in his *Annual Message to Congress on the State of the Union*, January 12, 1966, (Johnson 1966) said, in part:

"For that other nation within a Nation—the poor—whose distress has now captured the conscience of America, I will ask the Congress not only to continue, but to speed up the war on poverty. And in so doing, we will provide the added energy of achievement with the increased efficiency of experience."

"To improve the life of our rural Americans and our farm population, we will plan for the future through the establishment of several new Community Development Districts, improved education through the use of Teacher Corps teams, better health measures, physical examinations, and adequate and available medical resources."

"In some of our urban areas we must help rebuild entire sections and neighborhoods containing, in some cases, as many as 100,000 people. Working together, private enterprise and government must press forward with the task of providing homes and shops, parks and hospitals, and all the other necessary parts of a flourishing community where our people can come to live the good life."

Early in January 1966, Sargent Shriver, after six months of pleading with President Johnson to be relieved of either the Head of the Peace Corps or the Office of Economic Opportunity (OEO), became the Director of OEO only.

By the end of January more than 900 grants had been made for the establishment or planning of Community Action Programs in more than 1,000 counties (Moynihan 1969a).

Adam Clayton Powell defended the program, at the end of a six-month investigation by his committee's investigators into the operation of the anti-poverty program which visited 78 projects in 28 states and the District of Columbia at a cost of $250,000, and stated in *The New York Times*, February 28 1966 that:

"The Office of Economic Opportunity comes out smelling not of scandals, but of the sweet smell of success. The scandals are not in a misplaced penny here or an unrecorded dollar there. The scandals in the War on Poverty really are the scandals of America: 182 counties where the median family income is below $750 a year; the nine million families who earn less than $3,000 a year . . . Those are the scandals that should scorch our souls" (CSA 1969).

In the "Legislative Hearing, Washington Edition" program on WCBS-TV on the same day Powell said, in part:

"Out of the thousands of anti-poverty programs in America there has been a remarkable absence of outright dishonesty and corruption. There have been isolated – let me emphasize that word – cases of mismanagement, poor administration and bad judgement."

In the same month Shriver responded to a reporter from the *New York Times*:

"I suppose we shouldn't have started so many programs so fast and we wouldn't have gotten so many people excited . . . Maybe we should have limited the amount of programs we put out and waited six months longer to do some of the things we did. Things would have been quieter and calmer but the poor wouldn't have been helped so much."

Orshansky (1966) in March, wrote:

> There is still no all-embracing characterization that can encompass all the poor. Some are poor because they cannot work; others are poor even though they do. Most of the poor receive no assistance from public programs; others remain poor because they have no resources but the limited payments provided under such programs. And public programs to help the poor are in the main geared to serve those who cannot work at all or are temporarily out of a job. The man who works for a living but is not making it will normally find no avenue of aid.
>
> About half of all the Nation's poor families – one-seventh of the white poor and two-thirds of the nonwhite poor – lived in the south in 1966. Incomes in that area continue to be lower than elsewhere, by more than could possibly compensated for by any price differential.
>
> The Southern States today support a larger proportion of their population on public assistance than is true of the rest of the country. Indeed, of the 10 States with the highest OAA [Older Americans Act] recipient rate per 1,000 aged persons in

December 1966, eight were Southern States, although eligibility requirements are at least as restrictive in the South as anywhere else.

In our society it is a truism that work is the key to economic security. Yet though a job is usually necessary if one is to keep out of poverty, having one does not guarantee it.

The most poverty-prone calling for men was farming or unskilled labor; for women workers it was domestic service.

The Citizens Crusade Against Poverty held a national convention in April with the goal of expanding the War on Poverty and empowering the poor. Invited speakers were Shriver; Walter Reuther, Head, United Auto Workers Union; Dr. Eugene Carson Blake, Secretary-elect, World Council of Churches; and, Roy Wilkins, Executive Director, National Association of Colored People. Approximately 1,000 delegates from Watts, Harlem, Appalachia, the Mississippi Delta, as well as other impoverished regions, came to the two-day conference. Shriver's formal presentation and his unwillingness to stop for questions brought the audience's agitation to a head (Cazenave 2007). Speakers displayed disdain for the agency, the OEO; for failing the achieve participation by the poor; and during Shriver's luncheon speech booed and, in general, interrupted as he attempted to defend the agency, some shouting "You're lying!" and "He hasn't done anything for us!" Shriver replied that he was "not a bit ashamed of what had been done by the war on poverty; I don't apologize to anybody in or out of this room about the results." He finally left and stated that he would "not participate in a riot" (Clark 2000, Zarefsky 1986, Wofford 1969).

Goldstein (2012) suggested that: ". . . his bitter retort made the consequences of disloyalty explicit. To violate the protocols of participation, to disturb the polite and civil exchange between attendees at a conference who were all putatively committed to a common goal, was equivalent to violent insurrection. Poor people were expected to be thankful for the opportunity to voice their opinions, and their role was thus to assume the proper cadence of gratitude and to echo the policy priorities already articulated on their behalf. Outrage and indignation breached the confines of permissible expression and would not be sanctioned by the presence of the institution (embodied in this case by Shriver himself)."

Shriver asserted that the demonstrations had been organized, however Jack Conway and Richard Boone, former aids to Shriver disagreed, and said that Shriver's talk did not address the audience's "great tension, great unrest, a great sense of frustration" (Zarefsky1986, Clark 2000).

A week later it was announced by the OEO that it would no longer fund elections of the poor to antipoverty program boards unless the local government could demonstrate that there was no other way to involve the poor. The U. S. Justice Head of the Civil Rights Division stated that he expected organizations to "draw the line on protestors who assume that they have the unlimited right to protest at any time, any place, in any way, in any number" (Cazenave 2007).

In April there were moves in Congress to restrict the powers of the Director of the Office of Economic Opportunity and the mandate of the community action agencies. These were primarily liberal, urban, northern Democrats who were partly concerned for their own positions, positions threatened, or appeared to be threatened by the new agencies, and partly trying to forestall conservative members from doing worse (Moynihan 1969a).

Loftus of *The New York Times* (28 April 1966) wrote:

> Leading House Democrats have agreed on amendments that will alter the face and character of the Great Society's campaign against poverty.
>
> They are the majority of the Education and Labor Committee. They have been meeting secretly and will be ready in a few days to confront the Republicans with a Democratic consensus.
>
> The changes are aimed straight at the Community Action Program, which Sargent Shriver last month called "the prime offensive weapon in the war on poverty."
>
> It is one of eight major programs directed by Mr. Shriver. . . . Politically it is by far the most explosive program because it is the only one that requires "maximum feasible participation" by representatives of poverty areas . . .
>
> The issue of policy participation by the poor has generated "ugly problems of the political establishment" in the private language of one House Democrat who is supporting the changes.

"Extremist groups have seized it as a forum for dissent," he said (Moynihan 1969a).

In May the political pressure was rising from various sources.

The Associated Press (May 26) wrote:

> "A 'glorious victory against poverty' was cited in the House floor today – high school youths at Fort Lauderdale, Fla., can get tuxedos at government expense."

> "Rep. Robert M. Mitchell, R-Ill., quoted the Fort Lauderdale News of May 22 as reporting the government is footing the $250 bill to enable 16 boys in Dol Palos Union High School to attend a union prom."

> " 'In addition,' Mitchell said, 'the bill for dinner afterwards and tips will by courtesy of the taxpayers.' "

> " ' . . . I know that dancing and partying are very much in vogue in this administration but I am a little surprised to find that they are considered such vital areas in the War Against Poverty,' Mitchell told the house."

> " 'Perhaps it will be deemed equally

important to furnish mink stoles for those who want to attend the opera but wouldn't feel they were properly attired without a furpiece.' "

Shriver (26 May) suggested that Mr. Mitchell's assertions were complete nonsense and that no anti-poverty money would be used for such a purpose in Florida or in California where such a incident was previously reported, or anywhere else in the United States. He also predicted that the war on poverty would be won by 1976. He told the Senate Labor subcommittee:

> "What we can accomplish will depend, of course, on what the nation feels it can devote to this effort and the President and Congress believe it should appropriate to it. However, I am willing to say that with expenditure levels which are modest we can reduce poverty in the first five years to about 12 million people, 20 million fewer than we now have, and in the second five years we can eliminate it as a scourge of mankind."

Moynihan (1969a) suggested that the style of Congress was essentially Southern. That is, its essence is to conceal power, not to fault it. The style of the community action militants was utterly antipathetical to the Congressional style of operation and a serious political problem, or problems, in that the Democratic majority in the House, especially the ranking hierarchy consisted of mainly urban liberal Democrats and Southern rural conservatives. Both groups felt uniquely threatened by a seemingly governmental sponsored effort to politicize the black masses of the Northern cities and the Southern countryside.

Congress reacted as could be expected; it moved to limit and restrict funding to restrain the freedom of action of the program's administrators (Moynihan 1969a).

The Democrats planned to cut the size of the community action program, limit the salary levels that might be paid in it, and increase the amount local communities would have to contribute to obtain the Federal matching grant, which originally had been 90 percent. Chairman Adam Clayton Powell, House Education and Labor Committee had to deny this when it became public, which ended the plans for amending the Economic Opportunity Act in 1966. However, a proposal sponsored by Albert H. Quie, (R), Minnesota, was adopted which required that the poor make up one-third of the members on the boards of community action agencies. On February 18, 1958, he had been elected to Congress in a special election to fill a vacancy caused by the death of August H. Andresen. He served in Congress for ten successive terms. During his twenty years in office, he advocated and authored many legislative bills relating to education, agriculture, anti-poverty, and labor issues. He was a ranking minority member on the House Committee on Education and Labor.

The Office of Economic Opportunity in June submitted a national ten-year plan for the elimination of poverty in the United States. Its almost 400 pages represented the collaborative work of almost all the federal agencies along with the planning and analytic skill of the senior staff of the Office of Economic Opportunity. In his transmittal letter to the Bureau of the Budget, Shriver wrote:

The costs of this proposed program are

not trivial, but they are surprisingly modest. Building on the $24 billion base estimated by the Bureau of the Budget for fiscal 1967 anti-poverty expenditures, they would add in fiscal 1968, $6.4 billion for all federal anti-poverty programs, which is less than the expected increase of federal tax revenues from fiscal 1967-1968. The successive increments after 1968 would be substantially smaller – $3 billion from 1968-1969 and smaller amounts every year there after. I believe that at these costs we could achieve the realistic goal of ending poverty by 1976. I further believe that this country can afford to adopt this goal and that it should do so.

It was never fully implemented. However the program objectives remained as the national norms for most of the daily work in the local community action programs.

United Press International (3 June 1966) reported the following:

A Republican Congressman from Ohio complained today that California Democratic Congressman had been promised at a "secret meeting" that they would be given a 'preferential preview' of anti-poverty projects in their districts.

Rep. William H. Ayres, ranking GOP member of the House Education and

Labor Committee, asked in a letter to OEO Director Sargent Shriver that Republican lawmakers be given the same privilege.

"I can well understand the concern of these members," Ayres said. "For many of them have stated they themselves [are] blamed for ill-advised OEO projects over which they have no control."

June 3, the Office of Economic Opportunity replied:

"Sargent Shriver . . . said today that he had not as of late Friday received the letter which Representative William Ayres . . . announced in the press he had sent to Mr. Shriver."

"Mr. Shriver said that he wanted to make it clearly understood that there are no secrets or 'secret meetings' at the OEO, as Representative Ayres charged. This is a typical misrepresentation issued for political purposes," he said.

"Mr. Shriver said that the OEO has for months supplied governors and mayors with notification of all applications made to OEO as part of the routine practice of informing elected officials of OEO business at the earliest possible time . . . "

A *Chicago Tribune* (9 June) article *RIPS 'JOYRIDE' FOR JOB CORPS PICKERS* stated:

> Rep. Charles S. Gubser (R-Cal.) Charged today that the Office of Economic Opportunity spent 'at least $8,000', to fly 40 workers from a Job Corps camp in Hawaii in pick asparagus in the San Francisco area.
>
> " 'It is almost inconceivable that OEO would do this," said Gubser in a speech in the House. "It is stupid and ridiculous that the war on poverty uses money like this after the taxpayer has worked so hard to earn it. It almost seems like Sargent Shriver is trying to think up new ways of squandering it."

9 June, 1966, the Office of Economic Opportunity responded:

> "The statement by Rep. Charles S. Gubser of California . . . was completely in error."
>
> "Dr. Franklyn A. Johnson, Director of Job Corps, said that no Job Corpsmen have been flown from the Hawaiian center, Koko Head. 'A group of 14 young men, who formed the cadre for the center, were the only ones at the center on May, when

the trip allegedly was made,' Dr. Johnson said . . ."

"Airline representatives reported that on May 7 a group of 50 farm workers flew from Honolulu to San Francisco, destination, Stockton, to help harvest crops. The trip was privately financed."

As Head Start began its second summer, Shriver spoke of the enthusiasm for the program, from the public, from various organizations and from "both side of the (political) aisle." 680,000 children in 2,600 communities would be served in summer program that year; that 180,000 children between the ages of three and five would participate in year-round programs; that over 140 universities were cooperating in running training programs on and off campus. Reports from last summer's operation showed generally that children entered school "better prepared and with greater self confidence and greater intellectual capacity than children from similar backgrounds who did not have a Head Start experience."

The Office of Economic Opportunity presented to the Budget Bureau their second National Anti-Poverty Plan. The stated goal was to end poverty by 1976. The plan recognized that the ability of the United States to "end poverty at any moment we are willing to put resources to guarantee income at the poverty level," but the OEO approach remained that of an "income maintenance system," by which the present welfare structure would be replaced by an incentive system. Everything would depend on the economic health of the nation and its rate of growth as well as the opportunity programs to "maximize the anti-poverty effect of that growth."

The plan felt that economic growth "unaided" would diminish the number of poor by 7.3 million with another 26 million removed from poverty by the proposed opportunity programs as well as the phased income maintenance program. The remaining 12.5 million impoverished would be taken above the poverty line by 1976. The figures were based on the 1972 population numbers of those in poverty.

The plan proposed an increase in training programs on a large scale mainly administered by the Labor Department. This was prompted by what the plan saw as the current tight job market which necessitated a shift of emphasis from public to private employment.

This 1966 plan altered the 1965 program categories of jobs, social programs, transfer payments to more precisely express the new objectives.

Sam Gibbons, (D), Florida, acting chairman of the House Ways and Means Committee, opened the hearings on the Economic Opportunity Amendments of 1966 by stating: "This is not an administration bill. This is not the same bill which came to us from the agencies. This is a bill which is the work of Congress and the work of a committee." It was a move to stress a political independence from the executive branch. Shriver felt that cuts to the program(s) would mean that "The poor will feel they have been shortchanged. They will feel they have been double-crossed. The poor will feel that democracy is only for the rich" (Zarefsky 1986).

Adam Clayton Powell reversed his attitude and on 1 September 1966 mounted an attack on Shriver during his testimony before the Senate Subcommittee on Government Reorganization when Powell presented his plan, "Solving the Black-Urban Crisis in America."

Among the Senators who expressed their confusion in his

stance, Senator Robert F. Kennedy displayed a sheaf of newspaper clippings that reported Powell's praise of the Office of Economic Opportunity. "I thought," said Kennedy as he displayed a number of press clipping reporting Powell's praise of the OEO, "that was so impressive I relaxed a little." Powell replied that his comments were "campaign oratory" (CSA 1969).

Powell's swift reversal appeared to stem from Shriver's refusal to fund a project Powell was interested in and Shriver's unwillingness to make suggested programmatic changes.

Powell was increasingly being criticized for mismanaging his committee's budget, taking trips abroad at public expense, and missing meetings of his committee as well as for personal conduct—he had taken two young women at government expense with him on overseas travel. When he was questioned about this, he responded: "I wish to state very emphatically . . . that I will always do just what every other Congressman and committee chairman has done and is doing and will do." Opponents led the criticism in his District, where his refusal to pay a 1963 slander judgment made him subject to arrest; he spent increasing amounts of time in Florida.

In January 1967, the House Democratic Caucus stripped Powell of his committee chairmanship when the full House refused to seat him until completion of an investigation by the Judiciary Committee. On 1 March the House voted 307 to 116 to exclude him.

The Economic Opportunity Act amendments of 1966 (P.L. 89-794) made various changes impacting the Community Action Program (CAP). These added several new programs to the CAP umbrella: adult work and training programs to train and employ low-income adults in fields of community service; the establishment of health service centers; low-income family emergency loans; grants to adult basic education program. At the same time it identified Head Start and Legal Services as separate programs within the overall community action framework.

Legal Services role was to extend legal aid to poor people who otherwise could not afford to hire lawyers.

These 1966 amendments also created a work-training and experience program called New Careers (the Scheuer Amendment, $75 million for the Scheuer program of subprofessional jobs. The subprofessional employment concept envisioned training the poor to be aides to professionals in such fields as education, welfare, health and public safety. Such jobs and training were expected to provide the opportunity for at least some career advancement) to meet certain types of manpower shortages.

New Careers projects trained crops of skilled professional support personnel. Nurses, doctors, teachers, laboratory technicians, social workers, law enforcement officials, and counselors were freed to devote their limited time to duties requiring professional skill while the unemployed and underemployed adults (age 22 and older) were trained for careers in human services.

Special Impact, also a 1966 amendment, was designed to attack the critical problems facing urban areas that had a high concentration of low-income residents through projects that would serve as catalysts to bring together Federal, State and local resources to provide training, education, health, and community services for selected urban neighborhoods.

Title V projects sought to give previously unemployable heads of families the work experience, training, and education necessary for them to move into the work force. The amendment gave the Department of Labor and the Department of Health, Education and Welfare joint responsibility in administering the projects. The Department of Labor also provided counseling, testing, and related services.

The Amendments authorized $1.75-billion in new funds for fiscal year 1967.

Title I - Work Training and Work Study Programs – $696 million.

Job Corps - $211 million

Neighborhood Youth Corps - $410 million

Special Impact Programs - $75 million

Title II - Urban and Community Action Programs – $846 million.

Title III - Special Programs to Combat Poverty in Rural Areas – $57 million.

Title IV - Small Business Loan Program – $5 million.

Title V - Work Experience – $100 million.

Title VI - Administration and Coordination – $15 million.

Title VIII - Service to America – $31 million.

Shriver sent a memorandum to the entire Community Action Program organization (9 September) in which he said:

> "... our insistence on participation of 'the residents of the area' has not been limited to, and will not be limited to, membership on CAP governing boards. That particular "bone of contention' is for the most part now behind us."

> "A man from Watts told me: Sargent Shriver, you listen and listen good. I'll tell

you exactly how it is. We want to run the jobs. We want to run the programs. It is our lives. It is our future."

"We have no intention," Shriver continued, "of course, of letting any one group, even the poor themselves, 'run the jobs" or 'run the programs.' That's not Community Action. But it is crucial that all of us understand the intensity of poor people's determination to participate actively in programs designed specifically to help them help themselves" [emphasis in original].

" . . . The new elements in community affairs – involvement of the poor themselves – has not always been understood, and is still being registered. This is the reason for this memorandum. I will not consider any program a true community action program which does not have maximum feasible participation by all segments of the community – and that must include the intended beneficiaries of that program."

The Child Development Group of Mississippi (CDGM) had been given two Office of Economic Opportunity grants (summer 1965, February 1966) based on their having Head Start centers for more than 6,000 children in 28 counties.

Senator John Stennis, (D), Mississippi, senior member,

The Senate Appropriations Committee, a committed segregationist, claimed that the CDGM was mismanaging their funds (Adler 1994). Julius B. Richmond, discussing this, said that Senator Stennis had sent "an audit team down, and I think out of the million and a half dollars what we were expending that summer, there were about $26,000 that they couldn't identify receipts for. That became a great cause célèbre for the senator. . After all, $26,000 in a state where a black man couldn't ask a white vendor for a receipt and expect a response – so I was a little taken aback that it was that low. . . But to me, that was a ridiculously low figure not to have receipts for when you're expending a million and a half dollars, and particularly under those circumstances. So I viewed this as kind of a 'Star Chamber' proceeding." Donald M. Baker, Counsel to the Labor Subcommittee of the Senate Committee on Labor and Public Welfare, felt that, "Well, Stennis's main objection – he was reflecting accurately, I think, his white constituency, who was basically, if the thing had been run 100 percent by Uncle Toms, if they'd been all black, they would have objected to it because that's not the way it's done down there" (Gillette 2010).

The Office of Economic Opportunity (OEO) decided (27 September) based on audits, inspection reports, program analysis, and management reviews to not refinance the Child Development Group of Mississippi (CDGM) and to shift the funding to a newly formed biracial group, Mississippi Action for Progress which had the governor's backing.

Unable to arrange a meeting with the CDGM Board, OEO mailed their report, 11 pages plus a 3 page legal opinion by OEO General Counsel, Donald Baker, to the board, 1 October.

The decision started a major reaction of political argument that must have been unanticipated. After two months of pressure from civil rights groups, The Rev. James F. McCree,

Chairman of CDGM announced at a mass meeting (around 8,000 Negroes) in Jackson, Mississippi, that he was pledged to fight against "political tricks and manipulations" until the funds were restored. He had received a supporting telegrams from the Rev. Martin Luther King and the Citizens Crusade Against Poverty. Mrs. Fanie Lou Hamer of the Mississippi Freedom Democratic Party Stated: "We aren't ready to be sold out by a few middle-class bourgeoisie and some of them Uncle Toms who couldn't care less." The National Council of Churches as well as opponents argued that OEO had capitulated to Senator John Stennis, (D), Mississippi, political views.

Shriver, 2 November, stated, in support of CDGM: "because of this program, 5,280 Mississippi children received the education, the medical care, the social welfare services, and in some cases even the clothes, the like of which they never before enjoyed" (Adler 1994).

The Citizen's Crusade Against Poverty, a private organization representing more than 100 religious, civil rights, labor, academic, student, and farm groups, funded by a 1966 $37,000 grant (Ford Foundation 1966) and contributions from the United Auto Workers union, (headed by Richard Boone, former OEO CAP Deputy Director), appointed a 10-member Board of Inquiry which concluded that there was no evidence to support the OEO charges against CDGM. On the board were: Dr. Robert Coles, Harvard psychiatrist; A. Philip Randolph, elder statesman of the civil rights movement; and, Dr. Kenneth B. Clark, social scientist (Clark 2000).

Gerald Ford, (R), Nebraska, minority leader of the House, was quoted in an article in *The Washington Post*, 24 August 1966, where he called for President Johnson's resignation for what he felt was a connection between the Community Action Programs and urban riots (Goldstein 2012).

The Presbyterian Church, the United Church of Christ, and Episcopal Church urban specialists, 70 clergymen in all, picketed OEO headquarters in Washington, D.C. on 15 October, claiming that OEO was "throwing road-blocks in the way of maximum feasible participation of the poor in anti-poverty programs." Shriver met with them, 17 October. He strongly denied the charges they brought and that he would meet the Board of Directors of CDGM to discuss a possible relocation of their program, which he did in Atlanta, Georgia on 25 October. Afterwards he stated that OEO funds would not be allocated to them without "comprehensive reorganization."

By the end of the Congressional session, Johnson's teams had passed 181 out of 200 major pieces of legislation (Harward 2016).

That same month, 27 October, the *Christian Science Monitor* had its correspondents assess the first 18-months of the federal anti-poverty program. William C. Selover wrote a series of articles based on their reports. In his fifth one he wrote:

> "Nobody's amazed that problems and potential scandals have turned up. In the bright lights of vast publicity the war on poverty is being watched for every false move, by newspapers, by OEO itself, by the Administration, by local and State governments, and by the political opposition. What is remarkable is not that such instances have cropped up, but that there have been so few of them, and that in the sizable majority of local programs, there hasn't been a whisper of scandal."

The OEO renewed the CDGM grant, somewhat reduced in funding, as a pass through to Mary Holmes Junior College, which was operated by the National Board of Missions of the Presbyterian Church (Levitan 1969). Jack Conway, Director, Community Action Program (October 1964-February 1965), Deputy Director, OEO (February 1965-October 1965), said, "[Governor] Ross Barnett went out of his mind when we put that big Head Start grant into Mary Holmes Junior College in Mississippi and made it administrator of the program. But we did because he would have vetoed that." (Gillette 2010).

OEO announced a grant to Rust College, Holly Springs, Mississippi, a 12-month, $1.2 million for a Head Start program for 600 pre-school children in two counties, and, a grant to Southwest Mississippi Opportunity, Inc., Woodville, $713,00 to provide programs for 935 children in three counties.

Shriver stated in his decision, that no single group "has a monopoly on running any of the War on Poverty programs in Mississippi."

Mississippi Governor Paul B. Johnson, Jr., (D), vetoed the grant of $713,000 to the Southwest Mississippi Opportunity, Inc. Operation in November. He claimed that it had been infiltrated by 20 former members of CDGM. Shriver vetoed the Governor's veto as was permitted under the law.

Jule Sugarman, instrumental in the creation of Project Head Start, then Associate Director Head Start, said, "Part of the problem here was that, when we reached the decision that we could not continue with CDGM, we were reluctant to see a program disappear from Mississippi altogether, so we actively supported the formation of another group called Mississippi Action for Progress [MAP], which would develop programs to replace CDGM. . . . So the net results of all of this – you have to add up the fact that Mississippi now has the largest Head Start program in the country. There are some 30,000 children in Head Start in Mississippi in the full-year programs, which is one-seventh of all the kids in the country in full-year Head Start, in Mississippi. And that's roughly fifty percent of all the children that are in the first grade in Mississippi" (Gillette 2010).

The Mississippi Action For Progress, Inc. received a grant of $3,020,906 to conduct a full-year program for 1,500 children. The organization was to be administered by an 18-member Board of Directors, including: Aaron Henry, President of the Mississippi State Conference of NAACP Branches; Hodding Carter III, Editor, *The Greenville Delta Democrat Times,* as well as prominent labor leaders, businessmen, clergy, and six representative of the poor who were residents of the area and members of the groups to be served.

Shriver, in November, replaced Jack Conway, his Deputy, with Bernard Boutin. Conway had become involved in a private organization, the Citizens Crusade Against Poverty (Clark 2000).

The Johnson administration was frequently placed in a difficult position by threatened budget cuts. In its own internal budget process it repeatedly limited the amount of money allocated to the anti-poverty program because of the requirements of the Vietnam war. This was well known, so its protests against further cuts were less than convincing.

The Republican Party decided to focus on the failures of community action programs and "racial disorder" as central talking points in the midterm election (Goldstein 2012).

The Permanent Subcommittee On Investigation, Chairman John D. McClellan, (D), Arkansas, started hearings in November on riots, civil and criminal disorders. The bulk of the testimony was a rehash of accusations made by Newark officials before Senator Eastland's 2 August hearings (CSA 1969).

During the November 8 mid-term elections, the

Democrats lost forty-seven seats in the House of Representatives and three seats in the U.S. Senate to the Republicans. Forty-five in favor of the Office of Economic Opportunity were among the defeated, forty-five of the newly elected Republicans were known to oppose any increase in anti-poverty spending. The Democrats, however, retained control of both chambers of Congress. Republicans won a large victory in the gubernatorial elections, with a net gain of seven seats (Zarefsky 1986).

The GOP's victory in this election strengthened the conservative coalition including Ronald Reagan, Governor of California (who soon became the leader of the right-wing of the Republican Party); George H. W. Bush from Texas; and future vice president Spiro Agnew, Governor of Maryland; and, brought Richard Nixon forward as a front-runner for the 1968 Republican nomination (CSA 1969).

Melvin R. Laird, (R), Wisconsin, Chairman of the House Republican Conference and ranking minority member of the Health, Education and Welfare subcommittee of the Appropriations Committee, publically taunted Shriver, December 1966, to persuade the President to ask for more money for the anti-poverty program, guaranteeing his own support if such a request was made. None was.

As committed to the Vietnam War as he was, Johnson had no, or little extra funds, to respond to what was manifestly the problem of poverty. Instead he created commissions of various types. The commissions usual response was to tell him that he required more money to spend while at the same time Johnson's Secretary of the Treasury was telling him that there was no more money.

6 December, the Office of Economic Opportunity announced approval by 21 Governors for the first Job Corps Centers.

16 December, Shriver announced approval of 18 additional Job Corps centers in 15 states and the OEO announced that an "agreement in principle" had been reached between CDGM Board of Directors and OEO. A joint communique stated, in part:

> 1. The Board of Missions and Mary Holmes College agreed to assume full financial responsibility . . .
> 2. Mary Holmes College has agreed to assign its Vice President for Development . . . as administrator of the grant . . .
> 3. CDGM has completed the enlargement of its Board of Directors to a total of 19 of whom 6 will be white . . .
> 6. The Board of Directors of CDGM has taken action to make it clear to all employees that they are prohibited during working hours from participating in voter registration or partisan political activities, the organization of civil rights activity as defined . . . the organization of economic boycott or any other activity not essential to the approved purpose of the grant . . .

17 December, President Johnson announced a package totaling $482.6 million for 162 separate War on Poverty projects: the first three urban Job Corps Centers, each of them to train 1,250 and 2,500 enrollees per years when in operation; a near $4 million grant to Chicago for implementing an anti-poverty campaign; and, a $6,000 small business loan to a former

Pittsburgh steelworker to expand his 12-seat luncheonette.

The heavy political pressure stemming from the zealous application of "maximum feasible participation" by the Community Action Programs finally caused a reaction within the Executive Office of the White House that made the front page of the *New York Times*, 5 November 1966, which stated in clear terms a redefinition of that troublesome piece of terminology:

> The budget Bureau, fiscal arm of the White House, has told the Office of Economic Opportunity that it would prefer less emphasis on policy-making by the poor in planning community projects.
>
> "Maximum feasible participation" by the poor in the anti-poverty program is called for by law. In the bureau's view, this means primarily using the poor to carry out the program, not to design it.

Another page-one story in the *New York Times* (12 December 1966) stated:

> Without a word of debate, the House voted to give the Office of Economic Opportunity $370 million less than it had authorized for the agency yesterday.
> Regarding funds for the anti-poverty program, the Office of Economic Opportunity said that the House not only

cut its funds but also cut its discretion. As a result, it said, the community action programs would have to bear the brunt of the money reduction.

William P. Kelley, Task Force Against Poverty member, later Director, Job Corps, felt:

> The War on Poverty moved out very rapidly . . . . The operation of the War on Poverty during the period of 1965 and 1966 was just one of the most enormously successful undertakings . . . that I'd ever seen . . . [It] was a period of great building, a period of creation of resources that are going to be around for a long time in this nation" (Clark 2002).

The year 1967 would be a year of debate, conflict, and budgetary warfare. Administration decisions and the slow erosion of local programmatic responsibility led to what had been the keystone of the federal anti-poverty program into a less central but politically embarrassing force on both the local and national levels (Wofford 1969).

No program had been so controversial or so threatened and beleaguered (Selover 1969).

Congress would spend the entire year working on authorizations and appropriations. This would stand in contrast to 1966 when they spent about half as much time doing the same job.

Johnson gave his *State of the Union* address on 10 January 1967 and stated (Johnson 1967b), in part:

As President Abraham Lincoln said, "We must ask where we are, and whither we are tending."

The last 3 years bear witness to our determination to make this a better country.

We have struck down legal barriers to equality.

We have improved the education of 7 million deprived children and this year alone we have enabled almost 1 million students to go to college.

We have brought medical care to older people who were unable to afford it. Three and one-half million Americans have already received treatment under Medicare since July.

We have built a strong economy that has put almost 3 million more Americans on the payrolls in the last year alone.

We have included more than 9 million new workers under a higher minimum wage.

We have launched new training programs to provide job skills for almost 1 million

Americans.

We have helped more than a thousand local communities to attack poverty in the neighborhoods of the poor. We have set out to rebuild our cities on a scale that has never been attempted before. We have begun to rescue our waters from the menace of pollution and to restore the beauty of our land and our countryside, our cities and our towns.

We have given 1 million young Americans a chance to earn through the Neighborhood Youth Corps – or through Head Start, a chance to learn.

So together we have tried to meet the needs of our people. And, we have succeeded in creating a better life for the many as well as the few. Now we must answer whether our gains shall be the foundations of further progress, or whether they shall be only monuments to what might have been - abandoned now by a people who lacked the will to see their great work through.

Three years ago we set out to create these new instruments of social progress. This required trial and error – and it has produced both. But as we learn, through success and failure, we are changing our strategy and we are trying to improve our tactics. In the long run, these starts – some rewarding, others inadequate and disappointing – are crucial to SUCCESS.

One example is the struggle to make life better for the less fortunate among us.
On a similar occasion, at this rostrum in 1949, I heard a great American President, Harry S. Truman, declare this: "The American people have decided that poverty is just as wasteful and just as unnecessary as preventable disease."

I recommend that we intensify our efforts to give the poor a chance to enjoy and to join in this Nation's progress.

I shall propose certain administrative changes suggested by the Congress – as well as some that we have learned from our own trial and error.

The 88th and the 89th Congresses passed more social and economic legislation than any two single Congresses in American history. Most of you who were Members of those Congresses voted to pass most of those measures. But your efforts will come to nothing unless it reaches the people.

Federal energy is essential. But it is not enough. Only a total working partnership among Federal, State, and local governments can succeed. The test of that partnership will be the concern of each public organization, each private institution, and each responsible citizen.

We must eliminate by law unjust discrimination in employment because of age.

We should embark upon a major effort to provide self-help assistance to the forgotten in our midst--the American Indians and the migratory farm workers. And we should reach with the hand of understanding to help those who live in rural poverty.

And I will propose these measures to the 90th Congress.

On the same day 10 January 1967, Johnson gave his *Economic Report of the President* (1967a) to Congress in which he said, in part:

"Economic progress still left far too many behind.
• Nearly 3 million workers were without jobs at the end of 1966.

Perhaps two-thirds of them were "frictionally" unemployed: new entrants to the labor force in the process of locating a job; persons who quit one job to seek another; workers in the "off" months of seasonal industries; those temporarily laid off but with instructions to return. Their unemployment will be temporary; many were drawing unemployment insurance.

•But most of the remaining third will wait a long time for a steady job. They are the "hard-core" unemployed—lacking the necessary skills to find other than intermittent work; the victims of past or present discrimination; those unable or unwilling to move from depressed areas and occupations; the physically or emotionally handicapped.

•Another half million to one million potential workers were not even counted as unemployed. Many had long ago abandoned any search for a job. Some had never tried.

• But even among those who worked year-round, some 2 million breadwinners — particularly the low-skilled with large families — earned incomes insufficient to support a minimum standard of decent subsistence.

•And 6½ million families were poor because the heads of their households were unable to work: either aged, severely handicapped, or a widowed or deserted mother with young children. Those left behind used to be called the "invisible poor." But an awakened public conscience has sharpened the vision of most Americans. We will move this year toward solutions for these problems and others. But they cannot all be completely solved in 1967.

• The United States is the first large nation in the history of the world wealthy enough to end poverty within its borders. There are many fronts in the War on Poverty. We are moving forward on them all.

• There must be full employment so that those qualified and able to work can find jobs. . . . The unemployment rate last year was the lowest in 13 years.

• Those not now fully qualified must be given the education and training, the health and guidance services which will enable them to make their full contribution to society. . . . We have greatly increased our aid to education and enlarged our training programs, and we will expand them further.

• For those who will be unable to earn adequate incomes, there must be help—most of all for the benefit of children, whose misfortune to be born poor must not deprive them of future opportunity. . . . We have increased our income support, and we will increase it further.

• Wherever the poor and disadvantaged are concentrated, intensive and coordinated programs to break the cycle of deprivation and dependency must continue and be reinforced. . . . We instituted these programs in hundreds of cities and rural areas; we are expanding them and designing others.

• The coexistence of job vacancies and idle workers unable to fill them represents a bitter human tragedy and an inexcusable economic waste. One of society's most creative acts is the training of the unemployed, the underemployed, or the formerly unemployable to fill those vacancies. A dynamic economy demands new and changing skills. By enabling workers to acquire those skills, we open opportunities for individual development and self-fulfillment. And we make possible higher production without inflationary pressures.

I shall ask the Congress for funds to support a new and special effort to train and find jobs for the disadvantaged who live in urban ghettos.

These two reports apparently didn't say what some

commentators felt was enough.

On January 21, *The New Republic, A Journal of Opinion* (1967a) argued:

> Mr. Johnson proceeded to make clear that he suspects the nation has lost interest in the war on poverty, even if he himself hasn't. Discussion of domestic problems occupied much of his speech (some hawks grumbled about the time he devoted to poverty when he should, according to them, have been talking about the war in Vietnam), but his proposals for advancing the war against want at home were so modest, and he put them forward so diffidently, that he seemed to be saying he knew the Congress is willing to vote him money for Vietnam but not for domestic rehabilitation.
>
> [The author felt that those] who make up this Congress [were] nodding their conservative heads in solemn unison (Hubert Humphrey's wagging head could be seen on the television screen, rhythmically affirming each presidential statement).
>
> What it amounts to is that President Johnson's timid consensus-seeking risks pushing the country back into the mire of

former error: cutting public spending (except for "defense") and trying to "balance" the administrative budget. That is Eisenhower's swampland.

Joseph A. Califano, Jr., Johnson's Assistant for Domestic Legislation, his top domestic aid, stated at a conference of news paper reporters that those who felt that the Administration had abandoned the anti-poverty program were wrong. "I might say that the stuff in the newspapers over the past several months about the President not fighting for the poverty program is just a lot of hogwash and trash. It's just not true. I think he spent as much time working with Sarge on putting together this program as he did on any other programs that's going up there this year" (CSA 1969).

On 14 March 1967, Johnson presented a *Special Message to the Congress: America's Unfinished Business, Urban and Rural Poverty* (Johnson 1967c) in which he stated, in part:

> "In the 1960's, we have begun to devise a total strategy against poverty. We have recognized that public housing, minimum wages and welfare services could not, standing alone, change the bleak environment of deprivation for millions of poor families.
> A successful strategy requires a breakthrough on many fronts: education, health, jobs and job training, housing, public assistance, transportation, clean air and adequate water supplies. The basic conditions of life for the poor must, and

can, be changed."

"The purpose of community action is to encourage those who need help to help themselves."

"A Community Action Agency should provide a voice in planning programs to mayors, local business and labor leaders, the citizens to be helped, teachers, lawyers, physicians – all those who give their time and efforts to relieve poverty in their communities and who know well the needs of their neighbors. It may be established as a private, non-profit corporation or created by local government. Each agency analyzes the problems its community faces and develops a strategy for its anti-poverty, self-help effort. This strategy may include any combination of Federal, State and local programs which will assist the poor in their fight against poverty."

"Community action agencies should devote their energies to self-help measures and new initiatives that will advance their communities in the war against poverty. To be effective, it is essential that they be non-partisan and totally disengaged from any partisan political activity. This Administration, the

National Advisory Council on Economic Opportunity and, I am confident, the Congress, will be constantly alert to the danger of partisan political activity and will take the necessary steps to see that it does not occur."

"If the attack on poverty is to mean anything, it must reach all the poor--including those whose educational experience and past behavior make them difficult to teach, motivate and discipline."

"The Job Corps is a response to that moral imperative. Its success must be measured against the difficulties of its task."

"There are 113 Job Corps centers in America. More than 60,000 youths have passed through them in the last two years."

"I have asked the Director of the Office of Economic Opportunity, in cooperation with the Secretary of Housing and Urban Development and other federal departments, to expand and strengthen the development of Neighborhood Multi-Service and Multi-County Centers in the coming fiscal year. These Centers have become the focal point of many local efforts in their attack on poverty, and I expect that local communities will seek some $120 million for them in fiscal 1968."

"The Director of the Office of Economic Opportunity, in cooperation with the Secretary of Health, Education, and Welfare, will encourage local communities to establish additional Health Centers in the coming fiscal year, so that up to 50 will be in operation by the end of fiscal 1968."

"Two hundred and twenty-four public and private universities and private secondary schools are taking part in Upward Bound this year. More than 20,000 poor young men and women are today headed for high school graduation and college study through Upward Bound. We estimate that 78 percent of these youngsters – as compared to 8 percent of poor youth generally – will go on to college."

"Applications for Upward Bound far exceed the funds presently available. Those funds must be increased – for America needs the trained and competent citizens these poor children can become."

"If the attack on poverty is to mean

anything, it must reach all the poor – including those whose educational experience and past behavior make them difficult to teach, motivate and discipline."

"By this June, more than 4,000 Volunteers in Service to America – VISTA volunteers – will be in the field. They will be living and working in the hollows of Appalachia, on Indian reservations, in migrant camps and city slums – to teach skills, care for the sick, and help people to help themselves."

"Poverty cannot be eliminated overnight. It takes time, hard work, money and perseverance."

"It has been only two years and three months since we decided to embark upon a concentrated attack on poverty. We have made progress. But victory over poverty will not quickly or cheaply be won."

"We do not have all the answers. But we have given a great many people – very young children, restless teenagers, men without skills, mothers without proper health care for themselves or their babies, old men and women without a purpose to fill their later years – the opportunity they needed, when they needed it, in a way that called on them to give the best of themselves."

"Millions more Americans need – and deserve – that opportunity. The aim of this Administration is, and will be, that they shall have it."

"It is difficult for most Americans to understand what it is to be desperately poor in today's affluent America. More than half our population was born after 1940. Less than half can remember the depression on the farms of the twenties, or the bread-lines of the thirties. "The Grapes of Wrath" is ancient literature – not a living record – to most Americans."

"Yet for more than 31 million Americans, poverty is neither remote in time, nor removed in space. It is cruel and present reality. It makes choices for them. It determines their future prospects – despite our hope and belief that in America, opportunity has no bounds for any man."

"Poverty was universally tolerated until a century or so ago. But like disease, war and famine, it gained nothing in acceptability because it was prevalent. As soon as men saw that they might escape it, they fought and died to escape it."

"Poverty denies to most of those born into it a fair chance to be themselves, to be happy in life. Federal funds or services, and the opportunities they provide, cannot permanently free a man from the trap of poverty if he does not want to be free. He must use the ladders that circumstance, native ability, and his Nation may create."

"Let it be said that in our time, we pursued a strategy against poverty so that each man had a chance to be himself."

"Let it be said that in our time, we offered him the means to become a free man – for his sake, and for our own."

Joseph A. Kershaw, stated before the Senate Committee on Employment, Manpower and Poverty, 18 March, that the war on poverty, recognizing the existence of political conditions that perpetuated poverty, did not aim for conflict or overthrow. Rather, OEO aimed at changing the causative conditions of poverty, which included, but was not limited to, the political organization of the poor.

The *New Republic*, 25 March, wrote that "The President has officially bid farewell to the original poverty program by asking Congress . . . to tie local community action programs to city hall."

The New Republic article, 27 March, (1967b) felt that:

> Congress is waiting with knives for Mr.
> Johnson's trimmed poverty program.
> Senator Dirksen led a successful floor
> fight last year to cut back poverty funds.
> The conservatives are all set again this
> year. This is one of the things we find
> hardest of all to understand in
> Washington. Did you realize, for
> example, that in 1950 only five nations
> had lower infant mortality than we did
> but that in 1960 we were behind 10
> countries and that now there are 13 ahead
> of us? We are getting richer and we are
> falling behind.
> These countries ahead of us nearly all
> have national health plans. By contrast in
> the US 65 percent of children from low-
> income families have never seen a dentist.

In April the Administration submitted their bill (S. 1545), a joint product of the White House and the Office of Economic Opportunity staff, a heavily revised Economic Opportunity Act of 1964, to Congress.

Their approach was to strengthen the language of the programs to be explicit and well-defined in case Congress decided to dismantle the OEO. This, they felt, would guarantee that the programs would remain intact, regardless of which other agency they were moved to (CSA 1969).

Shriver, reacting to negative comments about the various

programs, said to the House Committee: ". . . some people felt the Declaration of Independence was an incendiary document, that it raised false hopes, and the Constitution of the United States when it was written, that it raised false hopes that never will be fulfilled." The basic approach to Congress was a matter of convincing its members that the program was a success. If Congress judged a program to be a success, then it was a success. Elmer J. Holland (D), Pennsylvania, stated: ". . . if keeping the promises of the Constitution and spreading the good news of human equality was revolutionary, then I would say hooray for the revolution." William S. Moorhead, (D), Pennsylvania pointed out "Many of those who are quick to denounce the War on Poverty are equally quick to defend its specific component programs . . . These people seem to feel that by removing the specific programs from the jurisdiction of OEO criticism of the antipoverty programs will end." Whitney Young, Executive Director of the National Urban League, argued: "The nation's promise to the poor as enunciated in 1964 is embodied in the OEO and to destroy the OEO is to destroy that promise" (Zarefsky 1986).

Carl Perkins, Chairman, House Committee on Education and Labor, introduced, 10 April, the Administration's poverty bill, H.R. 8311

The *New York Times*, 11 April, felt that all the politicians had been listening "from racists who object to special help for minorities, from politicians who want to run the program all by themselves and from bureaucrats yearning for bigger bureaus."

Senator Joseph Clark, (D), Pennsylvania, introduced, 13 April, the Senate equivalent of the Administration's poverty bill, S. 1545.

Bookbinder responded to written opinions (Bookbinder 1967), 15 April:

"By crudely lifting out of context a few words in the President's message, *The New Republic* claims that the poverty programs have now been turned over to city hall. The fact is that the President was merely reiterating what has always been the concept and the goal of community action: the involvement of the poor themselves, the involvement of the private sector (labor, business, education, social agencies, etc.), *and* the involvement of local government. . . . There are mayors who will probably continue to prefer to stay out. The President's message states that 'community action agencies should devote their energies to self-help measures and new initiatives that will advance their communities in the war against poverty.' In the development and implementation of such measures and initiatives, over 90 thousand poor people in over 1,000 community action agencies have found a voice, a role, a power they never dreamed of achieving only three years ago. . . . These changes may not look like the social revolution *The New Republic* dreams about, but thousands of institutions have already felt the impact of OEO programs. And millions of poor Americans have started to feel the impact of programs on their lives and their children's lives."

The Administration requested, 2 May, that the Senate amend the Second Supplement Appropriations Bill, passed by the House, to include $75 million. It was aimed at short-term programs for "idle youths in our teeming cities." The funds were to go to New York City and the Community Action Programs. It was approved in June.

Albert H. Quie, (D), Minnesota, and Charles E. Goodsell, (R), New York, introduced, 8 June, H.R. 10682, the "Opportunity Crusade," the Republicans alternative poverty program. Goodsell argued that this would increase money for poverty programs, maximize the involvement of the poor in community action, and transfer some OEO programs, Head Start and Vista, to HEW, under the direction of an Assistant Secretary. This was because of the confusion of "national innovation with spontaneous spending," and that OEO was in a phase of "Administrative adolescence," with a "regressive tendency" portending a "calcified adulthood" (CSA 1969).

Hyman Bookbinder said that the "Crusade would destroy the agency that did the innovating . . . It would cut the top off – creating a sort of topless poverty program." House members saw a film "Beyond the Hills," which showed Shriver and the Reverend Billy Graham touring a Job Corps Center."

Graham stated at a Congressional luncheon: ". . . now, when this program started, I was somewhat against it . . . But I am a convert . . . I believe we have a moral and spiritual responsibility as a people to attack this problem with even greater vigor that we have thus far" (CSA 1969).

The findings of the Senate Subcommittee on Employment, Manpower and Poverty, Authorized February 1967, made their findings public, 11 June. Joseph S. Clark, (D), Pennsylvania, stated:

"I would comment that we found a number of strengths in the program, in particular there are a number of splendid community action programs underway throughout the country. With respect to many of them, there is intense controversy – what mighty be called a struggle between the poor and the power structure in the particular communities."

"One hope has been, and the hope has been realized in several communities, that these struggles of the power structure to assure adequate administration are gradually but slowly being ironed our or hammered out on the anvil of controversy."

"We have learned that in these areas OEO speaks for the poor, and this, I believe, to be helpful. It is sometimes charged it speaks for the poor too strongly, and not enough for the power structure. This is a controversial matter which we will not resolve and on which we need to get more testimony."

"Every witness we heard, no matter where we went, would continue the OEO as an independent, high-level agency charged with the over-all responsibility of directing that part of the war on poverty which comes within the purview of the basic legislation, and also every witness we heard believed that OEO should have its finger in the large poverty pie where the many billions of dollars which are not under the direction of OEO and are done by other agencies, would nevertheless be affected in the philosophy and in their administration by the advice of the OEO agency."

"Great expectations have been aroused in America for the poverty program and those great expectations have largely been aroused by the work of the OEO and its dynamic director, Mr. Shriver."

"The poor are participating in their own programs, sometimes clumsily, sometimes ineffectively, but these expectations have been aroused, and in my judgement they will not be satisfied until many more significant victories over poverty have been won than have been won so far" (CSA 1969).

Moynihan (1967) wrote:

"The physical isolation of Negro housing is so near complete in the United States that it is possible to live in the same city with a million Negro Americans and have only the faintest awareness that they live in distinct neighborhoods and communities that have vastly greater 'urban' problems than those faced by the community-at-large ... I assume that the problem of objectivity evaluating urban problems must even become greater now the Federal government is moving beyond is original concern to improve the physical equipment of cities toward an effort to improve the human beings who live in them. No one need be told that people are harder to rehabilitate than buildings, although we have begun to learn that the process is expensive and frustrating in buildings as well ... We have set ourselves goals that are, in some ways, unique in history: not only to abolish poverty and ignorance, but also to become the first genuinely multi-racial and, we hope, in the end non-racial democracy the world has seen. I believe that in moving toward these goals, and in seeking to change present reality, an unflinching insistence on fact will be a major asset."

Through June and July both the House and the Senate held hearings on the amendments being proposed by the Administration. In the Senate the hearings consumed over 33 days, 144 hours of testimony of 401 witnesses, 7 executive sessions, 18 reports by staff, 15 studies by consultants, 11 inspections trips around the county. In the House, 6 weeks of 100 witnesses, produced 6 volumes and over 4,00 pages (CSA 1969).

During all this activity, Shriver also spent almost 41 hours in front of both the Senate Subcommittee on Employment as well as the House Committee as well as an investigation of his agency checking rumors and charges from mayors as well as newspaper articles stating that some of the people employed by the Office of Economic Opportunity had taken part in riots in the cities where there was an OEO program and violence (CSA 1969).

After the July riots in Detroit and Newark, Johnson created, 28 July 1967, the National Advisory Commission on Civil Disorders, Executive Order 11365, often called the Kenner Commission. The Commission released its 426 page report 26 February 1968. The report felt that "our nation is moving toward two societies, one black, one white – separate and unequal." The report felt that federal and state governments had failed in housing, education, and social-service policies. It also suggested that the mainstream media was ignoring the problem and that it "has too long basked in a white world looking out of it, if at all, with white men's eyes and white perspective." The report recommended government programs to provide needed services, more diverse hiring and sensitive police forces, and to invest billions to break up housing programs as a means of changing residential segregation. The government response was, in the main, a greater expenditure for police and weaponry (Trattner 1994).

Gaither observed, "Now, you don't read anything in the paper about some Social Security beneficiary who goes out and commits a robbery. You don't read anything about some schoolchild who happens to be getting $300 a year from the federal government through an HEW education program and that kid goes out and tries to burn the school down. John Gardner doesn't get blamed for it, nor does the President. But that's what happens [to] OEO. During the rioting in Detroit, in Watts, and elsewhere, there were always rather extravagant claims by some politicians that it was incited by OEO people. Every investigation proved that this not true" (Gillette 2010).

Shriver wrote, 20 July, to all Regional Directors:

> "There will be absolute insistence that every OEO employee and every employee of an OEO be scrupulously avoid and resist participation by OEO funded resources in any activities which threaten public order in any community . . . I shall insist upon the withholding of OEO funds from any grantee or delegate agency which is shown to be encouraging or tolerating such behavior" CSA 1969).

There were 12,128 persons that were direct employee of OEO that lived in or near ghettos: neighborhood works, health aides, clerical staff, community organizers. There were twenty-seven cities were riots occurred. Shriver pointed out that "In these twenty-seven cities a total of 6,733 person were arrested. In the same twenty-seven cities, six of the 12,128 paid poverty workers were arrested. To date, none of the six has come to trail, and none has been convicted" (CSA 1969).

During the House Committee on Education and Labor hearings, 1 August 1967, Congresswoman Edith Green said:

> "I have a very serious question, in fact, I

would heartily disapprove of the expenditure of Federal funds to finance people who are outside government and who are working for the express purpose of changing the political structure and changing the democratic process and upsetting or overturning the decisions which are made by mayors or duly elected officials or council people or anyone else that has been chosen by the majority of the people through the democratic process . . . if this is being done and if it is being done in a lot of places, then Congress most certainly – and when the bill gets to the floor – I think they would certainly want to take a look at it" (CSA 1969).

On 2 August, the Judiciary Committee, Senator James Eastland, (D), Mississippi, Chairman, began hearings on an anti-poverty bill (H.R. 421), passed by the house after the Newark riot.

Senator John D. McClellan, (D), Arkansas, on 9 August, in referring to the riots, stated that there was: "enough indication," of involvement on the part of OEO workers to warrant a thorough investigation. An article in the *Hartford Times*, 11 August, 1967 suggested: "There is little need and less wisdom in dispatching Senator McClellan's committee to ferret out a handful of radical anti-poverty workers . . . It is painfully obvious that the national interest would be best served by upgrading the material for the war on poverty, not be setting up senatorial snipers against the war's generalship" (CSA 1969).

In Mid-August, Herman Short, Police Chief of Houston, Texas, informed the press that a Harris County Community Action Committee employee had submitted a request for seven 22-inch telescopic rifle sights, $111.00 each, from the Kelly Air Force Base Gas surplus depot as well as a dozen walkie-talkies and four radios for monitoring police broadcasts, purportedly to be used in civil rights demonstration(s). Within days, Senator John Tower, (R), Texas. and Representative George H. Bush, (R), Texas, demanded Congressional investigation.

Shriver sent a letter to Senator Ralph Yarborough, (D), Texas, on 16 August saying that this episode was a perfect example of the "charge now – someone else will pay later" technique, which "typifies many malicious allegations against OEO. . . Because of the obvious hysteria potential of such an order, OEO cancelled it immediately, but let it appear that we had allowed the order to stand so that we could find out whether any one or any group of a subversive character was involved." He finally concluded:

> "All of this had been done a full week before Houston's Chief of Police 'disclosed' the requisition to the public. The Houston police, without checking with the local poverty program, OSI, the FBI, or with OEO/Washington, evidently could not resist the temptation of releasing the information to the press. Fortunately, this didn't make any difference as there was no wrongdoing. But the incident illustrates once again now intemperate and ill-advised people can raise suspicions and doubts about

perfectly innocent activities. Totally false charges are repeated and repeated and repeated. Hitler called this the technique of 'the big lie.' "

On 16 August 1967, the Senate met, Senator Walter Mondale, (D), Minnesota, President pro tempore presiding. Senator Joseph S. Clark, (D), Pennsylvania, had incorporated inside the Congressional Record (1967) a recent Washington Post written by Joseph Alsop in which Alsop stated: "If President Johnson wants to start an action-program inside the urban Negro ghettos, all he has to do is change the Federal priorities. Lunatic is a very mild word for the existing priorities, when you consider that the Negro ghettos in our great cities have long constituted a problem like a social-political version of near-terminal cancer . . . Urban renewal, in the ghettoes, is often called "Negro removal"– and with justice, for urban renewal projects have resulted in a net decrease of low income housing units over the years." Then Robert C. Byrd, (D), West Virginia, had inserted a newspaper article from the News-Register from Wheeling, West Virginia, wherein the author wrote: "The Office of Economic Opportunity in Washington recently took issue with a News-Register editorial linking some of the rioting in the Nation's cities withe activities of certain anti-poverty workers. . . Now we would like to refer the OEO officials to the testimony last week before the Senate Judiciary Committee given by a Negro detective from Newark. Detective William Millard told the committee that poverty workers "contributed" to the atmosphere that led up to Newark's five-day riot. The police officer even displayed a photograph in which he identified several individuals as being involved in the riots . . . we have a man – whom I could name to a congressional committee – who heads up a program designed to rehabilitate criminals, to prevent them from sliding back. Invited to an Episcopalian church on the night of Monday, July 17, a man by the name of Rap Brown. And that night – the Newark riot was still going on – Rap brown told the congregation that they should – literally, now, he said this – go out and burn Jersey City down. 'You built the city; go out and burn it down.' " [Question and answer with City Mayor Thomas J. Whelan] Q. Is the Federal government financing some of these people who incite others to riot? A. In the case I have cited, the man is on the anti-poverty program payroll. Q. Financed by the Office of Economic Opportunity? A. Yes. The program is sponsored by the Council of Churches in Jersey City, which is a Negro and white Protestant church group. The program has a federal grant, I believe, of $142,000. [continuation of the article's author] And that's not all. How about this case? A young man by the name of Marion Barry has been employed as a $50-per-day consultant by the United Planning Organization, top anti-poverty agency for the District of Columbia. Mr. Berry in August 1965, took part in a protest demonstration organized by the so-called Assembly of Unrepresented People. He was arrested and charged with disorderly conduct while leading demonstrations on the Capitol grounds. 'Riot power and rebellion power,' he was quoted as saying the other day, 'might make people listen now.' So there you have, more testimony from reliable public officials linking federally financed anti-poverty programs with discontent and rebellion in our cities. Officials of the Office of Economic Opportunity can deny all they want and hide their heads in the sand, the American people have a right to know these facts and we shall to endeavor to bring them to the attention of the public whenever the opportunity presents itself. Maybe in time our citizens will have had enough of these ill-conceived schemes which do little or nothing to alleviate true poverty conditions, and the people will demand that the Congress put an end to this 'gravy train' which stirs discontent and hatred among a segment of our population." Senator Byrd then had inserted into the Senate Congressional Record another editorial from the Jackson Herald, Ripley, West Virginia, entitled '"Disgusting, Isn't It?" The author of the editorial wrote: "We have always had poor white people but they have not rioted, burned the property of a neighbor, or stolen his property. What this country needs and must have is officials who will enforce the laws. That is all we need. We have laws against these things, some of them dating back to Moses and the Ten Commandments." Senator Vance Hartke, (D), Indiana, then had inserted into the record a letter he had received, discussing a woman's son's service in the military. She the mentions the National League of Cities meetings and says: "These leaders, it may be assumed, are not opposed to meeting needs. Rather, they doubtless sense that the Great Society methods – taking it away from those who work for their money and giving it to those who don't – is doomed to fail. This way kill the incentive in the worker and leaves the poor in perpetual dependency on governmental handouts." Senator Wayne Morse, (R), Oregon, gave a lengthily speech with which he stated: "What is it going to profit us if we spend these hundreds and hundreds of millions of dollars out of the humanitarianism of our hearts for the disadvantaged children in the underdeveloped areas of the world unless we are willing to do even more for the disadvantaged children of the United States? Does a difference in skin color at home justify our neglect? The color of the skin of those in underdeveloped areas of the world does not seem to cause us not to help them, even though their color is not white in most instances . . . However, first things have to come first, and we have a great domestic crisis in this country. One of the reasons we had this domestic crisis in this country is that we, as a people – and I speak generically – have been looking too far away from our own national backyard" (Congressional Record 1967a).

Other than Senator Morse, all the statements were presented by proxy voices rather than the politicians own voice, but it does present an image of the actual thought of the moment.

Mayor of Jersey City until 1953, Kenny remained the power behind the throne in Hudson County until 1971, when he and Mayor Thomas J. Whelan, during his second term, in 1971, was indicted by the U.S. Attorney's Office for the District of New Jersey as a member of the "Hudson County Eight," and was convicted in federal court of conspiracy and extortion in a multimillion-dollar political kickback scheme connected to city and county contracts, for taking $3.5 million in kickbacks in exchange for county construction contracts (Bonamo 2006).

Shriver sent the Director of the Office of Inspection, Edgar May journalist and politician, Inspector General of the Office of Economic Opportunity, to put together a comprehensive evaluation of all OEO community action programs. He had helped establish the Head Start Programs and was the Deputy Director of VISTA. His government service initiated a life long friendship with the Shriver and Kennedy families.

A summary of May's findings were published in the *Christian Science Monitor*, 21 August 1967, " . . . the major untold story of the riots is quite different [from accusations of inciting the riots on the part of people funded by the OEO programs] and deeply impressive. It is a story on constructive response to emergencies by anti-poverty workers in community after community." Efforts were being made in many cities, especially in areas where no rioting occurred, to keep the peace (CSA

1969).

On 8 September 1967, the Secretary of Labor had a lawsuit filed against him in California by the California Rural Legal Assistance (CRLA) organization. Their offices first appeared in the agricultural valleys of California in 1966. Their operating perspective was "that the problems of the poor result far less from unjust rules than from the inequitable distribution of wealth and power and that the lawyers serving them must focus on building legal institutions which can enhance the power of the poor client to economically and politically cope for himself." CRLA was neither staffed nor controlled locally; its early professional staff came almost entirely from big cities. In reference to the suit, O. W. Fillerup, Executive Vice President of the Council of California Growers, said: "The federal government, through the Office of Economic Opportunity, and the AFL/CIO now find themselves in a financial partnership in union organizing disguised as a legitimate social project for the poor." Senator George Murphy, (R), California, said: "The citizens of California have been horrified by the spectacle of CRLA lawyers, paid by their tax dollars, going to court against the Secretary of Labor and his Justice Department attorneys, also paid by the taxpayers, in an action which will inevitably result in losses to farmers and higher food prices to American consumers. Poor old John Q. Public is paying the bill three times for this absurd three-ring circus." Shriver told of receiving a telephone call from Secretary Wirtz who stated: "Those lawyers that work for you have just sued me in California." After discussing the suit, Shriver said: "Well, Bill, don't you think they're right? If the Department of Labor has failed to fulfill the requirements of the law, shouldn't a suit be brought to require that you fulfill it . . . what these lawyers in California have done is, in fact, to sort of hold you up, you might say, make sure you follow the legal process." . . . And I'm sure – well, I'm sure he agreed with that. And he said, as a matter of fact, "Now that I talk to you, I do." Shriver, then, in an effort to make the original grant to CRLA more palatable to the agricultural interest, imposed a special grant condition prohibiting CRLA from giving assistance to any collective bargaining group, whether or not the group met OEO financial eligibility standards, a unique prohibition which had never been imposed on a legal services grant before, but a condition for all grants for CRLA (Bennet and Reynoso 1972).

Baker stated, " . . . the California Rural Legal Assistance program out in California [have] probably done more to revolutionize within the legal structure of the society the operations of state, local, and federal government in the state of California than anything anybody has done in the last hundred years. They've challenged schools systems in the way they are treating kids. They have challenged the welfare system. They've challenged the Labor Department in the way that they use migrants and permit migrants in. They've challenged the governor. They've even undertaken a system of educating the justices of the peace out there" (Gillette 2010).

In late November, the California Rural Legal Assistance organization filed their application to OEO for 1968 funding. Newspapers throughout the state of California began speculating on whether Governor Reagan would veto that request. William P. Clark Executive Secretary to the Governor would not deny the possibility. When Shriver was asked about this, he said: "If I don't override that veto, we might as well turn the Country over to the John Birch Society" (Bennett and Cruz 1972).

The John Birch Society, was established in Indianapolis, Indiana, 9 December 9, 1958, by Robert W. Welch, Jr., a retired candy manufacturer from Belmont, Massachusetts. Welch named the new organization after John Birch, an American Baptist missionary and military intelligence officer who was shot and killed by communist forces in China in August 1945, shortly after the conclusion of World War II. It was built on two earlier groups: the National Association of Manufacturers which spent millions of dollars to try and convince the public that employers, not unions, were the natural allies of worker, and the Foundation of Economic Education whose libertarians views were so uncompromising that it bordered on anarchism. Harry Lynde Bradley, co-founder of the Allen Bradley Company and the Lynde and Harry Bradley Foundation; Fred C. Koch, founder of Koch Industries; and, Robert Waring Stoddard, President of Wyman-Gordon, a major industrial enterprise, were among the twelve founding members. It is a self-described conservative advocacy group supporting anti-communism and limited government. It motto was "Less government and more responsibility" (Perlstein 2001).

Congressman Carl D. Perkins, (D), Kentucky, Chairman, succeeding Adam Clayton Powell, House Education and Labor Committee, after four weeks of closed meetings, announced that all future sessions would be held in public. He stated "If they [the Republicans] want to kill this bill, then they're going to have to do it on the floor, out in the open and for the record. We're not going to let them do it behind closed doors." This was the appropriations bill for the poverty program. The critical point of a four-day mark-up session was the introduction of what became known as the Green Amendment. (Masters 2014, CSA 1969).

Edith Green stated:

"The original legislation did not intend to

create a new governmental structure of powerful political bodies with the luxury of millions of federal dollars to spend and none of the responsibilities of raising any of that money. Congress did not aim to create autonomous groups to displace the decision-making process of state, county, or local governments or to fund with federal dollars any group intent on reversing the decision of duly elected school boards or county or local governments. No one challenges the right to dissent, but many of us question the wisdom of requiring others to pay taxes to finance it. As I see it, the Congress clearly intended to attack this economic problem, but it did not intend to legislate a revolution in American politics by establishing another structure of government at the various levels of political action in the United States" (CSA 1969).

Kelley felt that, "She's an educator in the traditional sense. She thinks that education ought to be one of those powers reserved to the states and the local communities. If you're going to provide any kind of assistance to the states or local communities, what you ought to do is write them checks, establish guidelines, let them submit plans. If the plan meets the guideline, then write them a check and let them carry it out. That's her hang-up. You're not going to disabuse her of that notion, because that's pretty well ingrained. She's an ex-schoolteacher, and she's of the establishment. Mrs. Green's figures, at least all the figures she has ever given me, are not accurate. They're biased. She takes a snapshot, sampling, favorable to her point of view. . . . She's a very clever woman, very politically clever" (Gillette 2010).

The Green Amendment of 1967, mandated that the CAA boards would now require one third representation of public officials, and one third representation of business and civic groups. The "maximum" in "maximum feasible participation" was being cast aside in favor of a new claim to the meaning of "feasible". The Amendment also emphasized control by local public officials, mandating that CAA employees would not be allowed to protest or picket (Bae 2011, Zarefsky 1986, Selover 1969, Levitan 1969).

The essence of the Green Amendment was this:

> "A state or political subdivision of a state (having duly appointed governing officials), or a combination of such political subdivisions, or a public or private non-profit agency or organization which has been designated as such by a State or political subdivision . . . "

Green argued that this amendment would help insure that local officials would "be responsible for local successes and local failures . . . In fact, the bill demands engagement by local politicians so that they cannot avoid tough decisions on the battle lines of the war on poverty" (Clark 2000). Republicans and some liberal Democrats labeled the Green amendment "City Hall domination" and the "bosses and boll-weevil" amendment (Davidson 1969, Levitan 1969). The Green amendment gave greater structure in that it stated one-third of the board members of community action agencies were to be elected public officials or their representatives, at least one-third would be low-income people (Clark 2002).

Fewer than five percent of the communities elected political officials to do what the bill had stated (Sundquist 1969).

The Special Assistant to the President, Joseph A. Califano, Jr., determined that of the 898 community actions agencies put in place since the Green amendment 48 had been taken over by city hall (Moynihan 1969a).

The amendment was submitted 16 October and passed on 18 October, 18-11. It allowed the OEO Director to fund a private or public non-profit agency if the state or local government refused to be designated as a Community Action Agency (CSA 1969). Northern Democrats were not interested in doing deals with the Republican proposed "Opportunity Crusade" if they could get the majority to pass the administration bill with the acceptance of the Green amendment (Levitan 1968).

Perkins felt that this amendment took care of the complaint many of the southern members on the committee felt that community action efforts were the work of "power-grasping bureaucrats from Washington" and that, therefore they should help him out and pass the antipoverty program (Levitan 1968).

The outcome was a surprise to most observers. That the OEO was in trouble was no mere speculation.

The fiscal appropriations for FY 1966 had expired on June 30. A continuing Congressional budget resolution was delayed. November 8-28, the OEO was without authority to spend money on its programs. Congress had barred OEO from the federal pay raise given to all other agencies. Congressman Edward Gurney, (R), Florida, the sponsor of the prohibition of OEO from the pay raise was reviled. After a large backlash from private individuals, businessmen, such as Henry Ford, and those involved in the Urban Coalition, Congress renewed the funding resolution (CSA 1969).

Edith Green, 13 November 1967, offered an amendment (Congressional Record 1967b):

> (B) The Director shall take such action as may be necessary to insure that in recruitment efforts for the Job Corps, and in the selection for enrollment and enrollment of young men and women in the Job Corps there is no discrimination on account of race, color, religion, sex, or national origin. He shall administer the Job Corps in such a manner as to accommodate its programs and facilities to the make-up of the Job Corps recruiting from applicants of the proceeding sentence.

> She stated; "Mr. Chairman, the purpose of this amendment is to make it unmistakably clear that we intend to end any discrimination against women in the Job Corps Program."

Edith Green recommended Dr. Jeanne Noble, Associate Professor of Human Relations, New York University, to Shriver to head up the planning of Job Corps. Noble held a conference in Washington, 29-30 July, of educators, community organizers, leaders of women's groups, health experts, business executives, researchers, and other people who might be able to contribute ideas. She had also recruited the National Council of Catholic Women, the National Council of Jewish Women, the National Council of Negro Women, and the United Church Women. The groups created an instrumentality in the Job Corps, Women in Community Service, which did about fifty percent of the recruitment of women. Job Corps added to the recruitment packets a small folded postcard stating; "Get paid while you work, learn, and travel." It was to be filled out, name, address, age, colored coded, pink for girls, blue for boys. Cards flowed in. By January 1967, the rate was fifteen thousand a week. Within the initial eight months of operation, 893 girls were enrolled at women's centers. There were twenty approved centers out of twenty-one, the one selected by the Interior Department at Death Valley, California, was deleted (Weeks 1967, Gillette 2010).

Kelley said, "We published a code of conduct not only for the Job Corps enrollees but for the staff, and I ran into some flak on that. People were telling me that I couldn't tell grownups what they could do. Well, I figured if they were going to work in Job Corps, and if they're going to set an example for disadvantaged youth, that there ought to be some standards. So we prescribed the code. In the first six months, we fired twenty-right center directors. That's always a horrendous thing to have to do, but we did. I think that put a little spine into the Job Corps." Yarmolinsky felt: "I think it should be said in the defense of Job Corps that the Employment Service has done an absolutely miserable job of recruiting. The state employment services have connived with the courts and the police and everybody under the sun to get kids into the Job Corps that had no business of being there, who they had no hope of dealing with, who ran up bills at a phenomenal rate, led to exorbitant droput rates. They just did a lousy, lousy job, as they do in everything they put their hand to. But even so, some places are doing fantastically good jobs" (Gillette 2010).

The House of Representatives extended the Economic Opportunity Act, 11 December 1967, for two years. The vote of 247-149 was the greatest show of strength for the Act since its passage In 1964. Sixty-four Republicans – two of every five – strayed from their usual party position to join 183 Democrats (including 38 Southerners) to vote in favor of the Act. The final vote on appropriations was – 306-78 (Levitan 1968).

On 12 December, the Senate was presented a comprehensive anti-poverty bill by The Labor and Public Welfare Committee. It had a two-year authorization of $1.98 million increase over the administration's FY 1968 increase. One of the things the report from the committee said that "In the hearings held by the Committee . . . a clear consensus emerged that jobs are the single most important way to combat poverty." Senator Joseph F. Clark, (D), Pennsylvania, who once had called the Senate a "self-perpetuating oligarchy" in a 1963 address on the Senate floor, ushered a job program called an emergency job creation proposal through the Committee, $2.5 billion, designed to "provide meaningful employment opportunities in public service and other areas which will relieve severe unemployment and contribute to the national interest by filling unmet needs." Clark's amendment was eliminated on the Senate floor (CSA 1969).

In the Economic Opportunity Act of 1964, As Amended, Findings and Declaration of Purpose [part of the Economic Opportunity Amendments of 1967] it stated:

> Sec. 2. Although the economic well-being
> and prosperity of the United States have

progressed to a level surpassing any achieved in world history, and although these benefits are widely shared throughout the Nation, poverty continues to be the lot of a substantial number of out people. The United States can achieve its full economic and social potential as a nation only if every individual has the opportunity to contribute to the full extent of his capabilities and to participate in the workings of our society. It is therefore, the policy of the United States to eliminate the paradox of poverty in the midst of plenty in this Nation by opening to everyone the opportunity for education and training, the opportunity to work, and the opportunity to live in decency and dignity. It is the purpose of this Act to strengthen, supplement, and coordinate efforts in the furtherance of that policy.

It is the sense of congress that it is highly desirable to employ the resources of the private sector of the economy of the United States in all such efforts to further the policy of this act. [this last sentence was added as part of the Amendments]

Congress passed appropriations of $1.773 billion.

In January, 1968, the Bureau of the Budget and OEO came to an agreement on the allocation of funds.

President Johnson gave his *Annual Message to the Congress*

on the State of the Union, January 17, 1968, in which he (Johnson 1968a) said, in part:

"While we have accomplished much, much remains for us to meet and much remains for us to master."

"In some areas, the jobless rate is still three or four times the national average. Violence has shown its face in some of our cities.
Crime increases on our streets.
Income for farm workers remains far behind that for urban workers; and parity for our farmers who produce our food is still just a hope—not an achievement.
New housing construction is far less than we need—to assure decent shelter for every family.
Hospital and medical costs are high, and they are rising.
Many rivers—and the air in many cities—remain badly polluted. And our citizens suffer from breathing that air.
We have lived with conditions like these for many, many years. But much that we once accepted as inevitable, we now find absolutely intolerable."

"In our cities last summer, we saw how wide is the gulf for some Americans between the promise and the reality of our society."

President Johnson issued Executive Order 11399—Establishing the National Council on Indian Opportunity in which he stated (Johnson 1968c):

> Now, THEREFORE, by virtue of the authority vested in me as President of the United States, it is ordered as follows:

> SECTION 1. Establishment of Council. There is hereby established The National Council on Indian Opportunity (hereinafter referred to as the "Council"). The Council shall have membership as follows: The Vice President of the United States who shall be the chairman of the Council, the Secretary of the Interior, the Secretary of Agriculture, the Secretary of Commerce, the Secretary of Labor, the Secretary of Health, Education, and Welfare, the Secretary of Housing and Urban Development, the Director of the Office of Economic Opportunity, and six Indian leaders appointed by the President of the United States for terms of two years.

> SEC. 2. Functions of the Council. The Council shall: (a) Encourage full use of Federal programs to benefit the Indian population, adapting them where

necessary to be available to Indians on reservations in a meaningful way.

(b) Encourage interagency coordination and cooperation in carrying out Federal programs as they relate to Indians.

(c) Appraise the impact and progress of Federal programs for Indians.

(d) Suggest ways to improve such programs.

A comment on the August 27, 2011 by Ojibwa on *Native American Netroots* observed that:

> With the creation of the Office of Economic Opportunity, the BIA no longer had a monopoly on the economic future of the tribes. Tribes were eligible for funding for youth programs, community action programs, and other programs. Indian tribes and organizations participated in these programs along with other economically disadvantaged groups. Unlike the earlier BIA programs, these new programs emphasized the need for local involvement at all levels. Soon nearly every tribe in the United States was involved in the War on Poverty and local Indian people, not the BIA, were planning and running the programs. In

other words, the War on Poverty
provided tribal people with political
empowerment.

One of the key components of the War on
Poverty was the Community Action
Program (CAP). Each CAP was to utilize
and mobilize local people to determine
how best to deal with poverty in the local
community. On the reservations, the
CAPs often had better relationships with
the long-standing BIA administration.
The tribal CAPs dedicated the greatest
funding to programs such as Head Start,
educational development, legal services,
health centers, and economic
development.

On 22 March, President Johnson appointed Shriver to the
Post of Ambassador to France and that Bertrand M. Harding,
Deputy Director OEO would become Acting Director. Shriver
would hold that post 1968-1970. Harding felt that he was sure
that support for the war on poverty would continue as long as
Lyndon Johnson was in office. He stated that the agency has
"more of a mission than four years ago. . . . I don't think even a
Republican Administration – politically – could abolish or
seriously cripple this program."

31 March 1968, President Johnson addressed the nation
mainly about the Vietnam War (Johnson 1968b). At the end of
his address he said, in part:

"There is a division in the American

house now. There is a divisiveness among us all tonight. And holding the trust that is mine, as President of all the people, I cannot disregard the peril to the progress of the American people and the hope and the prospect of peace for all peoples."

"So, I would ask all American, whatever their personal interests or concern. To guard against divisiveness and all its ugly consequences."

"Fifty-two months and 10 days ago, in a moment of tragedy and trauma, the duties of this office fell upon me. I asked then for your help and God's, that we might continue American on its course, binding up our wounds, healing our history, moving forward in new unity, to clear the American agenda and to keep the American commitment for all of our people."

"United we have kept that commitment. United we have enlarged that commitment."

"Through all time to come, I think America will be a stronger nation, a more just society, and a land of great opportunity and fulfillment because of what we have all done together in these years of unparalleled achievement."

"Our reward will come in the life of freedom, peace, and hope that our children will enjoy through ages ahead."

"What we won when all of our people united just must not be lost in suspicion, distrust, selfishness, and politics among any of our people."

"Believing this as I do, I have concluded that I should not permit the Presidency to become involved in the partisan divisions that are developing in this political year."

"With America's son in the fields far away, with America's future under challenge right here at home, with our hopes and the world's hope for peace in the balance every day, I do not believe that I should devote an hour or a day of my time to and personal partisan causes or to any duties other than the awesome duties of this office – the Presidency of your country."

"Accordingly, I shall not seek, and I will not accept, the nomination of my party for another term as your President."

Johnson nominated Harding, who had worked in the

Bureau of the Budget, 11 years; the Revenue Service, rising to Deputy Director; then to be Director of OEO (Moynihan 1969a).

On April 4, 1968, Martin Luther King, Jr., was assassinated. A ground swell of outrage and rebellion swept across the country (Goldstein 2012).

The 1968 National Convention of the Republican Party met at the Miami Beach Convention Center in Miami Beach, Dade County, Florida, August 5 - 8, 1968. Nixon was nominated on the first ballot, by 692 votes, 277 votes for Nelson Rockefeller, 182 votes for California Governor Ronald Reagan, the rest scattered. Nixon selected as his running mate a perceived moderate, Spiro T. Agnew, Maryland Governor, former Baltimore County Executive in the Baltimore City suburbs (1963–1967). Nixon stated is his acceptance speech: "When the strongest nation in the world can be tied down for four years in Vietnam with no end in sight, when the richest nation in the world can't manage its own economy, when the nation with the greatest tradition of the rule of law is plagued by unprecedented racial violence, when the President of the United States cannot travel abroad or to any major city at home, then it's time for new leadership for the United States of America."

The 1968 National Convention of the U.S. Democratic Party met at the International Amphitheater in Chicago, Illinois, August26-29). Vice President Hubert H. Humphrey and Senator Edmund S. Muskie of Maine were nominated for President and Vice President.

The Presidential Election, was held on Tuesday, 5 November 1968. The Republican nominee, Richard Nixon tallied 43.5% of the vote; the Democratic nominee, incumbent Vice President Hubert Humphrey tallied 42.7% of the vote, and; American Independent nominee George Wallace tallied, 13.5% of the vote. Nixon received 301 electoral votes, Humphrey 191, and Wallace 46. The Wallace campaign won the electoral votes of several states in the Deep South.

Governor James Rhodes, (R), Ohio, sent a report written by members of Rhode's Cabinet under the direction of Denver L. White, Director, Ohio State Welfare. This report was alleged to call for the repeal of the Economic Opportunity Act; disestablishment of OEO; and, was critical of the Department of Health, Education and Welfare. White was quoted to have said: ". . . in recent years it has become apparent that the philosophy employed by the personnel in the Department of Health, Education and Welfare in the implementation of welfare laws bears no resemblance to the philosophy of the Congress that created the law." A Nixon aide stated he would be unable to say precisely what was in that report but it would "be studied closely" and receive "careful consideration" by staff and Nixon.

Johnson gave his last speech to Congress, the *Annual Message to the Congress on the State of the Union,* January 14, 1969 (Johnson 1969) and said, in part:

> "This is the richest nation in the world. The antipoverty program has had many achievements. It also has some failures. But we must not cripple it after only 3 years of trying to solve the human problems that have been with us and have been building up among us for generations."

> "I believe the Congress this year will want to improve the administration of the poverty program by reorganizing portions of it and transferring them to

other agencies. I believe, though, it will want to continue, until we have broken the back of poverty, the efforts we are now making throughout this land."

"I believe, and I hope the next administration — I believe they believe — that the key to success in this effort is jobs. It is work for people who want to work."

Nixon and The Start of The Unraveling

Nixon ran against the Great Society, Johnson's expansion of The New Deal and The Fair Deal. Like most Republicans since the thirties, he promoted a smaller and less intrusive government (Small 1999).

ON 8 August 1968, Nixon gave a prime-time television address to the nation in which he stated (Nathan 2011): "After a third of a century of power flowing from the people and the States to Washington it is time for a New Federalism in which power, funds and responsibility will flow from Washington to the States and to the people." His approach sought "a major reversal of the trend toward ever more centralization of Government in Washington." The speech covered welfare reform, revenue sharing, a new job training and placement program, and a "revamping" of President Johnson's Office of Economic Development that oversaw the anti-poverty programs.

The primary objective of New Federalism, unlike that of the eighteenth-century political philosophy of Federalism, was the restoration to the states of some of the autonomy and power which they lost to the federal government as a consequence of President Franklin Roosevelt's New Deal.

As a policy theme, New Federalism typically involves the

federal government providing block grants, called "revenue sharing," to the states to resolve a social issue. The federal government then monitors outcomes but provides broad discretion to the states for how the programs are implemented.

Revenue sharing had two parts: General Revenue Sharing; and, Special Revenue Sharing. General were monies distributed with no strings attached; Special consolidated 130 conditional grants-in-aid in six areas (urban development, rural community development, education, law enforcement, transportation, manpower training). However, for the bulk of the funds sent, the majority went into items like street and road repairs, fire protection, parks and other recreational areas. An early survey found that only 2.7% went into social programs, including health care (Trattner (1994).

Goldstein (2012) saw New Federalism as utilizing the "rhetoric of community to promote transferring federal resources to the so-called silent majority. Nixon sought to mobilize a majority built on working-class hostility to what he referred to as "special interests"– in other words, African Americans – supposedly courted by the Johnson administration's urban policies."

Daniel Patrick Moynihan, Director, Harvard-M.I.T. Joint Center for Urban Affairs, was appointed, 10 December 1968, to be Nixon's Assistant to the President for Urban Affairs. Moynihan took a two-rear leave from the Joint Center to work for the government (Anon 1968).

In President Nixon's *Inaugural Address*, 29 January 20, (Nixon 1969a) he said, in part:

> "In these difficult years, America has suffered from a fever of words; from inflated rhetoric that promises more than

it can deliver; from angry rhetoric that fans discontents into hatreds; from bombastic rhetoric that postures instead of persuading."

"We cannot learn from one another until we stop shouting at one another – until we speak quietly enough so that our words can be heard as well as our voices."

"For its part, government will listen. We will strive to listen in new ways – to the voices of quiet anguish, the voices that speak without words, the voices of the heart – to the injured voices, the anxious voices, the voices that have despaired of being heard."

"Those who have been left out, we will try to bring in."

"Those left behind, we will help to catch up."

"For all of our people, we will set as our goal the decent order that makes progress possible and our lives secure."

"As we reach toward our hopes, our task is to build on what has gone before – not turning away from the old, but turning toward the new."

"In this past third of a century, government has passed more laws, spent more money, initiated more programs than in all our previous history."

"In pursuing our goals of full employment, better housing, excellence in education; in rebuilding our cities and improving our rural areas; in protecting our environment and enhancing the quality of life – in all these and more, we will and must press urgently forward."

"We shall plan now for the day when our wealth can be transferred from the destruction of war abroad to the urgent needs of our people at home."

"The American dream does not come to those who fall asleep."

"But we are approaching the limits of what government alone can do."

"Our greatest need now is to reach beyond government, to enlist the legions of the concerned and the committed."

"What has to be done, has to be done by government and people together or it will not be done at all. The lesson of past agony is that without the people we can do nothing – with the people we can do everything."

"To match the magnitude of our tasks, we need the energies of our people – enlisted not only in grand enterprises, but more importantly in those small, splendid efforts that make headlines in the neighborhood newspaper instead of the national journal."

Donald Rumsfeld, (R), Illinois, was elected to Congress in 1963 and held the seat until he resigned and volunteered to be in Nixon's campaign, was seen as the one who would provide the Republican response to the Democrat's platform at the Democratic Convention being held in Chicago.

Rumsfeld was asked to taken on the job of Director OEO, a strong suggestion from Moynihan to Nixon. Rumsfeld said no and listed three points in a memo to Nixon stating why. He said (Rumsfeld 2011):

> 1) The probable reaction to the appointment of a white, Ivy League suburban, Republican Congressman from the wealthiest Congressional District in the Nation, with little visible [sic] management experience and little public identification with poverty programs, and who voted against the poverty program when it was first proposed would be harmful for the Nixon Administration . .
> 2) The job that the administration wishes

to have done on OEO, as I understand it,
is the liquidation of the Johnson poverty
approach. The development of the Nixon
approach to these problems would
essentially be the responsibility not of
OEO but of [other] departments . . .
3) In a political situation, which this is, it
would seem that the best approach would
be to use a person identified as a liberal
when one wishes to retrench and
reorganize.

In April 1969 Nixon phoned Rumsfeld and asked him to
meet with Nixon in Florida where Nixon occasionally
vacationed. Nixon persuaded him to take the position. ". . . to
take on an assignment I didn't want, at an agency I had voted
against, with a mission Nixon didn't like, for a purpose that was
still unclear" (Rumsfeld 2011).

The Constitution prohibits individuals from receiving a
government salary outside Congress if the salary for that
position was increased during their time in Congress. Congress
had raised salaries for federal posts while Rumsfeld was in
Congress. The decision, made by William Rehnquist, in the
White House was that he not receive a salary as Director of OEO
but be paid as an Assistant to the President and that he also be
made a member of the Cabinet (Rumsfeld 2011).

Rumsfeld was appointed, 21 April, by Nixon to be the
Director, Office of Economic Opportunity on Moynihan's
recommendation and was sworn in, 27 May. Nixon wanted
Rumsfeld, then a Republican member of Congress, to not only
head the OEO but to reform it. Rumsfeld cut non-performing
projects and worked with the states to develop more

economically feasible ones. "He saved it [the OEO], but he saved it by revolutionizing it, by changing it," stated his Deputy Director, Frank Carlucci. Rumsfeld had Carlucci, a former State Department Foreign Service Officer and Princeton room mate as well as a fellow member of the Varsity Wrestling Team at Princeton (1952), transferred to OEO from the State Department to be the Director of the Community Action Program. Rumsfeld hired Dick Cheney, as an Executive Assistant, urged by a good friend of Rumsfeld, Congressman Bill Steiger, (R), Wisconsin who had Cheney as an intern. Cheney had dropped out of a doctoral program in Political Science at the University in Madison (Nathan 2011, Clark 2000, Rumsfeld 2011, Perlstein 2014).

H.R. Haldeman, (R), California, was picked by Nixon to be his Chief of Staff. Haldeman had been an advance man on Nixon's 1956 and 1960 campaigns, managed Nixon's 1962 run for Governor of California. John Erhlichman was also involved in these campaigns. Nixon relied on Haldeman to filter information that came into his office and to make sure that information was properly dispensed.

Ehrlichman became the White House Counsel (later replaced by John Dean) and then the Chief Domestic Advisor for Nixon.

On 23 January 1969, Nixon created the Council for Urban Affairs by Executive Order, 11452. The Council would coordinate the existing programs and create new ones. Nixon was the Chairman of the Council. He assigned Moynihan to be the Executive Secretary.

Executive Order 11452—Establishing the Council for Urban Affairs (Nixon 1969b) stated:

By virtue of the authority vested in me by

the Constitution and statutes of the United States, and as President of the United States, it is ordered as follows:

SECTION 1. Establishment of the Council.

(a) There is hereby established the Council for Urban Affairs (hereinafter referred to as "the Council").

(b) The President of the United States shall preside over meetings of the Council. The Vice President shall preside in the absence of the President.

(c) The Council shall be composed of the following:

The Vice President of the United States
The Attorney General

Secretary of Agriculture

Secretary of Commerce

Secretary of Labor

Secretary of Health, Education, and Welfare Secretary of Housing and Urban Development Secretary of Transportation and such other heads of departments and agencies as the President may from time to time direct.

SEC. 2. Functions of the Council. The Council shall advise and assist the President with respect to urban affairs and shall perform such other duties as the President may from time to time prescribe. In addition to such duties, the Council is directed to:

(1) Assist the President in the development of a national urban policy, having regard both to immediate and to long-range concerns, and to priorities among them.

(2) Promote the coordination of Federal programs in urban areas.

(3) Encourage the fullest cooperation between Federal, State, and city governments, with special concern for the maintenance of local initiative and local decision making.

(4) Ensure that policies concerning urban affairs shall extend to the relations of urban, suburban, and rural areas, to programs affecting them, and to the movement of population between them.

(5) Seek constant improvement in the actual delivery of public services to citizens.

(6) Foster the decentralization of government with the object that program responsibilities will be vested to the greatest possible extent in state and local government.

(7) Encourage the most effective role possible for voluntary organizations in dealing with urban concerns.

(8) Meet with and advise the President on the occasion of emergency situations, or conditions threatening the maintenance of civil order or civil rights.

SEC. 3. Administrative Arrangements. (a) A person designated by the President shall serve as Executive Secretary of the Council. The Executive Secretary shall perform such duties as the President may from time to time direct.

(b) In compliance with provisions of applicable law, and as necessary to effectuate the purposes of this order, (1) the White House Office shall provide or arrange for supporting clerical administrative and other staff services for the Council, and (2) each Federal department and agency which is represented on the Council shall furnish the Council such information and other assistance as may be available.

SEC. 4. Construction. Nothing in this order shall be construed as subjecting any department, establishment, or other instrumentality of the executive branch of the Federal Government or the head thereof, or any function vested by law in or assigned pursuant to law to any such agency or head, to the authority of any other such agency or head or as abrogating, modifying, or restricting any such function in any manner.

Nixon on the next day issued Executive Order 11453, creating the Council for Urban Affairs, with some revisions from Executive Order 11452, which stated (Nixon 1969c):

By virtue of the authority vested in me by the Constitution and statutes of the United States, and as President of the United States, it is ordered as follows:
SECTION 1. Establishment of the Committee. (a) There is hereby established the Cabinet Committee on Economic Policy (hereinafter referred to as "the Committee").

(b) The President shall preside over meetings of the Committee. The Vice President shall preside in the absence of the President.

(c) The Committee shall be composed of the following:

The Vice President Secretary of the Treasury

Secretary of Agriculture

Secretary of Commerce

Secretary of Labor

Director of the Bureau of the Budget

Chairman of the Council of Economic Advisers Counselor to the President and such other heads of departments and agencies as the President may from time to time designate.

SEC. 2. Functions of the Committee. The Committee shall advise and assist the President in the development and coordination of national economic programs and policies and shall perform such other duties as the President may from time to time prescribe. In addition to such duties, the Committee shall:

(1) Assist the President in the formulation of the basic goals and objectives of national economic policy;

(2) Develop recommendations for the basic strategy of national economic policy to serve as guides for decisions concerning specific economic programs and policies;

(3) Promote the coordination of Federal economic programs;

(4) Consult with individuals from academic, agricultural, business, consumer, labor and other groups to assure the consideration of a wide range of views about national economic policy; and

(5) Recommend procedures for evaluating the effectiveness of Federal programs in contributing to our national economic objectives.

SEC. 3. Administrative Arrangements. (a) The Chair-man of the Council of Economic Advisers will coordinate the work of the Committee.

(b) In compliance with provisions of applicable law, and as necessary to effectuate the purposes of this order, (1) The White House Office shall provide or arrange for supporting clerical administrative and other staff services for the Committee and (2) each Federal department and agency which is represented on the Committee shall furnish the Committee such information and other assistance as may be available.

SEC. 4. Construction. Nothing in this order shall be construed as subjecting any department, establishment, or other instrumentality of the executive branch of the Federal Government or the head thereof, or any function vested by law in or assigned pursuant to law to any such agency or head, to the authority of any other such agency or head or as abrogating, modifying, or restricting any such function in any manner.

In Nixon's February *Special Message to the Congress on the Nation's Antipoverty Program* (Nixon 1969d) he stated, in part:

The blight of poverty requires priority attention. It engages our hearts and challenges our intelligence. It cannot and will not be treated lightly or indifferently, or without the most searching examination of how best to marshal the resources available to the Federal Government for combating it.

At my direction, the Urban Affairs Council has been conducting an intensive study of the nation's anti-poverty programs, of the way the anti-poverty effort is organized and administered, and of ways in which it might be made more effective.

That study is continuing. However, I can now announce a number of steps I intend to take, as well as spelling out some of the considerations that will guide my future recommendations.

The Economic Opportunity Act of 1964 is now scheduled to expire on June 30, 1970. The present authorization for appropriations for the Office of Economic Opportunity runs only until June 30, 1969.

I will ask Congress that this authorization for appropriations be extended for another year. Prior to the end of the Fiscal Year, I will send Congress a comprehensive proposal for the future of the poverty program, including recommendations for revising and extending the Act itself beyond its scheduled 1970 expiration.

From the experience of OEO, we have learned the value of having in the Federal Government an agency whose special concern is the poor. We have learned the need for flexibility, responsiveness, and continuing innovation. We have learned the need for management effectiveness. Even those most thoroughly committed to the goals of the anti-poverty effort recognize now that much that has been tried has not worked.

The OEO has been a valuable fount of ideas and enthusiasm, but it has suffered from a confusion of roles.

OEO's greatest value is as an initiating agency – devising new programs to help the poor, and serving as an "incubator" for these programs during their initial, experimental phases. One of my aims is to free OEO itself to perform these functions more effectively, by providing for a greater concentration of its energies on its innovative role.

Last year, Congress directed that special studies be made by the Executive Branch of whether Head Start and the Job Corps should continue to be administered directly by OEO, or whether responsibility should be otherwise assigned.

Section 309 of the Vocational Education Amendments of 1968 provides:

The President shall make a special study of whether the responsibility for administering the Head Start program established under the Economic Opportunity Act of 1964 should continue to be vested in the Director of the Office of Economic Opportunity, should be transferred to another agency of the Government, or should be delegated to another such agency pursuant to the provisions of section 602(d) of the aforementioned Economic Opportunity Act of 1964, and shall submit the findings of this study to the Congress not later than March 1, 1969.

I have today submitted this study to the Congress. Meanwhile, under the Executive authority provided by the Economic Opportunity Act, I have directed that preparations be made for the delegation of Head Start to the Department of Health, Education, and Welfare. Whether it should be actually transferred is a question I will take up in my later, comprehensive message, along with my proposals for a permanent status and organizational structure for OEO. Pending a final decision by the Secretary of HEW on where within the department responsibility for Head Start would be lodged, it will be located directly within the Office of the Secretary.

In order to provide for orderly preparation, and to ensure that there is no interruption of programs, I have directed that this delegation be made effective July 1, 1969. By then the summer programs for 1969 will all have been funded, and a new cycle will be beginning.

One of the priority aims of the new Administration is the development by the Department of Labor of a comprehensive manpower program, designed to make centrally available to the unemployed and the underemployed a full range of Federal job training and placement services. Toward this end, it is essential that the many Federal manpower programs be integrated and coordinated.

Therefore, as a first step toward better program management, the Job Corps will be delegated to the Department of Labor.

This delegation will also be made effective on July 1, 1969; and the Departments of Interior and Agriculture will continue to have operating responsibility for the Job Corps centers concerned primarily with conservation.

I have directed that preparations be made for the transfer of two other programs from OEO to the Department of Health, Education, and Welfare: Comprehensive Health Centers, which provide health service to the residents of poor neighborhoods, and Foster Grandparents program. In my judgment, these can be better administered at present, or in the near future, within the structure of the Department.

In making these changes, I recognize that innovation costs money – and that if OEO is to continue its effectiveness as an innovating agency, adequate funds must be made available on a continuing basis. Moreover, it is my intent that Community Action Agencies can continue to be involved in the operation of programs such as Head Start at the local level, even though an agency other than OEO has received such programs, by delegation, at the national level. It also is my intent that the vital Community Action Programs will be pressed forward, and that in the area of economic development OEO will have an important role to play, in cooperation with other agencies, in fostering community-based business development.

In the past, problems have often arisen over the relationship of State, county and local governments to programs administered by OEO. This has particularly been the case where the State and local officials have wanted to assume greater responsibility for the implementation of the programs but for various reasons have been prevented from doing so. I have assigned special responsibility for working out these problems to the newly-created Office of Intergovernmental Relations, under the supervision of the Vice President.

I have directed the Urban Affairs Council to keep the anti-poverty effort under constant review and evaluation, seeking new ways in which the various departments can help and better ways in which their efforts can be coordinated.

My comprehensive recommendations for the future of the poverty program will be made after the Urban Affairs Council's own initial study is completed, and after I have reviewed the Comptroller General's study of OEO ordered by Congress in 1967 and due for submission next month.

The men and women who will be valued

most in this administration will be those who understand that not every experiment succeeds, who do not cover up failures but rather lay open problems, frankly and constructively, so that next time we will know how to do better.

In this spirit, I am confident that we can place our anti-poverty efforts on a secure footing – and that as we continue to gain in understanding of how to master the difficulties, we can move forward at an accelerating pace.

In February, Nixon, following the advice of the Council for Urban Affairs, transferred to the Department of Health, Education and Welfare, the Head Start Program.

Transferring the Office of Economic Development programs to existing departments within the government had been something Republicans had been trying to obtain since 1966 when that Congress was working on the appropriations bill for anti poverty programs. Senator Paul J. Fannin, (R), Arizona, a hard-line conservative, often voting with Senator Goldwater on the issues, had proposed an amendment that would transfer the Job Corps from OEO to the Labor Department. It had failed 27 yes - 38 no.

Moynihan advocated against dismantling the OEO and other programs suggesting that doing so would exacerbate divisions in American society (Clark 2000).

The General Accounting Office (GAO), following the direction from the 1967 Act extending the OEO to examine and pay special attention to programs efficiency and success, issued a report on March 19 that concluded that many of the anti-poverty programs had suffered from poor administration and had attained varying degrees of success.

Gregory J. Ahart, Deputy Director, Civil Division, at the Conference on Federal Affairs, Sponsored by the Tax Foundation, Inc., stated (March 25,1969):

> About 15 months ago, in the 1967 Economic Opportunity Amendments, the Congress threw the Comptroller General two very tough questions. With reference to the various programs authorized by the Economic Opportunity Act, the Congress directed him to determine.
> (1) the efficiency of the administration of such programs and activities by the Office of Economic Opportunity and by local public and private agencies carrying out such programs and activities: and
> (2) the extent to which such programs and activities achieve the objectives set forth in the relevant part or title of the Economic Opportunity Act of 1964 authorizing such programs or activities.
>
> The accomplishments achieved under the Economic Opportunity Act must be appraised in the light of certain difficulties encountered by OEO and the other agencies involved. These difficulties include:
> -The urgency of getting programs underway as quickly as possible.

-Problems in the development of a new organization and in obtaining experienced personnel.

-Problems involved in establishing new or modified organizational
arrangements at the local level.

-The delays and uncertainties in obtaining congressional authorizations and appropriations.

-The problems of working out relationships with other agencies and with State and local governments.

-Lack of consensus as to the meaning of poverty.

Achievements of the programs authorized by the act can be assessed only in judgmental terms.

Criteria is lacking by which to determine at what level of accomplishment a program is to be considered acceptably successful.

-The methods for determining program accomplishments have not yet been developed to the point of assured reliability.

-The large volume and variety of pertinent data necessary to ascertain program results have been and still are either not available or not reliable.

-Program results may not be fully

perceptible for many programs within a relatively short time frame.

-Other programs-Federal, State, local, and private - aimed at helping the poor, as well as changes in local conditions - employment, wage scales, local attitudes- have their effect upon the same people who receive assistance under the programs authorized by the act.

-Amendments to the act and revisions in agency guidelines at various times have necessitated redirection of programs and other changes, which have affected the progress of programs in the short run.

This coordinating task was assigned to the Economic Opportunity Council created by the act and to the OEO, the former having the dominant role.

The Council has never functioned effectively and as recast by the 1967 amendments to the act has not been established.

OEO, preoccupied with setting up the machinery to get a new agency started and then with its responsibility for initiating and administering programs authorized by the act, was not able to devote as much effort to its coordinating function as that function demanded. This coordinating task was made difficult by the necessity of OEO's influencing the actions and policies of older established agencies; as a consequence, effective coordination has not been achieved. It was our conclusion that effective coordination cannot be achieved under the existing organizational machinery.

A careful reading of the criticism(?) just cited suggests that outside of the OEO's control is the usual behavior of Congress to "manage(?)" the agency and its programs by the usual process of changing the bill authorizing the function of the agency and then blaming the agency for poor performance as it adjusts to the new rules imposed during the usual Congressional process.

The President announced, 9 April, a new Office of Child Development inside the Department of Health, Education and Welfare (HEW), to oversee Head Start, day care and other early childhood programs, starting 1 July. Robert H. Finch, Secretary of HEW stated that fiscal 1970 allocations for Head Start would be $338 million, the level recommended by the Johnson Administration (CQ Almanac 1969).

George Schultz, Secretary of Labor from 1969 to 1970, felt that the independence of the Job Corps from other employment training programs was inappropriate. He felt that unskilled urban youth would be more effectively trained in small urban centers than in isolated rural conservation camps. On 11 April, Nixon announced the closing of fifty of the eighty-two conservation centers, two of the six large urban men's centers, seven of the seventeen women's centers with Job Corps enrollment being lowered from 32,000 to 22,000. He authorized the establishment of thirty urban centers to train unskilled youth. Schultz stated that this would save $100 million. (CQ Almanac 1969, Clark 2002).

Senator Gaylord Nelson, (D), environmentalist from Wisconsin, the founder of Earth Day, testified, April 18, before the Senate Labor and Public Welfare Committee, Subcommittee on Employment, Manpower and Poverty, that the difficulties of the Job Corps was that the average age of the enrollees were between 17 and 18, had spent nine years in school, and read at the 4th or 5th grade level.

Representative of the American Bar Association testified, May 23, in support of OEO's legal services program and stated that they felt that these programs to have been successful (CQ Almanac 1969).

Rumsfeld speaking, 2 June, to the House Education and Labor Ad Hoc Hearing Task Force on Poverty, said that President Nixon would ask Congress for a two-year extension of the antipoverty program. The long extension was not "a commitment simply to continue present programs." But rather a means for finding out "what works and what does not."

He viewed the OEO as an innovating agency – "an indicator for new programs." He was establishing study teams to review issues such as the relationship between community agencies under OEO and community demonstration agencies funded by the Department of Housing and Urban Development. Another question to be studied was how to bring the states into more active roles in OEO-sponsored programs. He wanted to devote greater attention to the problems of rural poverty. The OEO had undertaken little "hard analysis" of poverty issues during its history and had not accumulated a useful body of knowledge about its programs. "None could have expected the problem of poverty to be totally eradicated in four years." But people had a right to ask why so little was known about the effects of the programs (CQ Almanac 1969b).

On June 2, Nixon revised his earlier thought and recommended that the anti poverty program be funded for two years as this would allow longer-range planning, provide a better framework for necessary improvements in the program and make possible more efficient allocation of funds. "An innovative agency has a special need for both continuity and flexibility." The two-year extension would ensure that although a particular program might fail, "the lessons learned would be put to use."

Strom Thurmond, (R), South Carolina, not a member of the Senate Subcommitte was allowed to question Rumsfeld, 4 June, about an OEO grant to a black foundation in Durham, North Carolina, which Thurmond charged as being involved in campus riots. Rumsfeld said that the grant was being held up pending an investigation and that poverty funds would be spent "to help the poor and not to lead to subversion of society in any way" (CQ Almanac 1969).

Richard Nixon in his *Address to the Nation on Domestic Program* (Nixon 1969e) said, in part:

> "One common theme running through my proposals tonight is that of providing full opportunity for every American. A second theme is that of trying to equip every American to play a productive role and a third is the need to make Government itself workable – which means reshaping, reforming, innovating."

> "The Office of Economic Opportunity is basically an innovative agency, and thus

it has a vital place in our efforts to develop new programs and apply new knowledge. But in order to do so effectively what it can do best, OEO itself needs reorganization."

"This administration has completed a thorough study of OEO. We have assigned it a leading role in the effort to develop and test new approaches to the solving of social problems. OEO is to be a laboratory agency where new ideas for helping people are tried on a pilot basis. When they prove successful, they can be spun off to operating departments or agencies – just as the space agency, for example, spun off the weather satellite and the communications satellite when these proved successful. Then OEO will be free to concentrate on breaking even newer ground."

"The OEO reorganization to be announced next week will stress this innovative role. It also will stress accountability, a clear separation of functions, and a tighter more effective organization of field operations."

Nixon presented his *Statement on the Office of Economic Opportunity* (Nixon 1969f), released at San Clemente, California, 11 August, and stated, in part:

"The following are among the specific changes in OEO which I am announcing today:

--Creation of a new Office of Program Development.

--Revamping and strengthening the Office of Planning, Research,   and Evaluation.

--Strengthening and upgrading the Office of Health Services and the Office of Legal Services.

--Creation of a new Office of Program Operations to improve the administration of activities in the field."

"1. Office of Program Development. This new unit will be responsible for most of the experimental efforts which OEO will now emphasize and will include within it both totally new programs and some existing activities which previously were distributed throughout the agency.

2. Office of Planning, Research, and Evaluation. The Office of Planning, Research, and Evaluation will be reorganized and strengthened. Reporting straight to the Director, it will have responsibility for reviewing existing social programs, for comparing the results of projects with the objectives which have been set for them, for commenting on the adequacy with which both programs and objectives are formulated, and for

recommending alterations in existing programs as well as new experiments. It will seek to establish more precise standards for measuring performance than OEO has used in the past. The Office of Planning, Research, and Evaluation will provide a regular source for that independent appraisal of Federal social programs which often is not available at present.

3. Office of Health Services. A strengthened Office of Health Services will also report directly to the Director of OEO. Many of the problems of the poor are the product of ill health and many have serious medical consequences. We have already begun to develop new mechanisms for helping the poor pay medical costs. But now we must further improve our methods of delivering health services so that all the poor will have ready access to doctors, diagnosis, treatment, and hospital care. The Neighborhood Health Center program is one experimental effort which is working in this direction; OEO will initiate other activities in this area. The 1970 budget will also show increases in food and nutrition programs, family planning services, and other health related activities.

4. Office of Legal Services. The Office of

Legal Services will also be strengthened and elevated so that it reports directly to the Director. It will take on central responsibility for programs which help provide advocates for the poor in their dealings with social institutions. The sluggishness of many institutions--at all levels of society – in responding to the needs of individual citizens is one of the central problems of our time. Disadvantaged persons in particular must be assisted so that they fully understand the lawful means of making their needs known and having those needs met. This goal will be better served by a separate Legal Services program, one which can test new approaches to this important challenge.

5. Office of Program Operations. More attention must be given to the way in which OEO policies are carried out at the local, State, and regional level. A new Office of Program Operations will work to improve the quality of field operations; it will be able to define more clearly the purposes for which grants and contracts are given and to apply higher standards of effective management.

Following the belief that the Office of Economic Opportunity should be an innovative agency, this administration has already moved the Job Corps to the

Department of Labor and the Head Start program to the Department of Health, Education, and Welfare. In addition, I am suggesting in my manpower training proposals that several OEO-funded manpower programs which have been administered by the Department of Labor be transferred to that Department. These are on-going programs which have passed the trial stage and should now be seen as parts of our established manpower strategy."

"I believe that the goal of full economic opportunity for every American can be realized. I expect the Office of Economic Opportunity to play a central role in that achievement. With new organizational structures, new operating procedures, and a new sense of precision and direction, OEO can be one of the most creative and productive offices in the government. For here much of our social pioneering will be done. Here will begin many of our new adventures."

In June 1969, OEO Pamphlet 4100-7 was released. It was written (Mar and Heine 1969) by a VISTA volunteer who tutored in a totally segregated school during the academic year 1966-1967. The document gives clear picture of what poverty looked like in such a deprived area as where Heine worked. Heine wrote, in part:

The school build "was constructed in 1995, immediately after the Supreme Court decision . . . The windows were broken and the children had to sit with their coats on (those who had any) while the rain and snow came through the open holes." Speaking of her co-author, Hattie Mar, who illustrated the Pamphlet, "None of the local poverty programs touched her life nor that of several hundred children . . . About midway through the morning we had milk, graham crackers and raisins. For most of them this was the only food until evening since 'Mama don't cook but one meal a day.' For all of her [Hattie's] years her diet had consisted mainly of cold biscuits dipped in grease, an occasional hotdog on payday and when she got hold of a quarter, a bottle of pop and potato chips . . . During the summer she found wild plums and berries in the woods. At this writing she is unable to eat a balanced meal and rich milk nauseates her . . . Now 13 years old she attended fifth grade and had become painfully aware of her inadequacies. School had become a chamber of stark horror."

In September, 1969, Rumsfeld sent a memorandum to the 1,100 headquarters personnel notifying 900 of them that they would have new assignments, the rest now had questionable careers.

The Senate Subcommittee on Employment, Manpower and Poverty held hearings, 7-9 October, on the proposed reorganization of the Legal Services program of the Office of Economic Opportunity (OEO) (CQ Almanac 1969b).

On 7 October, Rumsfeld, Director, OEO, said:

> The operations of legal services were temporarily centralized in Washington to develop necessary management procedures. It was intended that when the reorganization process was complete and the program was in order, legal services would again be handled the same as other operational programs.

> Under the present arrangement, responsibility for funding, evaluation, monitoring, technical assistance and program policy rests with the headquarters legal services office.

> "It may well be desirable to move responsibility for one or more of those activities to the agency's Federal regional directors who are charged with the principal responsibility for the operational programs in their regions." When one talks of regionalization of legal services, or of decentralization, it is not a matter of weakening the program but rather improving the way it is administered.

On October 10, the full Senate Committee on Labor and Public Welfare passed a two-year extension for the program authorized under the Economic Opportunity Act of 1964 and authorized advance funding for those and other programs. California Senator George Murphy, (R), added an amendment to allow governors to have an absolute veto over Legal Services programs in their states increasing the Governors power by giving state executives the authority to disapprove portions of programs. On a roll-call vote it passed, 45-40. On 14 October the full bill was passed by a role-call vote, 72-3, and sent to the House (CQ Almanac 1969a).

Rumsfeld called the amendment "most unfortunate .. . The Congress properly saw when establishing the Legal Services Programs, that to be successful local communities should have an opportunity to develop Legal Services Programs to meet their local needs. A balance was carefully devised by the Congress and it has worked well. It should not be changed lightly. I will strongly oppose this amendment in the House. It is my hope that the House of Representatives will see the wisdom of maintaining the Legal Services Program and will not risk denying the benefits of Legal Services Programs to the poor in major sections of the Nation."

By the end of October there had been 70 vetoes of poverty programs by Governors. Of the total, 19 vetoes were subsequently withdrawn by the Governors, 25 were sustained by the OEO director, 15 were overridden, and 11 were still pending. California had registered the highest number of vetoes–15–all exercised by California Governor Ronald Reagan. Six vetoes were withdrawn by the Governor, four were overridden, four sustained by the OEO director And one was pending. Alabama had 13 vetoes, made by three different Governors, Mississippi had nine and Louisiana and Florida each had four. A total of 30 states were responsible for the 70 vetoes (CQ Almanac 1969a).

In the House Representatives Albert H. Quie, (R), Minnesota; Edith Green, (D), Oregon; Robert N. Giaimo, (D), Connecticut; William H. Ayres, (R), Ohio; and, Joe D. Waggoner, (D), Louisiana proposed an amendment to give control over plans and grant proposal to the states. It was defeated 12 December, 167-183. The largest piece of the OEO budget was put in "reserve by the conference committee. It was $328.9 million for community action, "local initiative." Reserve funds could not be subject to reduction if the $100 million cut is the OEO budget request stood.

On 20 December 1969, Congress (bill S 3016) extended the anti poverty program for two years through fiscal 1971. On December 30, 1969, the President signed the Economic Opportunity Amendments of 1969 (Public Law 91-177, 83 Stat. 827).

In January 1970 Rumsfeld announced that:

> "We are going to be doing some additional work in the family planning area . . . trying to develop some better approach, particularly in rural areas. We are continuing the development of neighborhood health system which is something that I think is a very exciting and a very interesting effort to try to improve the delivery of health services. This includes, of course, the use of subprofessionals and paraprofessionals in the delivery of health services."

This would provide backup for the welfare reform system that President Nixon wanted. Nixon stated that the passage of welfare reform would be the most significant domestic social legislation since enactment of social security in 1935 (Aaron 1973).

Rumsfeld further stated that the new bill gave state and local governments a higher preference in choosing sponsors for federally financed job training programs. The bill would also tend to eliminate an existing priority for community action agencies as program sponsors. Funds for agencies were cut off because, among "many factors" involved, they refused to follow the policy of ending programs that duplicated available local services. That it was "absolutely ridiculous" for a community action agency to make a decision "that any government units, federal, state, or local, is the enemy."

Phillip Victor Sanchez was appointed, 2 February 1970, Assistant Director, Operations (OEO). The Senate Labor & Public Welfare held their hearings, 27 April, on the nomination for Phillip V. Sanchez to be Assistant Director of OEO. He was confirmed on 3 May.

OEO issued, 5 March 1970, "The Role of State Economic Opportunity Office" (OEO Instruction 7501-1) which stated that the Governor, at his discretion, might rely on the advice and assistance of the State Economic Opportunity Office in exercising his veto authority over proposed OEO grants and contracts and that the State Economic Opportunity Office should also seek to develop other anti-poverty resources, advocate for the poor at the state level, provide information on poverty conditions, and coordinate with other state agencies in the effort to overcome poverty (Clark 2000).

Aaron (1973) suggested that the most basic reason why welfare reform is difficult to achieve is that welfare recipients are politically unpopular and weak, and socially set apart from the great mass of the population . . . welfare recipients are less likely to vote than other groups, a fact well known to elected officials.

President Nixon in his *Special Message to the Congress on Indian Affairs*, 8 July (Nixon 1970) said, in part:

> "The first Americans – the Indians – are the most deprived and most isolated minority group in our nation. On virtually every scale of measurement – employment, income, education, health – the condition of the Indian people ranks at the bottom."

> "Because termination is morally and legally unacceptable, because it produces bad practical results, and because the mere threat of termination tends to discourage greater self-sufficiency among Indian groups, I am asking the Congress to pass a new Concurrent Resolution which would expressly renounce, repudiate and repeal the termination policy as expressed in House Concurrent Resolution 108 of the 83rd Congress. This resolution would explicitly affirm the integrity and right to continued existence of all Indian tribes and Alaska native governments, recognizing that cultural pluralism is a source of national strength."

"To this end, I am proposing legislation which would empower a tribe or a group of tribes or any other Indian community to take over the control or operation of Federally-funded and administered programs in the Department of the Interior and the Department of Health, Education and Welfare whenever the tribal council or comparable community governing group voted to do so."

"Under this legislation, it would not be necessary for the Federal agency administering the program to approve the transfer of responsibility. It is my hope and expectation that most such transfers of power would still take place consensually as a result of negotiations between the local community and the Federal government. But in those cases in which an impasse arises between the two parties, the final determination should rest with the Indian community."

"I speak with added confidence about these anticipated results because of the favorable experience of programs which have already been turned over to Indian control. Under the auspices of the Office of Economic Opportunity, Indian communities now run more than 60 community action agencies which are located on Federal reservations. OEO is planning to spend some $57 million in Fiscal Year 1971 through Indian-controlled grantees. For over four years, many OEO-funded programs have operated under the control of local Indian organizations and the results have been most heartening."

"The BIA's responsibility does not extend to Indians who have left the reservation, but this point is not always clearly understood. As a result of this misconception, Indians living in urban areas have often lost out on the opportunity to participate in other programs designed for disadvantaged groups. As a first step toward helping the urban Indians, I am instructing appropriate officials to do all they can to ensure that this misunderstanding is corrected."

"But misunderstandings are not the most important problem confronting urban Indians. The biggest barrier faced by those Federal, State and local programs which are trying to serve urban Indians is the difficulty of locating and identifying them. Lost in the anonymity of the city, often cut off from family and friends, many urban Indians are slow to establish new community ties. Many drift from neighborhood to neighborhood; many shuttle back and forth between reservations and urban areas. Language and cultural differences compound these problems. As a result, Federal, State and local programs which are designed to help such persons often miss this most deprived and least understood segment of the urban poverty population."

"This Administration is already taking steps which will help remedy this situation. In a joint effort, the Office of Economic Opportunity and the Department of Health, Education and Welfare will expand support to a total of seven urban Indian centers in major cities which will act as links between existing Federal, State and local service programs and the urban Indians. The Departments of Labor, Housing and Urban Development and Commerce have pledged to cooperate with such experimental urban centers and the Bureau of Indian Affairs has expressed its willingness to contract with these centers for the performance of relocation services which assist reservation Indians in their transition to urban employment."

"Many of the new programs which are

outlined in this message have grown out of this Administration's experience with other Indian projects that have been initiated or expanded during the last 17 months."

"The Office of Economic Opportunity has been particularly active in the development of new and experimental efforts. OEO's Fiscal Year 1971 budget request for Indian-related activities is up 18 percent from 1969 spending. In the last year alone – to mention just two examples – OEO doubled its funds for Indian economic development and tripled its expenditures for alcoholism and recovery programs. In areas such as housing and home improvement, health care, emergency food, legal services and education, OEO programs have been significantly expanded. As I said in my recent speech on the economy, I hope that the Congress will support this valuable work by appropriating the full amount requested for the Economic Opportunity Act."

Britten (2017) noted:

While the Nixon administration had broached the idea of expanding federal funding for seven "model" urban Indian centers in the president's July 8, 1970 message to Congress, the American Indian Policy Review Commission (AIPRC) dedicated an entire section of its final report to the problems facing urban and rural non-reservation Indians. The two-year (1975-1977) $2.6 million study provided nearly one hundred separate recommendations for change in U.S. Indian policy. During the 1960s-70s, Native American "capacity to meet and cope" did not come merely from the act of relocating to urban centers but from urban Indian communities that organized Indian centers to provide newcomers with critically needed social services and a place to go where . . . they could feel safe, understood, and respected.

In the November 3, 1970, California elections, John Tunney, (D) defeated George Murphey, (R).

In the fall of 1970, Nixon instructed his aids to downplay the Administrations handling of the economy and instead put the emphasis on: anti-crime, anti-demonstrations, anti-drug, anti-obscenity, to get in touch with the mood of the country which is fed up with liberals (Small 1999).

OEO issued, 16 November 1970, "The Mission of the Community Action Agency" (OEO Instruction 6320-1) which stated that the purpose of the community action agency was to stimulate a better focusing of all available . . . resources on behalf of the poor. The effectiveness of a community action agency, therefore, is measured not by the services it provides directly but "by the improvements and changes it achieves in the community's attitudes and practices toward the poor . . . " (Clark 2000).

The Arizona Republic, 22 November 1970, wrote:

> Frank Jones and Terry Lenzner fired from the Office of Economic Opportunity's legal services program asserted yesterday that the antipoverty agency is "being run by southern bigots and right-wing politicians across the nation." Terry F. Lenzner, former chief of the embattled program, and his deputy, Frank N. Jones, told a news conference that their dismissals came at Rumsfeld's buckling under to Nixon administration political pressures. But a Rumsfeld spokesman said Friday that Lenzner and Jones had been dismissed because they condoned actions that violated the laws governing OEO and that were not in the best interest of the poor. Under the circumstances, Rumsfeld said, he had no choice but to replace them with "individuals who will effectively administer the program." He then named Arthur L. Reid, 40, OEO deputy general counsel, as counsel, as acting director of the program which involves about 2,000 attorneys in 850 neighborhood offices across the nation.

Jet magazine, 10 December, 1970, reported: "Americans

for Democratic Action said the firings mean that "the White House has bluntly told the poor that they will have no real chance of access to the legal system so that laws can be tested and changed." The article also noted that both Arthur L. Reid and Frank Jones were Black.

On 11 December 1970, Rosenthal (1970) wrote in *The New York Times*:

> WASHINGTON, Dec. 10—The Office of Economic Opportunity appears to have retreated for the second time from heatedly opposed plans to revise the administration of the legal services program for the poor.
>
> Arthur J. Reid, acting director of the poverty law program, disclosed today that O.E.O. had suspended, for at least two weeks, new guidelines that would have shifted authority over the program from lawyers to regional administrators.
>
> Such a change has been one of several issues that have stirred sharp and continuing criticism of the agency in recent weeks. Word that the guidelines had been suspended promptly won praise today from a leading critic.
>
> The suspension "is an encouraging step which the National Legal Aid and Defender Association has been urging for

some time," said John W. Douglas, president of the broad based organization. "We trust that the suspension will lead to permanent changes restoring proper authority to the legal services program."

"There was no intent in the guidelines to harm legal services in any way. If someone can show us a better way to coordinate the program with the rest or the agency, we'll do it," he said.

On Nov. 13, the poverty agency announced that it had abandoned the regionalization plan. The next day, the new guidelines were issued.

Rumsfeld's wife, Joyce, wrote him a poem and tacked it to the front of the refrigerator which he saw one day when he came home late. It said:

"He tackled the job that couldn't be done; with a smile he went right to it. He tackled the job that couldn't be done—and couldn't do it" (Rumsfeld 2011).

Shortly before Rumsfeld resigned, in 10 December 1970, as Director of OEO to work as a few-time Counselor to President Nixon in the White House, he announced a grant award to the California Rural Legal Assistance (CRLA), Inc.

Frank Carlucci was named acting director. Mr. Carlucci

answered during his testimony to be Acting Director, saying, "I am a Foreign Service officer, available for assignment by the President anywhere in the Government."

On December 19, The Conference Report on the bill (S 3016) extending the antipoverty program for two years was filed. The report dropped the Senate-passed amendment to allow Governors to veto legal services projects in their state, but it retained a House amendment which restricted legal services projects to strictly legal matters. The bill was cleared for the President's signature on December 20.

California Governor Ronald Reagan once again vetoed, 26 December, the refunding for CRLA.

The CRLA stated that the Governor's charges were ludicrous and listed three reasons for the veto.

> One – He was ideologically opposed to allowing the poor full access to the courts.
>
> Two – We were too successful. The Governor had lost every major piece of litigation CRLA had brought against him.
>
> Third – The Governor was doing the bidding of large California growers upon whose financial backing he heavily relied (Bennett and Cruz 1972).

Fifteen members of the California Congressional delegation sent, 28 December, a letter to Carlucci urging an immediate override of Reagan's veto.

On 2 January Carlucci was nominated as Director of OEO.

The Senate Committee of Labor and Public Welfare stalled Carlucci's nomination from 30 December until 24 March 1971 when it was reported and approved by the full Senate (Clark 2000). During the hearings Senator Walter Mondale, (D), Minnesota stated: "If he [Carlucci] doesn't [override], there would be nothing left of OEO's legal services. CRLA is the best in the country" (Bennett and Cruz 1972).

Howard Phillips, (R), Massachusetts, was appointed, 6 January 1971, to be Assistant to Acting Director OEO. Carlucci received a recess appointment as Director OEO on 19 January, 1971.

The Commission on California Rural Legal Assistance was created by OEO to investigate charges, starting in March, brought against the CRLA by Reagan and supporters. They concluded that CRLA was operating within the terms of its federal grant and in accordance with profession norms, and recommended refunding the organization. Carlucci announced, June 28, funds to extend CRLA through 1971. It was accepted by the Governor's office, 1 July, 1971, because Carlucci attached twenty-two conditions to the funding. This was the only Legal Services program in the United States to ever have this happen as a function of their funding, once again. It was basically a deal between a Republican President and a Republican Governor with a large political establishment (Bennett and Cruz 1972; Clark 2000, 2002).

During the political activities between Nixon and Reagan over the grant to CRLA, Carlucci resigned his position as Director of OEO. Nixon appointed Phillip V. Sanchez, a Mexican-American with first-hand experience with migratory poverty in childhood. The Senate confirmed his position as Director, 17 November 1971 and he became the highest ranking Mexican-American in the administration. (Clark 2000, 2002).

Sanchez favored broadening the "meaningful involvement" of the poor in the programs that affected them. He said that he favored "maximum feasible participation" and the Community Action Program should shift their emphasis to the "intangibles," such as increased involvement of the poor in the processes of government.

Nixon, 22 January 1971, gave his *Annual Message to the Congress on the State of the Union* in which he said, in part (Nixon 1971c):

> "The sixth great goal is a complete reform of the Federal Government itself."

> "Based on a long and intensive study with the aid of the best advice obtainable, I have concluded that a sweeping reorganization of the executive branch is needed if the Government is to keep up with the times and with the needs of the people."

> "I propose, therefore, that we reduce the present 12 Cabinet Departments to eight."

> "I propose that the Departments of State, Treasury, Defense, and Justice remain, but that all the other departments be consolidated into four: Human Resources, Community Development, Natural Resources, and Economic Development. Let us look at what these would be:
> --First, a department dealing with the concerns of people – as individuals, as members of a family – a department focused on human needs.
> --Second, a department concerned with the community – rural communities and

urban communities – and with all that it takes to   make a community function as a community.

--Third, a department concerned with our physical environment, with the preservation and balanced use of those great natural resources on which our Nation depends.

--And fourth, a department concerned with our prosperity – with our jobs, our businesses, and those many activities that keep our economy running smoothly and well."

"Under this plan, rather than dividing up our departments by narrow subjects, we would organize them around the great purposes of government. Rather than scattering responsibility by adding new levels of bureaucracy, we would focus and concentrate the responsibility for getting problems solved."

"With these four departments, when we have a problem we will know where to go – and the department will have the authority and the resources to do something about it."

"Over the years we have added departments and created agencies at the Federal level, each to serve a new

constituency, to handle a particular task –
and these have grown and multiplied in
what has become a hopeless confusion of
form and function."

"The time has come to match our
structure to our purposes – to look with a
fresh eye, to organize the Government by
conscious, comprehensive design to meet
the new needs of a new era."

Om March 24, 1971 Nixon gave his *Message to the Congress Transmitting Reorganization Plan 1 of 1971 To Establish ACTION* (Nixon 1971d) and said, in part:

"Recognizing that private channels of
voluntary action are a vital source of
strength in our national life, I have
supported the establishment and
development of the National Center for
Voluntary Action. The National Center is
a private, non-profit partner in the effort
to generate and encourage volunteer
service. The Center works to promote the
establishment of local Voluntary Action
Centers, as well as to assist in the
expansion of voluntary action
organizations already in existence. It
stimulates voluntary action by providing
information on successful voluntary
efforts, and it assists in directing those
who wish to volunteer services to areas

and endeavors in which their services are needed. The National Center for Voluntary Action is functioning now to fill a vital need in the private voluntary sector. Now we must turn our attention to bringing government volunteer programs into line with new national priorities and new opportunities for meeting those priorities. We must take full advantage of the lessons of the past decade, and we must build on the experience of that period if we are to realize the full potential of voluntary citizen service. This is no longer a matter of choice. We cannot afford to misuse or ignore the considerable talents and energies of our people. In the coming years, the continued progress of our society is going to depend increasingly upon the willingness of more Americans to participate in voluntary service and upon our ability to channel their service effectively."

"Under the reorganization plan Action would administer the functions of the following programs:
--Volunteers in Service to America: VISTA volunteers work in domestic poverty areas to help the poor break the poverty cycle.
--Auxiliary and Special Volunteer

Programs in the Office of

Economic Opportunity: At present the National Student Volunteer   Program is administered under this authority. This program stimulates student voluntary action programs which deal with the problems of the poor.

--Foster Grandparents: This program provides opportunities for the   elderly poor to assist needy children.

--Retired Senior Volunteer Program:

--RSVP provides opportunities for retired persons to perform voluntary services in their communities.

--Service Corps of Retired Executives:

--SCORE provides opportunities for retired businessmen to assist in the development of small businesses.

--Active Corps of Executives: ACE provides opportunities for working businessmen to assist in the development of small businesses."

"After investigation I have found and hereby declare that each reorganization included in the accompanying reorganization plan is necessary to accomplish one or more of the purposes set forth in section 901 (a) of title 5 of the United States Code. In particular, the plan is responsive to section 901(a)(1), "to promote the better execution of the laws, the more effective management of the executive branch and of its agencies and functions, and the expeditious administration of the public business;" and section 901 (a) (3), "to increase the efficiency of the operations of the Government to the fullest extent practicable."

"Upon the establishment of Action, I would delegate to it the principal authority for the Peace Corps now vested in me as President and delegated to the Secretary of State. In addition, the function of the Office of Voluntary Action, now operating in the Department of Housing and Urban Development, would be transferred to the new agency by executive action."

"Finally, I will submit legislation which would include the transfer of the functions of the Teacher Corps from the Department of Health, Education, and Welfare to the new agency. This legislation would expand authority to develop new uses of volunteer talents, it would provide a citizens' advisory board to work with the director of the new agency, and it would provide authority to match private contributions."

May 21, 1971, the White House released the transcript of a news briefing on the trip by Robert H. Finch and Donald Rumsfeld, Counselors to the President, who made a 23-day trip to Europe and North Africa to discuss drug abuse prevention and control with foreign officials.

President Nixon gave a *Special Message to the Congress on Drug Abuse Prevention and Control*(Nixon 1971f) in which he said, in part:

> "A large number of Federal Government agencies are involved in efforts to fight the drug problem either with new programs or by expanding existing programs. Many of these programs are still experimental in nature. This is appropriate. The problems of drug abuse must be faced on many fronts at the same time, and we do not yet know which efforts will be most successful. But we must recognize that piecemeal efforts, even where individually successful, cannot have a major impact on the drug abuse problem unless and until they are forged together into a broader and more integrated program involving all levels of government and private effort. We need a coordinated effort if we are to move effectively against drug abuse."

> "To help expedite the prosecution of narcotic trafficking cases, we are asking the Congress to provide legislation which

would permit the United States Government to utilize information obtained by foreign police, provided that such information was obtained in compliance with the laws of that country."

"Finally, I am asking the Congress to provide a supplemental appropriation of $25.6 million for the Treasury Department. This will increase funds available to this Department for drug abuse control to nearly $45 million. Of this sum, $18.1 million would be used to enable the Bureau of Customs to develop the technical capacity to deal with smuggling by air and sea, to increase the investigative staff charged with pursuit and apprehension of smugglers, and to increase inspection personnel who search persons, baggage, and cargo entering the country. The remaining $7.5 million would permit the Internal Revenue Service to intensify investigation of persons involved in large-scale narcotics trafficking."

On the same day, 17 June, 1971, Nixon gave a White House announcement, *Remarks About an Intensified Program for Drug Abuse Prevention and Control,* in the White House Briefing room, in which he said, in part (Nixon 1971g):

"America's public enemy number one in the United States is drug abuse. In order to fight and defeat this enemy, it is necessary to wage a new, all-out offensive."

"I have asked the Congress to provide the legislative authority and the funds to fuel this kind of an offensive. This will be a worldwide offensive dealing with the problems of sources of supply, as well as Americans who may be stationed abroad, wherever they are in the world. It will be government wide, pulling together the nine different fragmented areas within the government in which this problem is now being handled, and it will be nationwide in terms of a new educational program that we trust will result from the discussions that we have had."

"If we are going to have a successful offensive, we need more money. Consequently, I am asking the Congress for $155 million in new funds, which will bring the total amount this year in the budget for drug abuse, both in enforcement and treatment, to over $350 million."

Baum (2016) wrote, in part, in *Harper's Magazine*:

The term "War On Drugs" was popularized by the media shortly after the press conference which he declared drug abuse "public enemy number one". That message to the Congress included text about devoting more federal resources to the "prevention of new addicts, and the rehabilitation of those who are addicted", but that part did not receive the same public attention as the term "war on drug."

At the time, I was writing a book about the politics of drug prohibition. I started to ask Ehrlichman a series of earnest, wonky questions that he impatiently waved away. "You want to know what this was really all about?" he asked with the bluntness of a man who, after public disgrace and a stretch in federal prison, had little left to protect. "The Nixon campaign in 1968, and the Nixon White House after that, had two enemies: the antiwar left and black people. You understand what I'm saying? We knew we couldn't make it illegal to be either against the war or black, but by getting the public to associate the hippies with marijuana and blacks with heroin, and then criminalizing both heavily, we could disrupt those communities. We could arrest their leaders, raid their homes, break up their meetings, and vilify them night after night on the evening news. Did we know we were lying about the drugs? Of course we did."

Hanson (2016) wrote, in part, in *Huffpost, Politics* that:

That Nixon Aides stated: ". . . that Ehrlichman was "known for using biting sarcasm to dismiss those with whom he disagreed, and it is possible the reporter misread his tone . . . John never uttered a word or sentiment that suggested he or the President were "anti-black."

Erhlichman may have never said anything to suggest this, but Nixon himself was taped referring to the "little Negro bastards" on welfare and stating that they "live like a bunch of dogs."

The former officials also noted that the Nixon administration established drug education and addiction treatment programs. While this is true, Nixon also signed the Comprehensive Drug Abuse Prevention and Control Act of 1970, which gave law enforcement the right to conduct "no-knock" searches, allowing them to enter premises without notifying occupants. This is presumably what Ehrlichman was referring to when he allegedly said the drug war gave authorities the license to "raid [the] homes" of black people and hippies."

As part of the War on Drugs initiative, Nixon increased federal funding for drug-control agencies and proposed strict measures, such as mandatory prison sentencing, for drug crimes. He also announced the creation of the Special Action Office for Drug Abuse Prevention (SAODAP), which was headed by Dr. Jerome Jaffe.

Vecsey (1971) wrote in *The New York Times* that:

> ATLANTA, June 5 — A bus load of mountain people went home to eastern Kentucky to day, its occupants hoping they had persuaded the Office of Economic Opportunity not to terminate their million dollar a year poverty program.
>
> The regional director of the antipoverty agency, Roy E. Batchelor [Regional Director of the Southeastern Region of OEO], has threatened to abolish the Jackson Clay Community Action Group because of disruptions on the board of directors. After 12 hours of testimony yesterday, Mr. Batchelor said he would need several weeks before reaching a decision.
>
> The embattled executive director of the Jackson Clay group, Flem Messer, had previously argued that Mr. Batchelor should not be the hearing official because

he had twice suspended various functions of the agency during the four month struggle. Mr. Messer has asserted that Mr. Batchelor is under pressure from the Nixon and Kentucky Administrations to let politicians take over the agency for patronage purposes.

On 29 June, Nixon sent a Message to the Senate a *Message From The President of the United States returning Without Approval the Bill (S. 575) Entitled "To Extend the Public Works Acceleration Act, the Public Works and Economic Development Act Of 1965, and the Regional Appalachian Development Act of 1965.* He wrote, in part:

> Title II—the Public Works and Economic Development Act of 1965 until June 30, 1973, and extends—by Title III—the Appalachian Regional Development Act to June 30, 1975. I agree that our present economic development programs should be extended while the Congress is considering my revenue sharing proposals. But most importantly, the Congress must act immediately to insure that there is no gap in service, to the people in Appalachia and in the economically depressed areas served by EDA. In this connection, I am pleased to note that the House has already provided for the temporary continuance of these programs until new legislation can be

enacted. I urge the Senate to do likewise. I know the problems of these areas. I met with the Appalachian Governors last year for a full half day to discuss the best ways in which we could meet the needs of the people of Appalachia. When I met with the Governors of Virginia, West Virginia, and Kentucky last week, I emphasized that even if I would have to veto the Accelerated Public Works bill, I support the Appalachian program 100 percent.

The Appalachian Regional Commission has been a very useful experimental development program which can be improved upon and can serve in many respects as a model for a national program. This is essentially what I have done in proposing to the Congress Rural and Urban Community Development Revenue Sharing. The record of the Appalachian Regional Commission goes a long way in proving that State and local governments do have the capacity to make revenue sharing work.

The revenue sharing proposals will insure that States and localities will get their fair share of the funds automatically without having to play grantsmanship games. Furthermore, those proposals would eliminate Federal red tape and local share requirements. State and local officials could more quickly provide public projects which are most responsive to local needs. The gap between Federal resources and local needs would be bridged in a way that would strengthen State and local responsibilities and decision-making. These proposals deal with problems which simply will not yield to the old approaches, no matter how they are reworked or expanded. I again urge upon

Title II—the Public Works and Economic Development Act of 1965 until June 30, 1973, and extends—by Title III—the Appalachian Regional Development Act to June 30, 1975. I agree that our present economic development programs should be extended while the Congress is considering my revenue sharing proposals. But most importantly, the Congress must act immediately to insure that there is no gap in service, to the people in Appalachia and in the economically depressed areas served by EDA. In this connection, I am pleased to note that the House lias already provided for the temporary continuance of these programs until new legislation can be enacted. I urge the Senate to do likewise. 1 know the problems of these areas. I met with the Appalachian Governors last year for a full half day to discuss the best ways in which we could meet the needs of the people of Appalachia. When I met with the Governors of Virginia, West Virginia, and Kentucky last week, I emphasized that even if I would have to veto the Accelerated Public Works bill, I support the Appalachian program 100 percent.

The Appalachian Regional Commission has been a very useful experimental development program which can be improved upon and can serve in many respects as a model for a national program. This is essentially what I have done in proposing to the Congress Rural and Urban Community Development Revenue Sharing. The record of the Appalachian Regional Commission goes a long way in proving that State and local governments do have the capacity to make revenue sharing work.

The revenue sharing proposals will insure that States and localities will get their fair share of the funds automatically without having to play grantsmanship games. Furthermore, those proposals would eliminate Federal red tape and local share requirements. State and local officials could more quickly provide public projects which are most responsive to local needs. The gap between Federal resources and local needs would be bridged in a way that would strengthen

State and local responsibilities and decision-making. These proposals deal with problems which simply will not yield to the old approaches, no matter how they are reworked or expanded. I again urge upon the Congress the early enactment of my revenue sharing programs.

On 30 June 1971, OEO's legal and fiscal authority expired. Nixon requested a two year extension. In July a Child Development program was added and created a new National Legal Services Corporation with a seventeen-member board.

On June 30, 1971, the President signed *Executive Order 11603 — Assigning Additional Functions to the Director of ACTION* further implementing the reorganization plan (Nixon 1971e) in which he stated:

> SEC. 101. Authority. The Peace Corps, established as an agency in the Department of State pursuant to Executive Order No. 10924 of March 1, 1961 (26 F.R. 1789), and continued in existence in that Department under the Peace Corps Act (hereafter in this part referred to as the Act) pursuant to section 102 of Executive Order No. 11041 of August 6, 1962 (27 F.R. 7859), is hereby transferred to the agency created by Reorganization Plan No. 1 of 1971 and designated as ACTION. The Director of ACTION (hereinafter referred to as the

Director) shall provide for its continuance under the Act as a component of that agency.

SEC. 401. The National Voluntary Action Program to encourage and stimulate more widespread and effective voluntary action for solving public domestic problems, established in the Executive Branch of the Government by section 1 of Executive Order No. 11470 of May 26, 1969, is hereby transferred to ACTION. That program shall supplement corresponding action by private and other non-Federal organizations such as the National Center for Voluntary Action. As used in PARTS IV and V of this Order, the term "voluntary action" means the contribution or application of non-governmental resources of all kinds (time, money, goods, services, and skills) by private and other organizations of all types (profit and nonprofit, national and local, occupational, and altruistic) and by individual citizens.

SEC. 606. The Order shall become effective on July 1, 1971.

On July 1, the White House announced the nomination of Joseph H. Blotchford, Director, Peace Corps, as Director of ACTION.

In the last week of July Congress passed a continuing resolution to finance Federal agencies until October15.

Carlucci moved, 28 July, from OEO to the Office of Budget and Management.

Nixon in his *Statement on Signing Bill Extending Special Assistance to Depressed Rural Areas,* 6 August, Senate Bill S 2317,(Nixon 1971b) said:

> It is essential that we encourage and maintain balanced economic growth in rural areas, especially in those regions where special assistance is needed. The enactment of S. 2317, which I have today signed, contributes significantly to this effort.
>
> This bill provides for the extension of two acts: the Public Works and Economic Development Act of 1965 and the Appalachian Regional Development Act of 1965. It extends for 2 years the Economic Development Administration (EDA), and the title V regional action planning commissions, while also expanding the special impact area criteria for the purposes of EDA eligibility. It provides for a 4-year extension of the Appalachian Regional Commission (ARC), and extends the Commission's highway program until June 30, 1978.
>
> The experience, leadership, and example

of the Appalachian Commission has been an important part of the basis for my proposal for a $1.1 billion program of rural community development special revenue sharing. The work of the Appalachian Commission has shown how effective regional cooperation and local initiative can be in planning and developing the economy of a depressed area.

It is both appropriate and necessary that the work of the Appalachian and other existing regional commissions, as well as the programs of EDA, be continued in the interim until the more comprehensive program of rural revenue sharing can be enacted. I again urge the Congress to enact my general and special revenue sharing proposals.

The Appalachian Regional Development Act, passed 1965 by Congress established the Appalachian Regional Commission (ARC) to plan and manage economic development in the region. The Act defines the region as the entire state of West Virginia and parts of twelve other states--Alabama, Georgia, Kentucky, Maryland, Mississippi, New York, North Carolina, Ohio, Pennsylvania, South Carolina, Tennessee and Virginia. It concentrates its efforts in two major areas. (1) The highway program, which annually receives about two-thirds of the ARC's funds, provides for construction of the Appalachian Development Highway System; (2) area development, grants for education and health care, water and sewer systems, housing, child development, enterprise development, natural resources development, and research on topics related to the region's economic development with grants often combining local and/or state funds. ARC is organized to ensure federal, state, and local participation. The Commission consists of fourteen members – the thirteen Appalachian governors and a Federal Co-Chair, appointed by the President. An executive director heads the Commission staff.

In August, The House Education and Labor Committee agreed to a compromise plan to remove from OEO the Legal Services Program and put it with board members appointed by The President with consent of Congress into a corporation run by a seventeen member Board of Directors. The Administration proposed to give the President sole authority for board appointment. The vote was 13-23 against this idea.

The Committee, 32-3, reported out the authorization bill for fiscal years 1972, 1973, $4.9 billion for the two years funding of for the Economic Opportunity Act. During the negotiations of the bill, Elliot Richardson, Secretary of Health, Education, and Welfare, emphasized that the administration was completely opposed to the Senate-approved child care section. The Senate passed the bill, 49-12, for $7.3 billion for the Economic Opportunity Act amendment of 1971.

It was reported in *The New York Times*, 23 September, that Arthur Fletcher, known to many as the father of affirmative action, Assistant Secretary of Labor for two years, refused a post at OEO.

In October, the House accepted a sweeping child development program amendment to the Economic Opportunity amendments. Sanchez named Howard Phillips, Associate Director OEO to a new Office of Program Review.

In November, the House committee authorized two new categorical programs: an Environmental Action Program providing jobs to low-income persons; and, a Rural Housing program. With the strict earmarking of funds and the new Child Development Program put in the Senate bill, a ranking White House official suggested that a White House veto was possible. The Staff Director of the Senate subcommittee said: "I think people have ceased to take veto threats from this Administration seriously." On 9 November, Senator Robert A. Taft, (R), Ohio, attempted to review the bill, to put it more in line with Nixon's recommendations, was rejected.

On 29 November, The Congressional Conference Committee agreed that $4,320 was the income level to be set for families to qualify for free services under the Child Development program. The House passed $4,320 or less; the Senate passed $6,960 or less.

Congress cleared the bill (HR 6283—PL 92-179) on December 1, 1971, extending for two years the President's authority to submit plans to Congress for reorganization of executive agencies. The President's reorganization authority, extended in March 1969 (PL 91-5), had expired April 1, 1971.

The Reorganization Act of 1949 authorized the President to submit to Congress plans to reorganize government agencies through transfer, abolition or consolidation of agency functions. Each plan would take effect within 60 days unless disapproved by either chamber.

On 2 December, by roll-call vote, 63-17, the Senate approved the OEO funding bill.

On 3-4 December, Roy E. Batchelor of Chattanooga, Tennessee, was nominated and confirmed for Assistant Director, Operations, OEO.

Nixon in his 9 December 1971 message on his *Veto of the*

Economic Opportunity Amendments of 1971 stated (Nixon 1971a):

> I return herewith without my approval S. 2007, the Economic Opportunity Amendments of 1971.
>
> Upon taking office, this administration sought to redesign, to redirect – indeed, to rehabilitate – the Office of Economic Opportunity, which had lost much public acceptance in the five years since its inception. Our objective has been to provide this agency with a new purpose and a new role. Our goal has been to make the Office of Economic Opportunity the primary research and development arm of the Nation's and the Government's ongoing effort to diminish and eventually eliminate poverty in the United States. Despite occasional setbacks, considerable progress has been made.
>
> That progress is now jeopardized. Two ill-advised and restrictive amendments contained in this bill would vitiate our efforts and turn back the clock.
>
> In the 1964 act the President was granted authority to delegate – by executive action – programs of OEO to other departments of the Government. That

flexibility has enabled this administration to shift tried and proven programs out of OEO to other agencies--so that OEO can concentrate its resources and talents on generating and testing new ideas, new programs and new policies to assist the remaining poor in the United States. This flexibility, however, would be taken away under amendments added by the Congress – and the President would be prohibited from spinning off successful and continuing programs to the service agencies.

If this congressional action were allowed to stand, OEO would become an operational agency, diluting its special role as incubator and tester of ideas and pioneer for social programs.

The provision creating the National Legal Services Corporation differs crucially from the proposal originally put forth by this administration. Our intention was to create a legal services corporation, to aid the poor, that was independent and free of politics, yet contained built-in safeguards to assure its operation in a responsible manner. In the Congress, however, the legislation has been substantially altered, so that the quintessential principle of accountability has been lost.

In re-writing our original proposal, the door has been left wide open to those abuses which have cost one anti-poverty program after another its public enthusiasm and public support.

The restrictions which the Congress has imposed upon the President in the selection of directors of the Corporation is also an affront to the principle of accountability to the American people as a whole. Under congressional revisions, the President has full discretion to appoint only six of the seventeen directors; the balance must be chosen from lists provided by various professional, client and special interest groups, some of which are actual or potential grantees of the Corporation.

With this message, I urge the Congress to act now to pass the OEO extension and to create the legal services corporation along the lines proposed in our original legislation.

Spangler (2012) felt "Despite the myriad of motivations for the veto, in his veto message, Nixon chose to emphasize just one primary motivation: the protection of the family. For Nixon, the veto message of the Comprehensive Childcare Act was an opportunity to recommit himself to the family agenda of the conservative Christians who had voted for him in 1968. Nixon's strong condemnation of the bill reinforced the negative social and political image that had been attached to day care in the United States from its inception. The stigmatization of childcare, solidified by Nixon's decision in this veto, set the development of a universal childcare system in the United States back for decades to come."

The Senate sustained the President's veto on December 10. The vote to override the veto obtained a simple majority, 51–36, but this was seven votes short of the two-thirds majority required to override a veto (CQ Almanac 1971). The veto forced the OEO to operate under a continuing resolution, introduced 13 December (Clark 2000).

Nixon gave his Address on the *State of the Union Delivered Before a Joint Session of the Congress,* 20 January 1972, and stated, in part (Nixon 1972c):

> "Nineteen hundred seventy-two is now before us. It holds precious time in which to accomplish good for the Nation. We must not waste it."

> "Our budget will help meet it by being expansionary without being inflationary – a job-producing budget that will help take up the gap as the economy expands to full employment."

> "Our program to raise farm income will help meet it by helping to revitalize rural America, by giving to America's farmers

their fair share of America's increasing productivity."

"We also will help meet our goal of full employment in peacetime with a set of major initiatives to stimulate more imaginative use of America's great capacity for technological advance, and to direct it toward improving the quality of life for every American."

"This second session of the 92d Congress already has before it more than 90 major Administration proposals which still await action."

"I have discussed these in the extensive written message that I have presented to the Congress today."

"They include, among others, our programs to improve life for the aging; to combat crime and drug abuse; to improve health services and to ensure that no one will be denied needed health care because of inability to pay; to protect workers' pension rights; to promote equal opportunity for members of minorities, and others who have been left behind; to expand consumer protection; to improve the environment; to revitalize rural America; to help the cities; to launch new initiatives in education; to improve transportation, and to put an end to costly labor tie-ups in transportation."

"The messages also include basic reforms which are essential if our structure of government is to be adequate in the decades ahead."

"They include reform of our wasteful and outmoded welfare system – substitution of a new system that provides work requirements and work incentives for those who can help themselves, income support for those who cannot help themselves, and fairness to the working poor."

"They include a $17 billion program of Federal revenue sharing with the States and localities as an investment in their renewal, an investment also of faith in the American people."

"They also include a sweeping reorganization of the executive branch of the Federal Government so that it will be more efficient, more responsive, and able to meet the challenges of the decades ahead."

"One year ago, standing in this place, I

laid before the opening session of this Congress six great goals. One of these was welfare reform. That proposal has been before the Congress now for nearly 2 1/2 years."

"My proposals on revenue sharing, government reorganization, health care, and the environment have now been before the Congress for nearly a year. Many of the other major proposals that I have referred to have been here that long or longer."

"Now, 1971, we can say, was a year of consideration of these measures. Now let us join in making 1972 a year of action on them, action by the Congress, for the Nation and for the people of America."

"We believe in independence, and self-reliance, and the creative value of the competitive spirit."

"We believe in full and equal opportunity for all Americans and in the protection of individual rights and liberties."

"We believe in the family as the keystone of the community, and in the community as the keystone of the Nation."

"We believe in compassion toward those in need."

"We believe in a system of law, justice, and order as the basis of a genuinely free society."

"We believe that a person should get what he works for – and that those who can, should work for what they get."

"We believe in the capacity of people to make their own decisions in their own lives, in their own communities – and we believe in their right to make those decisions."

"In applying these principles, we have done so with the full understanding that what we seek in the seventies, what our quest is, is not merely for more, but for a better quality of life for all Americans."

"We have been undergoing self-doubts and self-criticism. But these are only the other side of our growing sensitivity to the persistence of want in the midst of plenty, of our impatience with the slowness with which age-old ills are being overcome."

"If we were indifferent to the

shortcomings of our society, or complacent about our institutions, or blind to the lingering inequities – then we would have lost our way."

"But the fact that we have those concerns is evidence that our ideals, deep down, are still strong. Indeed, they remind us that what is really best about America is its compassion. They remind us that in the final analysis, America is great not because it is strong, not because it is rich, but because this is a good country."

"Let us reject the narrow visions of those who would tell us that we are evil because we are not yet perfect, that we are corrupt because we are not yet pure, that all the sweat and toil and sacrifice that have gone into the building of America were for naught because the building is not yet done."

"Let us see that the path we are traveling is wide, with room in it for all of us, and that its direction is toward a better Nation and a more peaceful world."

"Never has it mattered more that we go forward together."

On January 24, 1972, Sanchez was sworn into office, at the

White House, as Director OEO by Presidential Counselor Robert Finch. Sanchez pledged to reinstate credibility, audibility and visibility of the antipoverty agency.

The House Education and Labor Committee, 25 January, reacted angrily at Sanchez testimony when he suggested Congress pass a "clean" EOA bill, one containing no controversial amendments. "The administration considers it inadvisable to undertake substantive amendments to the act until Congress has acted on the President's proposals for government reorganization and revenue sharing which would have a significant bearing on the future of OEO."

Hearings started on the nomination of Bert A. Gallegos, from Colorado, to Assistant Director OEO.

In April, the Senate Employment, Manpower and Poverty Subcommittee passed a bill to provide $2.9 billion over three years for an extension of OEO and a separate three-year Child Development bill and then in June passed, 74-16, a $9.6 extension, which extended OEO and EOA programs through fiscal 1974.

The GAO issued a report 26 April which stated, in part:

B-175394

Dear Senator Proxmire

Pursuant to your request of February 24, 1972, we examined charges of improper practices regarding two contracts (B99-4889 and B99-5008) entered into In June 1969 between the Office of Economic Opportunity (OEO) and BOOZ, Allen and Hamilton, Inc (BAH), a management consulting firm The charges were made in a letter to you dated February 7, 1972, by

Mr, Barry A Willner, an employee of the Center for Study of Responsive Law Specifically, Mr Willner charged that

1 Mr Bruce Stevens, a BAH employee, could not have worked 45 days on contract B99-5008 between June 30 and September 30, 1969, because he worked every day at OEO during this period on contract B99-4889

2 Mr Paul Anderson, a White House fellow assigned to the Director, OEO, had initiated contract B99-4889 and had subsequently worked as a BAH employee under this contract.

*　　*　　*　　*　　*

Because of the significant amount of funds OEO spends each year on contracts with private firms, we previously made a comprehensive review of OEO contracting policies, practices, and procedures We issued three reports to the Congress on the results of our previous reviews (1) Contract Award Procedures and Practices of the Office of Economic Opportunity Need Improving (B-130515, December 15, 1971), (2) Improvements Needed in the Administration of Contracts for Evaluations and Studies of Anti-poverty Programs (B-130515, December 28, 1971), and (3) Improvements Needed in Training and Technical Assistance Services Provided to

Anti-poverty Agencies (B-130515, April 26, 1972).

In these reports we identified a number of OEO contracting weaknesses and made a number of recommendations for improving OEO contract administration. OEO has informed us that a number of positive measures have been undertaken, including the appointment in July 1971 of a high-level task force to help improve and strengthen OEO's contract administration.

Copies of these reports are enclosed.

In May, OEO, and three other federal agencies, announced that they would set up a network of Urban Indian Centers to work with existing social organizations in order to make them more responsive to that population.

June 16, Nixon in his budget included no funds for OEO because, he stated, Congressional rules require that authorizing legislation be passed for a program to be enacted before funds can be voted.

On June 17, 1972, five men were arrested for illegally entering the Democratic National Committee headquarters in an office building at the Watergate complex in Washington, D.C. On September 15, they were indicted by a Federal grand jury on charges which included conspiracy to use illegal means to obtain information from the Democratic headquarters, intent to steal property of another, and intent to intercept willfully, knowingly, and unlawfully, oral and wire communications.

Nixon (Nixon 1972a) held *The President's News Conference*, 22 June, and was asked, in part:

Q. Mr. O'Brien [Lawrence F. O'Brien was chairman of the Democratic National Committee] has said that the people who bugged his headquarters had a direct link to the White House. Have you had any sort of investigation made to determine whether this is true?

THE PRESIDENT. Mr. Ziegler [Ronald L. Ziegler, the White House press secretary] and also Mr. Mitchell [Former Attorney General John N. Mitchell was campaign director of the Committee for the Re-Election of the President], speaking for the campaign committee, have responded to questions on this in great detail. They have stated my position and have also stated the facts accurately.

This kind of activity, as Mr. Ziegler has indicated, has no place whatever in our electoral process, or in our governmental process. And, as Mr. Ziegler has stated, the White House has had no involvement whatever in this particular incident.

As far as the matter now is concerned, it is under investigation, as it should be, by the proper legal authorities, by the District of Columbia police, and by the FBI. I will not comment on those matters, particularly since possible criminal charges are involved.

The Senate approved, 29 June, a $9.6 billion authorization for anti-poverty programs over a three-year period. The bill did not give the President free hand in handling or transferring programs.

On July 1, the Senate approved by roll-call the $9.6 anti-poverty bill and an amendment to keep Consumer Action program within OEO and defeated an amendment that would have continued the Legal Services program within OEO.

22 July, House and Senate Conferees agree on $9.6 two-year extension of anti poverty programs. The bill included a provision to establish an independent Legal Services Corporation.

28 July, Carlucci moved to Associate Director, Office of Budget and Management.

In August, the House and Senate passed a continuing resolution to maintain spending levels for OEO at present levels to the end of September. The two year extension was sent to the White House for signing. The Legal Services Corporation language was no longer in the bill.

Nixon signed, 21 September, a compromise $4.8 billion, two-year authorization for the OEO and EOA programs. Legal Services for the poor were still in the bill.

Toward the end of his 1972 Presidential election campaign Nixon stated in the interview with Garertt D. Horner, *Washington Star-News* of Washington, D.C., that he would "shuck off" and "trim down" social programs "set up in the 1960s" that he, Nixon, considered massive failures largely because they "just threw money at problems." He criticized "the limousine liberal set" of the northeast and the "liberal establishment." He wanted to end "the whole era of permissiveness." and there would be "few social goodies" in his second administration (Nathan 2011, Jansson 1977).

Nixon held *The President's News Conference* on 5 October 1972 and addressed questions from the press (Nixon 1972b), some of which were:

> [1.] Q. Mr. President, what are you planning to do to defend yourself against the charges of corruption in your Administration?
>
> THE PRESIDENT. Well, I have noted such charges. As a matter of fact, I have noted that this Administration has been charged with being the most corrupt in history, and I have been charged with being the most deceitful President in history.
>
> The President of the United States has been compared in his policies with Adolf Hitler. The policies of the U.S. Government to prevent a Communist takeover by force in South Vietnam have been called the worst crime since the Nazi extermination of the Jews in Germany. And the President who went to China and to Moscow, and who has brought 500,000 home from Vietnam, has been called the number one war-maker in the world.

Needless to say, some of my more partisan advisers feel that I should respond in kind. I shall not do so – not now, not throughout this campaign. I am not going to dignify such comments.

In view of the fact that one of the very few Members of the Congress [Representative Jerome R. Waldie of California] who is publicly and actively supporting the opposition ticket in this campaign has very vigorously, yesterday, criticized this kind of tactics, it seems to me it makes it not necessary for me to respond.

I think the responsible members of the Democratic Party will be turned off by this kind of campaigning, and I would suggest that responsible members of the press, following the single standard to which they are deeply devoted, will also be turned off by it.

[7.] Q. Mr. President, don't you think that your Administration and the public would be served considerably and that the men under indictment would be treated better, if you people would come through and make a clean breast about what you were trying to get done at the Watergate?

THE PRESIDENT. One thing that has always puzzled me about it is why anybody would have tried to get anything out of the Watergate. But be that as it may, that decision having been made at lower levels, with which I had no knowledge, and, as I pointed out –

Q. But, surely you know now, sir.

THE PRESIDENT. Just a minute. I certainly feel that under the circumstances that we have got to look at what has happened and to put the matter into perspective.

Now when we talk about a clean breast, let's look at what has happened. The FBI assigned 133 agents to this investigation. It followed out 1,800 leads. It conducted 1,500 interviews.

Incidentally, I conducted the investigation of the Hiss case. I know that is a very unpopular subject to raise in some quarters, but I conducted it. It was successful. The FBI did a magnificent job, but that investigation, involving the security of this country, was basically a Sunday school exercise compared to the amount of effort that was put into this.

I agreed with the amount of effort that was put into it. I wanted every lead carried out to the end because I wanted to be sure that no member of the White House Staff and no man or woman in a position of major responsibility in the Committee for the Re-Election had anything to do with this kind of reprehensible activity.

Now, the grand jury has handed down indictments. It has indicted incidentally two who were with the Committee for the Re-Election and one who refused to cooperate and another who was apprehended. Under these circumstances, the grand jury now having acted, it is now time to have the judicial process go forward and for the evidence to be presented.

I would say finally with regard to commenting on any of those who have been indicted, with regard to saying anything about the judicial process, I am going to follow the good advice, which I appreciate, of the members of the press corps, my constant, and I trust will always continue to be, very responsible critics.

I stepped into one on that when you recall

I made, inadvertently, a comment in Denver about an individual who had been indicted in California, the Manson case. I was vigorously criticized for making any comment about the case, and so, of course, I know you would want me to follow the same single standard by not commenting on this case.

On October 1972 Public Law 92-512, known as General Revenue Sharing, was
passed by the Congress and signed into law by President Nixon.

Nixon, 20 October, released at Philadelphia, Pa., in his *Statement About the General Revenue Sharing Bill*, said, in part (Nixon 1972d):

In my State of the Union Address nearly 2 years ago, I outlined a program which I described as "a new American revolution – a peaceful revolution in which power [is] turned back to the people . . . a revolution as profound, as far-reaching, as exciting as that first revolution almost 200 years ago."

The signing today of the State and Local Fiscal Assistance Act of 1972 – the legislation known as general revenue sharing-means that this new American revolution is truly underway. And it is appropriate that we launch this new

American revolution in the same place where the first American Revolution was launched by our Founding Fathers 196 years ago – Independence Square in Philadelphia. It is appropriate that we meet in this historic place to help enunciate a new declaration of independence for our State and local governments.

Even as we return today to the place where our Nation was founded, we are also returning to the principles of the Founding Fathers.

They came here in the 18th century to establish the federal system. We return here in the 20th century to renew the federal system.

They came here to create a balance between the various levels of government. We come here to restore that balance.

They came here "to form a more perfect Union." We come here to make it more perfect still.

But the most important point is this: In each case it will be local officials responding to local conditions and local constituencies who will decide what should happen, and not some distant bureaucrat in Washington, D.C.

The American people are fed up with government that doesn't deliver. Revenue sharing can help State and local government deliver again, closing the gap between promise and performance.

Revenue sharing will give these hard-pressed governments the dollars they need so badly. But just as importantly, it will give them the freedom they need to use those dollars as effectively as possible.

Under this program, instead of spending so much time trying to please distant bureaucrats in Washington – so the money will keep coming in – State and local officials can concentrate on pleasing the people – so the money can do more good.

Under revenue sharing, more decisions will be made at the scene of the action – and this means that more people can have a piece of the action. By multiplying the centers of effective power in our country we will be multiplying the opportunities for involvement and influence by individual citizens.

General Revenue Sharing lasted from 1972 until 1986.

Nixon, spoke, 20 January 1973, at 12:02 p.m. from the inaugural platform erected at the east front of the Capitol, after the oath of office was administered by Chief Justice Warren E. Burger, first to Vice President Spiro T. Agnew and then to President, broadcast live on nationwide radio and television with an advance text was released on the same day, and said in his *Oath of Office and Second Inaugural Address* (Nixon 1972e), in part:

> "We have the chance today to do more than ever before in our history to make life better in America – to ensure better education, better health, better housing, better transportation, a cleaner environment – to restore respect for law, to make our communities more livable – and to ensure the God-given right of every American to full and equal opportunity."

> "Because the range of our needs is so great, because the reach of our opportunities is so great, let us be bold in our determination to meet those needs in new ways."

> "Just as building a structure of peace abroad has required turning away from old policies that have failed, so building a

new era of progress at home requires turning away from old policies that have failed."

"And at home, the shift from old policies to new will not be a retreat from our responsibilities, but a better way to progress."

"Abroad and at home, the key to those new responsibilities lies in the placing and the division of responsibility. We have lived too long with the consequences of attempting to gather all power and responsibility in Washington."

"Abroad and at home, the time has come to turn away from the condescending policies of paternalism – of 'Washington knows best.'"

"A person can be expected to act responsibly only if he has responsibility. This is human nature. So let us encourage individuals at home and nations abroad to do more for themselves, to decide more for themselves. Let us locate responsibility in more places. And let us measure what we will do for others by what they will do for themselves."

"That is why today I offer no promise of

a purely governmental solution for every problem. We have lived too long with that false promise. In trusting too much in government, we have asked of it more than it can deliver. This leads only to inflated expectations, to reduced individual effort, and to a disappointment and frustration that erode confidence both in what government can do and in what people can do."

"Government must learn to take less from people so that people can do more for themselves."

"Let us remember that America was built not by government, but by people; not by welfare, but by work; not by shirking responsibility, but by seeking responsibility."

"In our own lives, let each of us ask-not just what will government do for me, but what can I do for myself?"

"In the challenges we face together, let each of us ask – not just how can government help, but how can I help?"

"Your National Government has a great and vital role to play. And I pledge to you that where this Government should act, we will act boldly and we will lead boldly. But just as important is the role that each and every one of us must play, as an individual and as a member of his own community."

"Above all else, the time has come for us to renew our faith in ourselves and in America."

"In recent years, that faith has been challenged."

"Our children have been taught to be ashamed of their country, ashamed of their parents, ashamed of America's record at home and its role in the world."

"At every turn we have been beset by those who find everything wrong with America and little that is right. But I am confident that this will not be the judgment of history on these remarkable times in which we are privileged to live."

"America's record in this century has been unparalleled in the world's history for its responsibility, for its generosity, for its creativity, and for its progress."

"Let us be proud that our system has produced and provided more freedom and more abundance, more widely shared, than any system in the history of the world."

Nixon made large cuts in the federal budget for compensatory education for poor student, urban renewal, the construction of hospitals, aid for school districts located near military bases, money for farmers for soil management, and funding for mental hospitals (Aksamit 2014).

Gruson wrote in *The New York Times*, 31 January, in part (Gruson 1987):

> The end of a Federal aid program that provided more than half the money for some municipal budgets has caused a severe financial crisis in small and medium-size cities around the country and is forcing larger cities to make hard choices between cutting services and raising taxes.

> The elimination of the program of general revenue sharing on Sept. 30, after several years of significant cuts in other Federal aid, has prompted layoffs, curtailment of police protection and other services, and higher taxes and user fees in thousands of counties, cities and villages.

> The program became the center of controversy in part because some share of the money went to communities with

little or no demonstrable need. Money for Beverly Hills, too

"In a very tight budget, it's hard to defend money going to places like Beverly Hills," said Robert W. Rafuse Jr., Deputy Assistant Secretary of the Treasury for state and local finances. "It's a welfare program with a 50 percent error rate. Sure, Beverly Hills gets much less money per capita than, say, Oakland. But the point is Beverly Hills shouldn't get a nickel. The only question is, should you throw the baby out with the bathwater?"

The ultimate answer was yes. Congress last year was unable to agree on a way to distribute the money without giving a share to well-to-do communities, the Reagan Administration's opposition carried the day and the program, which had survived several other attempts at elimination, was gradually ended after 14 years and $85 billion dollars.

Susskind wrote a review of Revenue Sharing and said, in part (Susskind 1974):

The basic thrust of the New Federalism, exemplified by the domestic assistance proposals of the Nixon Administration, is to reduce the federal government's impact on state and local policy-making. The principal tactic for achieving this reform will not be the withdrawal of federal support for key domestic programs; rather a concerted effort will be made to decategorize and broaden federal grants-in-aid. Although some inconsistencies are apparent (e.g., the President's attempts to further centralize income support and welfare programs and to impound certain funds appropriated by Congress), the fundamental characteristic of the New Federalism has been its emphasis on decentralization. Many arguments are made in favor of decentralization. By minimizing the federal government's size, the advocates of decentralization expect: (1) to reduce the concentration of power at the top; (2) to permit greater flexibility in problem-solving; (3) to acknowledge the different needs of each community; (4) to encourage innovation by allowing similarly situated communities to experiment with different solutions to public problems; and (5) to encourage the development of political subsystems that allow for widespread participation. To the extent that supporters of the New Federalism espouse a consistent philosophy, these arguments in behalf of decentralization provide a relatively firm ideological base. Their arguments are most often accompanied by the firm belief that the national government is not inherently more "liberal" on domestic issues than are states and localities.

Paradoxically, one effect of revenue sharing has been to reduce the amount of money available to the public sector. A portion of all revenue sharing funds is invariably used to reduce state or local taxes. Revenue sharing thereby inhibits the growth of state and local tax yield. One study estimates that an annual flow of 5.5 billion dollars in general revenue sharing funds will increase state and local expenditures by an average of only two to three billion dollars. The remainder of the money will probably be devoted to tax reductions.

The New Federalists want to change the balance of power in the federal system by strengthening the position of the states vis-a-vis the national government. They look upon revenue sharing as a tool for altering the entire structure of the federal system and providing a more independent and vigorous role for the states. The New Federalists are actually making three separate assumptions that need to be examined in light of the first few years experience with general revenue sharing and block grants. First, they assume that states and localities are closer to the people and are therefore better able to recognize public priorities. Secondly, they suggest that state and local officials can be trusted to use federal funds honestly and efficiently. Lastly, they expect decentralization to encourage innovation and ensure greater respect for the diverse needs and interests of minority groups.

Over half of the cities receiving revenue sharing funds did not hold public hearings prior to determining their revenue sharing expenditures. City officials may have been reluctant to encourage extensive public involvement since the amount of revenue could not, in most cases, have covered all the uses that would have been suggested. Revenue sharing funds accounted ultimately for less than 10% of most cities' annual income and less than six per cent of annual state revenue collections. When local governments were asked if they planned to hold public hearings in the future, 37.4% said yes, 38.4% said no, and 24.2% were unsure. The decentralists would have us believe that the power of the federal government ought to be minimized to achieve the goal of local self-determination. Yet how can there be local involvement and control when few cities are willing to make an effort to encourage citizen participation in the local budgetary Process?

In connection with the question whether local officials are responsive to pressing local needs, recall that one of the objectives of general revenue sharing is to provide state and local governments with greater flexibility in the use of federal funds. Accordingly, General Revenue Sharing contains only general guidelines delimiting how governmental units may spend their share. A local government may use the funds for any "ordinary and necessary capital expenditure authorized by law." In addition, funds are to be spent only within specified priority areas, one of which is described as "social services for the poor and aged." An analysis of general revenue sharing allocations in 250 governments (including the 50 cities and 50 counties that received the largest amounts of revenue sharing funds in 1972) prepared by the Comptroller General of the United States, indicates a minuscule response on the part of local governments to the needs of the poor and aged.

The fact that more than half of the governments receiving revenue sharing funds failed to allocate any of these funds during the first year or two should not be overlooked. This suggests that not only has the financial squeeze been exaggerated, but also that many communities may be unable to manage large amounts of unrestricted funds on short notice. The reduction in federal administrative requirements brought about by revenue sharing was supposed to achieve both increased efficiency at the local level and the stabilization of local administrative costs. Instead of monitoring administrative arrangements, it was expected that new city and state employees could devote their time to actual problem-solving. In reality, few if any new personnel were hired with general revenue sharing funds. Moreover, local investments in improved planning and management have not been forthcoming.

Congress continually initiates new grant-in-aid programs with no real sense of overall purpose. Individual programs and single-function agencies continue to proliferate at the federal and state levels along with local special districts and authorities. While new programs are continually added, existing grants are rarely eliminated. Contributing to the problem, perhaps, is the absence of a single congressional committee responsible for reviewing the whole array of grants-in-aid. Once a particular grant has continued for a number of years, it becomes an integral part of state and local budgets and constitutes one of the assumed sources of revenue in the state or local budgetary process. State and local officials are therefore reluctant to support any grant reduction. Should federal funds be reduced, a greater state or local appropriation would be needed to maintain a particular program at a given level.

Susskind's remarks are, in approach, very much in the same sense as earlier remarks made about the War on Poverty process during the Johnson administration, that is, that there is often a great gap between programmatic assumed behavior of the folk affected and the actual behavior of those same folk. This is, of course, a recurring problem of the Congressional desire to have their concepts put in place and the actual results of this or that law and/or program which may not, in practice, reflect those wished for behaviors.

In late October, Nixon signed the FY 73 Supplemental Appropriations bill for $790 million for OEO. It would be effective until Congress adjourned for the year.

Semple (1972) wrote in, in part, *The New York Times*:

The Mr. Dean to whom the press secretary referred is John W. Dean ... the White House counsel who conducted an internal investigation at the Presidents request following the arrest of several persons employed by the reelection campaign in the incursion into the Watergate offices of the Democratic National Committee.

After the investigation, Mr. Nixon told a news conference that he was satisfied that no one "presently employed" in the White House was involved in the Watergate bugging.

On 15 December, 53 officials at OEO was asked to submit proforma resignations after the November election. By the middle of the month they had not heard whether they would still be working during Nixon's second term.

Rumors were flying as to whether or not the agency, OEO, would be "dismantled." The Office of Management and Budget had not released a full-year allotment but was giving OEO monthly "allowances."

Bert Gallegos, OEO General Counsel, testified that the use of poverty agency funds for travel expenses was legally sound.

An article in *The New York Times* (1973), 29 December, in part, stated:

WASHINGTON, Dec. 28—President Nixon signed into law today legislation designed to give state and local governments a larger role in determining their need for a variety of employment and training programs.

The signing took place at Mr. Nixon's home in San Clemente, Calif., and was announced in a statement released here.

Mr. Nixon said that he had signed the Comprehensive Employment and Training Act of 1973 "with great pleasure," adding that the act would put an end to the patchwork system of individual rigid categorical manpower programs which began in the early nineteen sixties."

The act represents the first consolidation of the programs since the first manpower legislation was passed in 1962.

It also represents a compromise between the White House and Congress over the need for public service employment and for giving flexibility to the state and local authorities in using manpower funds

In the compromise, Congress retained the public employment program that the Administration wanted to drop. Last year the White House argued against renewing this program and provided no new funds for continuing it.

In the other part of the compromise, the White House gained its first legislation incorporating the principles of special revenue sharing. According to the President, the employment and training programs be available to states and communities "without any Federal strings as to what kind of services or how much of those services should be provided."

The approximately 10,000 contracts now let out for manpower programs around the country will be reduced to about 500 state and local programs with states, counties and cities acting as prime contractors.

In a press briefing here today, William H. Kolberg, Assistant Secretary of Labor for Manpower Administration, said that theoretically local and state governments could use all their allotted money for public, service jobs. "I'm sure that will not happen," he said.

The 1974 fiscal budget proposals announced by Nixon late in January 1973 would transfer most programs to other agencies and eliminate direct federal funding for Community Action. The justification for this was that if the constituencies to local community action agencies wanted to continue financial support to local community action agencies, general and special revenue sharing funds could be used. There still were no announcements from the White House on the 53 agency officials who had submitted proforma resignations.

In December Nixon signed the fiscal 1974 appropriations for the Department of Labor and Health, Education and Welfare.

The Manpower Administration, Labor Department, began to implement the Comprehensive Employment and Training Act (CETA), January 1974, replacing The Manpower Development and Training Act and Title 1B of OEO, to be competed by 30 June (Jansson 1977).

On 7 February 1974, the newly-created House Subcommittee of Equal Opportunity began hearings on the proposed reorganization of OEO.

Howard J. Phillips, a paladin of conservatism who helped lead the New Right movement in the 1970s, a member of the conservative Young Americans for Freedom in college, was moved from Associate Director of Program Review to Acting Director OEO until 30 June when Nixon's budget proposals would eliminate OEO (Masters 2014, Clark 2002).

Speaker of the House, Carl Albert, (D), Oklahoma, who replaced Speaker John W. McCormack, (D), Massachusetts, when he retired in January 1971, said: "Congress will not permit the President to lay-waste the great programs and the precedents of compassionate government which we have created and developed the decades past."

Phillips wrote a private memorandum outlining a strategy to dismantle OEO before "critics of the administration can organize effective countermoves." While he stated that the memorandum was "not an official agency document" it offered a course of action to follow. It suggested that adverse public and Congressional reaction to the scattered, angry demonstrations would be inevitable when decisions are announced. Discussions of Community Action Agencies should stress "a picture of agitation, destructive unrest, diversion of Federal funds to support partisan political activity, administrative waste, criminal misuse of funds, and a program structure which exacerbated rather than resolved racial problems . . . Debate should be steered to the Appropriation Committees, whose interest most closely align with the President." A review should be done of House and Senate rules for points of order to block any attempts to continue OEO and Community Action under a continuing resolution . . . The issue might well hinge on whether Southern Democrats will be more moved by their fiscal conservatism and dislike for the laws at issue, or by their jealousy for Congressional power and opposition to the other party's President . . . A swift and successful dismemberment of the rest of OEO would also strengthen the administration's hand in pressing for its Legal Services Corporation. Disappearance of its present home would reenforce the Hobson's choice between the President's corporation and oblivion." If possible, it was suggested, try to steer Legal Services legislation to the more conservative Judiciary Committees. It "probably means prompt transfer of all surviving programs to new agencies and then completing arrangements for the GSA [General Services Administration] receivership by the end of this fiscal year . . . Under such a timetable it is unlikely that the opposition could muster enough strength (or will) to put Humpty-Dumpty together again."

This memorandum was leaked to Congress.

Phillips, in an interview in the *Washington Post*, said:

"I think in many ways OEO has had a negative impact. When we spend dollars we have to decide not merely whether they're being spent effectively, but whether there are some ways in which they've been harmful. And to the extent to which that we have promoted the welfare ethic out of OEO, to the extent that some people funded by us have advanced the notion that the main values of American life are without merit, then I think OEO has done a great disservice to this country. And unfortunately there have been a number of instances of that . . . To me OEO has come to symbolize a number of unfortunate things. It's come to symbolize challenges to the importance of family. It's come to symbolize the seeking of change beyond the ken of orderly democratic process. Boycotts and demonstrations and riots and so forth and so on these things may be legal. They shouldn't be subsidized by the Federal government. And even if they're conducted privately, they tend to erode the kind of normal majoritarian democratic safeguards that are incident to the electoral process."

On 4 February 1973, Phillips said in a *New York Times* article that he believed that OEO had become a vehicle for achieving political ends and that "It's based on the wrong notion that the poor should be treated as a class apart . . . That's a Marxist notion" (Clark 2002).

Alvin Arnett, (R), was moved from Executive Direction, Appalachain Regional Commission, to Phillip's Chief Deputy, OEO, 19 February.

Phillips set the target date for closing 10 regional office as 28 April. He said that keeping the office open would be a waste of public funds as the death of OEO was expected before the end of the fiscal year.

Ripley (1973) in an article in *The New York Times*, 28 February, wrote:

> WASHINGTON, Feb. 27 — A Congressional subcommittee today accused Howard J. Phillips, acting director of the Office of Economic Opportunity, of arrogance, subverting national policy, encouraging summer turmoil in the streets and using a "meat ax" on the program.
>
> It was the first appearance of Mr. Phillips before Congress since he was appointed head to the post a month ago. He stood his ground, saying that the drive against poverty had been a failure and that the steps he was taking were designed to improve and strengthen the program, not dismantle it.
>
> Mr. Phillips appeared before the Subcommittee on Equal Opportunity of the House Committee on Education and Labor.

Community Action Programs, which have boards of directors including local poor people and initiate new activities locally, will be turned over to cities and local supporting groups to fend for themselves, Mr. Phillips said.

He said these programs had been warned that "the day will come" when they would have to be self supporting.

"That day is here," he said.

He said that the Federal budget had contributed about one–third of the total funds to such Community Action Programs. In President Nixon's budget proposal for the fiscal year 1974, there is no money for continuing these programs, he said, adding that he was preparing for them to go out of business by June 30, when the fiscal year 1973 ends.

Enough money will be provided to carry them on six months more to complete an "orderly phase out," he said.

Representative Carl D. Perkins, Democrat of Kentucky, chairman of the Education and Labor Committee, who attended part of the four hour hearing, said, "The forum for poor people is being destroyed." He asserted that programs were being transferred to other departments that "are not going to do anything."

"I think you're rendering a great disservice to the poor of this nation," Mr. Perkins said.

Mr. Phillips replied that he thought American society had done "more than any society in the world" to eliminate poverty.

The subcommittee chairman, Representative Augustus F. Hawkins, Democrat of California, said that since President Nixon was first elected "5.5 million people have been added to the welfare rolls."

"I think it represents the success of some Legal Services lawyers, sir," Mr. Phillips replied.

"This is as arrogant an answer as I have ever heard given to the concrete problem of human suffering," Mr. Hawkins replied.

Lydon (1973) in an article in *The New York Times*, 28 February, wrote:

WASHINGTON, Feb. 27 —Four Democratic Governors protested to the Senate today that President Nixon's idea of revenue sharing was costing states money and his "New Federalism" was making chaos of their budgets.

Gov. Jimmy Carter of Georgia even threatened to sue the Federal Government for congressionally appropriated funds that the President has impounded.

"The meat ax approach which has been adopted this year," said Governor Carter, "is an open admission of inability to determine which parts of programs are effective and which are not."

If Congress had taken its own budgetary responsibility seriously, Mr. Holton said, the Administration's approach would not have been necessary.

Senator Muskie, the subcommittee chairman, said that Congress had been tricked out of its responsible role by the President's signing programs into law, like the anti-poverty program, and then sitting on the money.

"Senator, the President's patience has run

out," Mr. Holton [Linwood Holton of Virginia] said.

"Well, then, Governor," Mr. Muskie replied, "why didn't he used the constitutional veto power to indicate his impatience?"

"I don't know," Governor Holton replied.

Senator Muskie said that Mr. Nixon's handling of special, revenue sharing would make it "damn tough" to convince Congress to proceed to the consolidation of Federal grants in special revenue sharing.

"If you can't get me to sell it," said Mr. Muskie, one of revenue sharing's early advocates, "you're going to have hard time getting anyone to sell it."

On 2 March Nixon held *The President's News Conference* and was asked a number of questions including these (Nixon 1973a):

[15.] Q. Mr. President, now that the Watergate case is over, the trial is over, could you give us your view on the verdict [On January 30, 1973, G. Gordon Liddy and James W. McCord, Jr., were convicted in the United States District

Court for the District of Columbia on charges of burglary, wiretapping, and conspiracy in connection with the illegal entry into the Democratic National Committee headquarters on June 17, 1972. Earlier in January, five other defendants had pleaded guilty to charges connected with the break-in before Chief Judge John J. Sirica of the court] and what implications you see in the verdict on public confidence in the political system?

THE PRESIDENT. NO, it would not be proper for me to comment on the case when it not only is not over, but particularly when it is also on appeal.

I will simply say with regard to the Watergate case what I have said previously, that the investigation conducted by Mr. Dean, the White House Counsel, in which, incidentally, he had access to the FBI records on this particular matter because I directed him to conduct this investigation, indicates that no one on the White House Staff, at the time he conducted the investigation--that was last July and August--was involved or had knowledge of the Watergate matter. And, as far as the balance of the case is concerned, it is now under investigation by a Congressional committee and that committee should go forward, conduct its investigation in an even-handed way, going into charges made against both candidates, both political parties. And if it does, as Senator Ervin has indicated it will, we will, of course, cooperate with the committee just as we cooperated with the grand jury.

CONGRESSIONAL HEARINGS AND EXECUTIVE PRIVILEGE

[16.] Q. Mr. President, yesterday at the Gray hearings, Senator Tunney suggested he might ask the committee to ask for John Dean to appear before that hearing to talk about the Watergate case and the FBI-White House relationship. Would you object to that?

THE PRESIDENT. Of course.

Q. Why?

THE PRESIDENT. Well, because it is executive privilege. I mean you can't – I, of course – no President could ever agree to allow the Counsel to the President to go down and testify before a committee.

On the other hand, as far as any committee of the Congress is concerned, where information is requested that a member of the White House Staff may have, we will make arrangements to provide that information, but members of the White House Staff, in that position at least, cannot be brought before a Congressional committee in a formal hearing for testimony. I stand on the same position there that every President has stood on.

FRANK CORMIER [Associated Press]. Thank you, Mr. President.

Q. Mr. President, on that particular point, if the Counsel was involved

THE PRESIDENT. He always gets two. [Laughter]

Q. if the Counsel was involved in an illegal or improper act and the prima facie case came to light, then would you change the rules relative to the White House Counsel?

THE PRESIDENT. I do not expect that to happen, and if it should happen, I would have to answer that question at that point.

Let me say, too, that I know that, since you are on your feet, Clark [Mollenhoff], that you had asked about the executive privilege statement, and we will have that available toward the end of next week or the first of the following week, for sure, because obviously, the Ervin committee is interested in that statement, and that will answer, I think, some of the questions with regard to how information can be obtained from a member of the White House Staff, but consistent with executive privilege.

MR. CORMIER. Thank you again.

Phillips commenced wrecking the agency. He said, "At OEO I was confronted with evil, pure and simple," in the *National Review*, referring to what he and conservative colleagues regarded as the agency's record of funding liberal organizations. "I was not there very long when I discovered that OEO was the warroom for those that were trying to overturn what had once been America." He purged the moderate Republicans replacing them with colleagues from the YAF [Young America's Foundation the principal outreach organization of the Conservative Movement], who reportedly received $100 a day to serve as assistants. YAF staff were in charge of: Operations (Randall Teague, with Michael Thompson, Special Assistant), Legal Services (Laurence McCarty), Program Review (Dan Joy), and the General Counsel's Office (Alan McKay), as well as a number of consultant positions and lower level administrative positions. Budget funds were withheld. OEO employees started getting termination notices. Phillips believed that if he acted fast enough that he could eliminate

OEO before the libs had a chance to stop him (Frank 2008).

Nixon held *The President's News Conference*, 15 March, and responded to questions some of which were (Nixon 1973b):

WHITE HOUSE AIDES AND THE ERVIN COMMITTEE

[10.] Q. Mr. President, does your offer to cooperate with the Ervin committee include the possibility that you would allow your aides to testify before his committee? And if it does not, would you be willing to comply with a court order, if Ervin went to court to get one, that required some testimony from White House aides?

THE PRESIDENT. In answer to your first part of the question, the statement that we made yesterday answered that completely-not yesterday, the 12th I think it was – my statement on executive privilege. Members of the White House Staff will not appear before a committee of Congress in any formal session.

We will furnish information under the proper circumstances. We will consider each matter on a case-by-case basis.

With regard to the second point, that is not before us. Let me say, however, that if the Senate feels at this time that this matter of separation of powers – where, as I said, this Administration has been more forthcoming than any Democratic administration I know of – if the Senate feels that they want a court test, we would welcome it. Perhaps this is the time to have the highest Court of this land make a definitive decision with regard to this matter.

I am not suggesting that we are asking for it. But I would suggest that if the Members of the Senate, in their wisdom, decide that they want to test this matter in the courts, we will, of course, present our side of the case. And we think that the Supreme Court will uphold, as it always usually has, the great constitutional principle of separation of powers rather than to uphold the Senate.

EXECUTIVE PRIVILEGE COMPARISON

[11.] Q. Mr. President, isn't there an essential difference really between your investigation of the Hiss case and the request of this subcommittee to Mr. Dean to appear? In the former, foreign affairs was involved and possibly security matters, where here they only wish to question Mr. Dean about the breaking into the Watergate?

THE PRESIDENT. Yes, I would say the difference is very significant. As a matter of fact, when a committee of Congress was investigating espionage against the Government of this country, that committee should have had complete cooperation from at least the executive branch of the Government in the form that we asked. All that we asked was to get the report that we knew they had already made of their investigation.

Now, this investigation does not involve espionage against the United States. It is, as we know, espionage by one political organization against another. And I would say that as far as your question is concerned, that the argument would be that the Congress would have a far greater right and would be on much stronger ground to ask the Government to cooperate in a matter involving espionage against the Government than in a matter like this involving politics.

Theodore Tetzlaff, Acting Director of OEO Legal Services program, was dismissed. He was one of the proforma letter of resignations employees. He was the third Legal Services head to leave under fire during the past 27 months. Tetzlaff said that Phillips had installed a number of officials "of questionable qualification" into important positions. He pointed out that Marshall Boarman, Chief of Evaluation, was not a lawyer and that the Acting Director of Legal Services, was recruited from a New England life insurance company

The same day as Tetzlaff's dismissal, Nixon scrapped the Legal Services advisory committee sponsored by the American Bar Association (ABA). ABA President Robert Messerve and 34 members of the committee had received letters stating that this was Nixon's decision to make "Community Action a local option."

Nixon submitted a Budget to Congress requesting no money for OEO.

A number of organizations and four Senators filed various suits over Phillips' and Nixon's actions.

After three years, the House-Senate Conference Committee agreed, May 1974, to establish an independent Legal Services Corporation.

11 June, Judge William Jones, United States District Court for the District of Columbia, ruled that the dismantling of OEO must cease forthwith. He declared Phillips and others acts "unauthorized by law, illegal and in excess of statutory authority" and ordered the agency "restored to its normal mode and level of operation." and that the President's budget was "nothing more than a proposal" and could not be used as legal authority for phasing out OEO. He found that Phillips had violated the reorganization act by not filing the required plan to abolish a federal agency by not publishing termination announcements and instructions in the Federal Register at least thirty days before their effective date. Jones halted the reduction-in-force, the closing of regional offices, and the transfer of functions from OEO to other agencies. He stated that Phillips was serving illegally, that his actions as Acting Director

were null and void (Masters 2014, Clark 2002, Langer 2013).

26 June, Nixon announced his intent to submit Alvin Arnett as Director OEO. Phillips had resigned on that same day.

As he left Phillips issued a final statement:

> "During the period immediately following July, I expect to witness the completion of the actions we set in motion following the President's budget message of January 25: the transfer of programs and personnel to other departments, the enactment of legislation which will lead to reform of the legal services programs and will place OEO's economic development activities at the Department of Commerce, the complete reassignment of decision-making concerning community action to local elected officials, and the general discontinuation of OEO's operations activities. Just as OEO itself came to symbolize the Great Society's unsuccessful and unwise reliance on centralized bureaucratic power, so shall our effort be recalled as an historic turning point toward the disaggregation of unaccountable bureaucratic authority, and its dispersal back to the people, from whom it derives."

Judge William Jones ruled, 27 June, that a "state of emergency" existed at OEO. He ordered Arnett to process some 600 grant applications before 30 June, before the fiscal year ended. He stated:

> That any applicant whose grant had been
> denied by OEO had to be notified
> immediately that they had one hour to file
> a complaint.
> The agency had to conclude public
> hearings on the complaints within 24
> hours of the ruling (by noon June 28).
> By 3 p.m., June 28, the agency must have
> completed notification of applicants as to
> the findings regarding the complaint. Any
> applicant they turned down was then
> allowed to file suit with Jones.
> The agency had to complete action on all
> pending grant applications by June 30.

Jones noted that Arnett had authority to act only because of the emergency situation; that Congress could have prevented the entire situation "by providing for an orderly succession of power at OEO in the case of a vacancy."

An article in *The Washington Post* in June stated that conservative critics of OEO were beginning to pressure Nixon to fire Arnett due to Arnett's lobbying for continuing funding of OEO.

Senators Jacob Javitts, (R), New York, Edward Kennedy, (D), Massachusetts, Robert Dole, (R), Kansas, and Bennet Johnson, (D), Louisiana, co-sponsored a bill to create a new independent agency to replace OEO.

On 29 June, Arnett signed the agreements that would transfer all OEO programs to other agencies with the exception of Community Action, Economic Development, and Legal

Services.

Arnett stated in the hearing of the Senate Labor and Public Welfare Committee, Harrison Williams, (D), New Jersey, Chairman, that the agency was in "shambles" when he took over on June 26 and that he did not want to be associated with Phillips statement as he left the agency. He said: "At this moment I have no reservations about any of OEO's programs."

Edward Kennedy, (D), Massachusetts, asked Arnett why he should be confirmed to a $42,500 a year job just to administer a zero funded agency? Arnett replied that there must be a Director OEO to serve as "liaison" with other agencies that receive OEO programs.

Kennedy suggested that the administration was not asking for a liaison office, not a Director of a viable agency. Arnett said that he supported funding for the agency for an additional year and that he had "a high level of discomfort" with the administration's budget requests.

"What do you think the level of discomfort for the poor has been?" asked Kennedy.

Arnett replied, "I've done everything I could to ease the effects of the confrontation [between Congress and the administration of OEO] on the poor."

"Will you be a voice within the administration for OEO?" continued the questioning.

"I already have been and will continue to be," replied Arnett. "I'm very strong on advocacy for the poor. I have not been in a position to deal with the future, I've had to concentrate my time on healing the wounds of the past few months." He stated that he had funded all Community Action Programs with one-half of the CAPs funded through the first quarter of fiscal 1974, the other half through the second quarter.

Senator Richard Schweiker, (R), Pennsylvania, asked if he

would advise the President to submit a revised budget to include funds for OEO and CAP? He agreed.

Schweiker asked if Arnett agreed that many CAAs couldn't survive if forced to rely on revenue sharing as proposed by the administration. Arnett said "Yes."

Schweiker then asked if he would stop the harassment of CAAs and comply with the law concerning proper procedure for defunding agencies? He agreed.

Senator Walter Mondale, (D), Minnesota, suggested that the only difference between Arnett and Phillips, as he saw it, was the type of "funeral director" each man wanted to be. Phillips "wanted to bury the patient [OEO] alive while Arnett wanted a funeral with sad music and flowers." Arnett said that he would support all programs until they were terminated by law.

A Senate vote on Arnett's confirmation was held up until after the August recess by Senator Carl Perkins, (R), Nebraska. There was strong feeling that Phillips had played a key role in this as he was working to have the nomination defeated.

Starting on 1 July, OEO began operating under a continuing resolution through 30 September.

Arnett outlined his plans in a letter to one of the attorneys for the Community Action Agencies group which filed the successful challenge to Phillip's actions. He said:

> "Under the Continuing Resolution (P.L. 93-52) OEO is now entertaining applications for the refunding of community action agencies under Section 221 and will continue to do so. As you know, only the exceptional community action agency will require funding on

September 30, 21973. However, beginning with grantees in this status OEO will resume the awarding of three-month program grants.

In addition, OEO is resuming normal processing of community action agency grants in a manner consistent with standing OEO instructions governing the orderly award of funds to grantees. Consequently it is our hope to adhere to a relatively normal processing cycle, i.e., the awarding of a new three-month grant well in advance of the existing grant.

Under ideal conditions, the new grant is made 60 day prior to the expiration of the new grant. In the past, though, OEO often has not been able to adhere to the administratively-established timetable for a variety of reasons. Thus, in the present case, I would hope to begin the release of funds to grantees expiring at the end of October by mid-September. The awards to October grantees will also be for a period of three-months. Similarly, we would then proceed with awarding three-month grants to November grantees assuming conditions have not changed in the meantime.

By this calendar point we will be in a period beyond that now governed by the current Continuing Resolution. We will then be governed by subsequent legislative action, whether that be enactment of another Continuing Resolution or a final disposition of the issues surrounding OEO funding for 1974.

Since the question of an OEO appropriation in 1973 still remains to be legislatively resolved, I believe these procedures to be fair and consistent with the Congressional intent as expressed thorough the Continuing Resolution. I further believe them to be in harmony with the April 11 decision of the U.S. District Court."

Later in the month, Dean Birch, Presidential Counselor, assured Arnett that his job was not in jeopardy and pledged White House non-intervention in OEO operations. On 15 July Arnett was asked to resign. In the letter Birch sent to Arnett he stated: "This is to notify you that your service as Director of the Office of Economic Opportunity is terminated effective at the close of business to day. Being a Presidential appointment whose status is derived from a deliberate confidential relationship between yourself and the President, please know that the President no longer has confidence in that relationship." Arnett resigned 31 July.

Nixon named Bert Gallegos, OEO's General Counsel, to be acting Director OEO.

Nixon signed HR 7824, legislation that established an independent Legal Services Corporation.

John Thomas Flanney, nominated to the U. S. District Court by President Richard Nixon on November 18, 1971, to a seat vacated by Leonard Walsh, confirmed by the Senate on December 1, 1971, and received commission on December 6, found, 3 August that delegations "are not integral to the abolition of OEO or its programs . . . " that they were "consistent with the past actions of delegating OEO programs to other Executive agencies either at the point that they have matured into operational programs or when the OEO programs can enhance the activities and functions of such agencies . . . The current delegations are fully supportable on a rational basis: the achievement of maximum economy and efficiency in the administration of Federal programs, the enhancement of the statutory missions of the receiving agencies, and the assurance of continued program operation under current Congressional appropriations."

Direct program support people were transferred for payroll purposes, 5 August, indirect program personnel on 17-18 August.

OEO would administer: Community Action Agencies, Senior Opportunities and Services, National Summer Youth Sports Programs, State Economic Opportunity Offices, and Community Economic Development

Kilpatrick (1974) wrote in *The Washington Post*, 9 August:

> Richard Milhous Nixon announced last night that he will resign as the 37th President of the United States at noon today.
>
> Vice President Gerald R. Ford of Michigan will take the oath as the new President at noon to complete the remaining 2 1/2 years of Mr. Nixon's term.

"By taking this action," Nixon said in a subdued yet dramatic television address from the Oval Office, "I hope that I will have hastened the start of the process of healing which is so desperately needed in America."

After two years of bitter public debate over the Watergate scandals, President Nixon bowed to pressures from the public and leaders of his party to become the first President in American history to resign.

Public confidence in him had waned; the House Judiciary Committee, July 1974, had adopted three articles of impeachment against President Nixon: obstruction of justice, abuse of presidential powers, and hindrance of the impeachment process.

On July 30, under coercion from the Supreme Court, Nixon finally released the Watergate tapes. On August 5, transcripts of the recordings were released. In one segment the president was heard instructing Haldeman to order the FBI to halt the Watergate investigation. With Nixon's loss of political support coupled with near-certainty of impeachment and removal, he resigned on August 9, 1974, after addressing the nation on television the previous evening in which he stated, from the Oval Office and carried live on radio and television, that he was resigning for the good of the country and asked the nation to support the new president, Gerald Ford.

Ford and the Transition To CSA

On August 9, 1974, Ford assumed the presidency. On August 20, Ford nominated Nelson Rockefeller, former New York Governor, to be the vice president. Ford appointed J. F. terHorst as the President's Press Secretary. TerHorst was a veteran journalist, respected member of the White House press corps, and an "old friend" of Gerald Ford's, whom he had known since Ford's first Congressional race in 1948. *The Detroit News* allowed him to take a leave of absence to serve as Press Secretary.

John O. Marsh, appointed, 10 August, Counselor to the President, said: "When Ford came into the Presidency the executive power was very much under attack. If Ford had given in to Congress the executive branch might have simply been overwhelmed within the federal system" (Reichley 1981).

The overall problem facing the Ford administration was the economy (Congressional Quarterly 1974).

Ford issued, 10 August 1974, *Memorandums on the Transition of the Presidency* in which he said, in part (Ford 1974a):

> As I assume the new responsibilities of the Presidency, I want you to know how mindful I am of your past labors--and how grateful and indebted I am to you. You have contributed indispensably to

the successful operation of the Office of the Vice President and to my ability to assume my new responsibilities. Our staff has been close to one another, much as a family, and I hope all of you understand the depth of my appreciation and affection. Although I am moving to another office, my loyalty and esteem for you remain unchanged.

I have asked some old friends to come in and help us during this difficult period, which we all hoped would not come. I hope you will render all possible cooperation to those who will be here to facilitate the transition, as well as to those of Mr. Nixon's staff for whom this time is even more difficult than it is for us.

Ford, 12 August, at 9:06 p.m. in the House Chamber at the Capitol, introduced by Carl Albert, Speaker of the House, in his *Address to a Joint Session of the Congress*, set the focus of his administration, when he stated, in part (Ford 1974k):

"My first priority is to work with you to bring inflation under control. Inflation is domestic enemy number one. To restore economic confidence, the Government in Washington must provide some leadership. It does no good to blame the public for spending too much when the Government is spending too much."

"I began to put my Administration's own economic house in order starting last Friday. I instructed my Cabinet officers and Counselors and my White House Staff to make fiscal restraint their first order of business, and to save every taxpayer's dollar the safety and genuine welfare of our great Nation will permit. Some economic activities will be affected more by monetary and fiscal restraint than other activities. Good government clearly requires that we tend to the economic problems facing our country in a spirit of equity to all of our citizens in all segments of our society."

Ford remained preoccupied with issues like inflation at the national level almost to the disregard of other areas. Funding for anti-poverty programs remained relatively stable during his presidency (Clark 2002).

Ford spoke to the nation, 20 August 1974, at 10:04 a.m. in the Oval Office at the White House about his *Remarks on Intention To Nominate Nelson A. Rockefeller To Be Vice President of the United States* in which he said, in part (Ford 1974c):

"Mr. Speaker, members of the leadership of the House and Senate, members of the Cabinet:"

"After a great deal of soul searching, after considering the advice of Members of the Congress, Republicans as well as the

Democratic leadership, after consulting with many, many people within the Republican Party and without, I have made a decision which I would now like to announce to the American people."

"This was a difficult decision, but the man that I am selecting as nominee for Vice President is a person whose long record of accomplishment in the Government and outside is well known. He comes from a family that has long been associated with the building of a better America. It is a family that has contributed significantly to many accomplishments, both at home and abroad, for the American people."

"His achievements in Government are well, well known. He served in the Department of State under former President Franklin Delano Roosevelt. He served under the Presidency of Harry Truman. He served in the Department of HEW under President Eisenhower."

"He has served as Governor of the great Empire State, the State of New York, for 15 years, the longest period of time in the history of the State of New York. He is known across the land as a person dedicated to the free enterprise system, a person who is recognized abroad for his talents, for his dedication to making this a peaceful world."

"It was a tough call for a tough job. The number of people who were considered by me in the process were all men and women of great quality. They came from those suggested to me who serve in the Congress, the Senate and the House of Representatives."

"The names included individuals who had served their respective States with great credit. The names included individuals who were in government, but not in Washington. The names included individuals who were not connected with government."

"But after a long and very thoughtful process, I have made the choice, and that choice is Nelson Rockefeller of New York State. It is my honor and privilege to introduce to you a good partner for me and, I think, a good partner for our country and the world."

"So, I now announce officially that I will send the name of Nelson Rockefeller to the Congress of the United States for confirmation."

Ford spoke, 28 August, at *The President's News Conference*, broadcast live on radio and to the nation, starting at 2:30 p.m. in the East Room, at the White House. He replied to various questions such as these (Ford 1974d):

> IMMUNITY OR PARDON FOR FORMER PRESIDENT NIXON
>
> [1.] Q. Mr. President, aside from the Special Prosecutor's role, do you agree with the bar association that the law applies equally to all men, or do you agree with Governor Rockefeller that former President Nixon should have immunity from prosecution? And specifically, would you use your pardon authority, if necessary?
>
> THE PRESIDENT. Well, let me say at the outset that I made a statement in this room a few moments after the swearing in. And on that occasion I said the following: that I had hoped that our former President, who brought peace to millions, would find it for himself.
>
> Now, the expression made by Governor Rockefeller, I think, coincides with the general view and the point of view of the American people. I subscribe to that point of view, but let me add, in the last 10 days or 2 weeks I have asked for prayers for guidance on this very important point.

In this situation, I am the final authority. There have been no charges made, there has been no action by the courts, there has been no action by any jury. And until any legal process has been undertaken, I think it is unwise and untimely for me to make any commitment.

OFFICE OF ECONOMIC OPPORTUNITY [21.]
Q. Do you have any plans to revive the Office of Economic Opportunity, and if so, in what areas?

THE PRESIDENT. As I am sure you know, the old poverty program has been significantly changed over the last several years. The Head Start program has been taken out of OEC [OEO] and turned over to the Department of HEW. The health aspects of the old poverty program are also over in HEW.

The Congress just approved, and Mr. Nixon approved, a Legal Services Corporation, which was another part of the old poverty program. So, we end up really with just the CAP program, community action program.

Now I think most people who have objectively looked at the community action program and the Model Cities program and maybe some of the other similar programs – there is duplication, there is overlapping.

And under the new housing and urban development bill, local communities are given substantial sums to take a look at the Model Cities programs and related programs, and they may be able to take up the slack of the ending of the community action programs.

Ford issued, 8 September 1974, *Proclamation 4311—Granting Pardon to Richard Nixon* in which he said (Ford 1974b):

It is believed that a trial of Richard Nixon, if it became necessary, could not fairly begin until a year or more has elapsed. In the meantime, the tranquility to which this nation has been restored by the events of recent weeks could be irreparably lost by the prospects of bringing to trial a former President of the United States. The prospects of such trial will cause prolonged and divisive debate over the propriety of exposing to further punishment and degradation a man who has already paid the unprecedented penalty of relinquishing the highest elective office of the United States.

Now, Therefore, I, Gerald R. Ford, President of the United States, pursuant to the pardon power conferred upon me by Article II, Section 2, of the Constitution, have granted and by these presents do grant a full, free, and absolute pardon unto Richard Nixon for all offenses against the United States which he, Richard Nixon, has committed or may have committed or taken part in during the period from January 20, 1969 through August 9, 1974.

J. F. terHorst resigned, 8 September 1974, after President Fords announcement that he would pardon former president Richard Nixon for any possible crimes connected with the Watergate scandal. Once the pardon was issued, terHorst felt that any credibility that he had earned with reporters had been undermined. His successor as Press Secretary was NBC reporter Ron Nessen, who had been a Washington, D.C. correspondent for NBC News.

21 September, Alexander Haig, Ford's Chief of Staff was replaced by Rumsfeld. Ford felt that Haig's "Nixon image" made it impossible to keep Haig on (Reichley 1981).

The 93rd Congress met from Jan 3, 1973 to Dec 20, 1974.

The Economic Opportunity Act of 1964 was terminated in 1973 and replaced with the Head Start, Economic Opportunity and Community Partnership Act of 1974. The new bill, introduced in the Senate (S. 3066) by John Sparkman, (D), Alabama, on February 27, 1974, to Senate Banking, Housing, and Urban Affairs, House Banking and Currency Committee, established the U.S. Community Services Administration as a successor to OEO. OEO would undergo the name change on 1 July 1975. The Community Services Administration (88 Stat. 2310) was funded through fiscal 1978. The agency remained an independent agency as Ford did not make it part of the Executive Office of the President. It was an option within the bill but not taken by the President (Clark 2002). The Joint conference committee, 12 August 1974, agreed to the Senate on August 13, 1974 (84-0) and by the House on August 15, 1974 (377-21). The bill was signed into law by President Ford, 22 August 1974.

The agency's purpose was to assist low and near-low income families and individuals, including persons of limited English speaking ability to attain the skills, knowledge, and motivations, and opportunities needed to become fully self-sufficient, available to the poor in both urban and rural areas. The basic technique of the agency was the combined use of federal, state, and local funds in the organization and operation of community action type programs which were directed and overseen by locally selected boards.

Funding for present programs was through an extension of the continuing resolution until Congress adjourned.

On 20 July 1974 a Turkish military invasion of the island of Cyprus was launched, following the Cypriot coup d'état, ordered 15 July 1974 by the military Junta in Greece and staged by the Cypriot National Guard in conjunction with EOKA-B. The coup intended to annex the island and create the Hellenic Republic of Cyprus. Turkish forces invaded and captured 3% of the island before a cease fire was declared. The Greek military junta collapsed and was replaced by a democratic government. In August 1974 another Turkish invasion resulted in the capture of approximately 40% of the island. The cease fire line from August 1974 became the United Nations Buffer Zone in Cyprus and was commonly referred to as the Green Line.

The Foreign Assistance Act of 1974 (Public law 93-559) added several amendments to the Foreign Assistance Act of 1961 that effectively eliminated aid and military funding for South Vietnam and included other amendments, including, among others, appropriation of funds to Israel, Egypt, and Jordan, and the suspension of funds to Turkey due to the conflict in Cyprus. It was a sharp challenge from Congress to President Ford and Secretary of State Henry A. Kissinger on their conduct of foreign policy (CQ Almanac 1974).

Ford in issuing a *Statement on House Action To Suspend United States Military Assistance to Turkey, 8 October,* stated, in part (Ford 1974e):

> YESTERDAY the House of Representatives, once again acting against the almost unanimous advice of its leadership, amended the continuing resolution granting funds for our foreign aid programs. The amendment requires an immediate cessation of all U.S. military assistance to Turkey and is, in my view, a misguided and extremely harmful measure.
>
> Instead of encouraging the parties involved in the Cyprus dispute to return to the negotiating table, this amendment, if passed by the Senate, will mean the indefinite postponement of meaningful negotiations. Instead of strengthening America's ability to persuade the parties to resolve the dispute, it will lessen our

influence on all the parties concerned. And it will imperil our relationships with our Turkish friends and weaken us in the crucial Eastern Mediterranean.

But most tragic of all, a cutoff of arms to Turkey will not help Greece or the Greek Cypriot people who have suffered so much over the course of the last several months. We recognize that we are far from a settlement consistent with Greece's honor and dignity. We are prepared to exert our efforts in that direction. But reckless acts that prevent progress toward a Cyprus settlement harm Greeks, for it is the Greek Government and the Greek Cypriots who have the most to gain from a compromise settlement. And it is they who have the most to lose from continued deadlock.

Thus I call upon the Senate to accept the original conference report language on Turkish arms aid and to return the bill to the House of Representatives once again. And I ask the House of Representatives to reconsider its hasty act and, working with the Senate, pass a bill that will best serve the interests of peace.

Ford threatened to veto the continuing resolution supporting major government agencies: OEO; Department of

Health, Education and Welfare; Department of Labor, over the congressional act affecting Turkish support. Congress postponed their recess and returned to session.

Ford at *The President's News Conference*, 9 October, replied to a question about the economy and said (Ford 1974f):

> Well, the first question. Dick Lerner [Richard E. Lerner, United Press International].
>
> QUESTIONS
> INFLATION AND RECESSION [2.] Q. Mr. President, a few things were left unsaid in your economic address yesterday. I was wondering if you could say now if the United States is in a recession, and how soon Americans can expect to see a meaningful reduction of inflation and unemployment?
>
> THE PRESIDENT. I do not think the United States is in a recession. We do have economic problems, but it is a very mixed situation, and that was the reason that we had some 31 specific recommendations in my speech yesterday.
> We have to be very, very careful to make sure that we don't tighten the screws too tightly and precipitate us into some economic difficulty. And at the same time, we had to have provisions and programs

that would meet the challenge of inflation.

I am convinced if the Congress responds, if the American people respond in a voluntary way, that we can have, hopefully early in 1975, some meaningful reduction in the rate of inflation.

On 10 October Ford send a *Memorandum on Fiscal Year 1975 Budget Cuts* which stated (Ford 1974g):

MEMORANDUM FOR
THE SECRETARY OF STATE
THE SECRETARY OF THE TREASURY
THE SECRETARY OF DEFENSE
THE ATTORNEY GENERAL
THE SECRETARY OF THE INTERIOR
THE SECRETARY OF AGRICULTURE
THE SECRETARY OF COMMERCE
THE SECRETARY OF LABOR
THE SECRETARY OF HEALTH, EDUCATION, AND WELFARE
THE SECRETARY OF HOUSING AND URBAN DEVELOPMENT
THE SECRETARY OF TRANSPORTATION

SUBJECT: Fiscal Year 1975 Budget Cuts

As I noted at the last Cabinet meeting, the suggestions which you and others have made for reducing 1975 spending are insufficient if we are to hold spending to $300 billion or below. I have asked Roy Ash and his staff to work with you and your staff in finding further reductions.

I recognize that this will be a very difficult task. There are few programs in which large cuts are desirable from the point of view of achieving agency missions. Nevertheless, under current economic conditions, it is essential that we present the Congress with a significant package of legislative and budgetary proposals that would allow us to reach our 1975 goal. Time is short. We are well into the fiscal year. It is essential, therefore, that we complete work on our proposals so that I can send them to the Congress at an early date. I attach special urgency to this effort and look forward to your support and cooperation.

GERALD R. FORD.

Ford sent his *Remarks on Signing Veto of Continuing Appropriations Resolution Containing an Amendment Suspending Military Aid to Turkey*, 14 October, in which he said (Ford 1974h):

TODAY, in the interest of preserving the ability of the United States to assist the Governments of Greece, Turkey, and

Cyprus to negotiate a peaceful settlement of the Cyprus dispute, I am returning to the Congress without my approval the continuing resolution which the Congress has amended to cut off military aid to Turkey.

In so doing, I want to clear the air of a number of misunderstandings concerning the U.S. position toward the Cyprus crisis.

Since the outbreak of the crisis, our objectives have been to establish a cease-fire, to provide humanitarian aid to the refugees, to assist the parties toward a negotiation and a settlement, and to strengthen and to improve our historically friendly ties with Greece, Turkey, and Cyprus.

I have discussed these goals with the bipartisan leadership of the Congress and have received their unanimous and vigorous support. Our ability to pursue these goals depends, however, on being able to maintain a constructive relationship with the parties involved. The cutoff of assistance to Turkey is destructive of that relationship.

Further, it in no way helps the Greek people or the people of Cyprus who have suffered so much in the past months. In fact, by dashing hopes for negotiations, it prolongs their suffering.

We recognize clearly the need to ensure that the honor and the integrity of the Greek people be maintained. We seek a settlement which ensures that fundamental requirement. United States friendship with Greece has been established through generations of cooperation and mutual respect, based on shared values and common goals. I intend firmly to carry on and strengthen that relationship.

I cannot, however, carry out this pledge if my ability to act in the current crisis is undercut by restrictions imposed by the Congress. We all seek a peaceful resolution of this problem; we all seek justice for the people of Cyprus; we all seek to maintain the strength and cooperation in our relationship that is a cornerstone to Western security in the Mediterranean.

It is for these reasons that I return this resolution to the Congress and ask that it thoughtfully reconsider its position.

I pledge to continue working closely in

partnership with the Congress to enable the United States to play a useful role in helping the parties toward a peaceful resolution of the Cyprus dispute.

I am now signing my veto message, which will be delivered today to the Congress.
Thank you very much.

The House of Representatives sustained the President's veto on October 15, 1974.

Ford, 15 October, in addressing his *Remarks to the Annual Convention of the Future Farmers of America, Kansas City, Missouri*, at 7:05 p.m. at the Municipal Auditorium, broadcast live on radio and television, said, in part: "Now some have said that instead of asking Congress and the Nation to bite the bullet, I offered only a marshmallow. Well, I had already asked the Congress to postpone for 3 months a 5.5 percent pay increase for Federal Government employees which would have saved $700 million. Congress wouldn't even chew that marshmallow. They haven't, as yet, shown much appetite for some of the other 'marshmallows' in my latest message. But if they don't like the menu, I may be back with some tough turkey."

Senator James Abourezk, (D), South Dakota held up, 16 October, the nomination of Gallegos as he felt that "enough questions have been raised to warrant looking again at Gallego's [sic] qualifications."

Public Law 93-448, A Joint Resolution of Congress, passed 17 October 1974 stated:

JOINT RESOLUTION

October 17, 1974

Making further continuing appropriations for the fiscal year
1975, and for other [H. J . Res. ii67]
purposes.

*Resolved by the Senate and House of
Representatives of the United States of
America in Congress assembled,* That (a)
clause (c) of section 102 of the joint
resolution of June 30,1974 (Public Law 93-
324), is hereby amended by striking out
"September 30,1974" and inserting in lieu
thereof "sine die adjournment of the
second session of the Ninety-third
Congress".

(b) Clause (a) of such section is amended
by inserting immediately
after "joint resolution" the following: "or,
in the case of the United
States Information Agency, enactment of
authorizations of appropriations for fiscal
year 1975 for that Agency".

SEC. 2. Section 101(e) of such joint
resolution is amended by striking out
"first quarter" and inserting in lieu
thereof "quarterly".

SEC. 3. The fourth unnumbered clause of
section 101(b) of such joint resolution,
relating to foreign assistance and related
programs appropriations, is amended by
striking out all that follows "as amended"
and inserting in lieu thereof ":*Provided,*
That in computing the current rate of

operations of military assistance there shall be included the amount of obligations incurred in Department of Defense appropriations during the fiscal year 1974 for military assistance to Laos;"

SEC. 4. Such joint resolution is amended by adding at the end

thereof the following new section:

"SEC. 112. Notwithstanding any other provision of this joint resolution or any other Act, the President is authorized to use funds made available for foreign assistance by this joint resolution but not to exceed $15,000,000, to provide, on such terms and conditions as he may determine, relief, rehabilitation, and reconstruction assistance in connection with the damage caused by floods in Honduras and Bangladesh and by civil strife in Cyprus."

SEC. 5. Such joint resolution is amended by adding at the end thereof the following new section:

"SEC. 113. None of the funds made available for foreign assistance by this joint resolution may be used to purchase fertilizer in the United States for export to South Vietnam.".

SEC. 6. None of the funds herein made available shall be obligated Turkey, military or expended for military assistance, or for sales of defense articles and services (whether for cash or by credit, guaranty, or any other means) or for the transportation of any military equipment or supplies to Turkey until and unless the President certifies to the Congress that the Government of Turkey is in compliance with the Foreign Assistance Act of 1961, the Foreign Military Sales Act, and any agreement entered into under such Acts, and that substantial progress toward agreement has been made regarding military forces m Cyprus: *Provided,* That the President is authorized to suspend the provisions of this section and said Acts if he determines that such suspension will further negotiations for a peaceful solution of the Cyprus conflict. Any such suspension shall be effective only until December 10, 1974 and only if, during that time, Turkey shall observe the ceasefire and shall neither increase its forces on Cyprus nor transfer to Cyprus any U.S. supplied implements of war.

Approved October 17, 1974.

Ford issued his *Veto of Second Continuing Appropriations Resolution Providing for Suspension of Military Aid to Turkey*, on 17 October, and stated (Ford 1974i):

To the House of Representatives:

I greatly regret that for the second time I must return without my approval the Continuing Resolution granting funds for the operation of several departments and agencies and for the temporary continuation of our foreign aid programs, H.J. Res. 1163.

My previous veto message and my public statements on this matter have clearly expressed our objectives with respect to the resolution of the Cyprus dispute as well as the dangers posed by legislative restrictions destroying our ability to assist the parties involved. The Congress, despite the best efforts of the bipartisan leaders of both Houses, has for the second time refused to recognize the realities of the situation.

While the language of this new bill is different, its effect is similar to the earlier Continuing Resolution which required my veto on October 14. I need not reiterate the extensive comments which I made at that time and which again compel a veto. The provisions of this bill as they would apply to Turkey would do nothing to bring an end to the suffering of the Cypriot people, would do nothing to encourage the two sides to resolve the dispute peacefully, and would bring a further deterioration of the posture of the NATO alliance in the crucial Eastern Mediterranean. It is for these reasons and those previously stated that I must reluctantly veto the bill before me.

In addition, I am compelled to point out again that should this measure become law, the United States would have lost the ability to play a useful role in this dispute and would in effect have to withdraw from the negotiations. Should the Congress force such an action, it must do so in the clear knowledge that it assumes full responsibility for the situation which would then prevail.

I ask that the Congress not choose that path but that it reconsider its action and provide a bill which will permit the continued execution of United States foreign policy in a constructive and responsible manner.

GERALD R. FORD
The White House,
October 17, 1974.

The House of Representatives sustained the President's veto on October 17, 1974.

Ford, during his time in office, delivered more vetoes, relative to his time in office, than only three other presidents. Most of these vetoes were related to national policy issues and issues affecting the federal budget (Reichley 1981).

After Ford reluctantly agreed in a telephone conversation with House Minority Leader John J. Rhodes, (R), Arizona, Oct. 17 to accept the third version of the aid cutoff provision, the House quickly passed H. J. Res 1167 by a 191–33 vote, the Senate passed it by voice vote and sent the measure to the President (CQ Almanac 1974).

Ford signed the Continuing Funding Resolution and said in his *Statement on Signing the Continuing Appropriations Resolution* the following (Ford 1974j):

> I HAVE signed, with serious reservations, the continuing resolution (H. J. Res. 1167) providing necessary funds after a 3-week delay for the operation of several departments and agencies and for the temporary continuation of our foreign aid programs.
>
> Despite two vetoes of similar versions of this bill and my public statements concerning the damage to our diplomacy that would result from its restrictions on military aid to Turkey, Congress has nevertheless persisted by clear majorities in a course which I consider ill-advised and dangerous.
>
> The restrictions imposed in this bill on our military assistance to Turkey create serious problems. Without substantial benefit to any other country, these

restrictions threaten our relations with a country which is a close ally, which is the eastern anchor of an alliance vital to the security of the United States, and which plays a fundamental role in the strategic interests of the United States in the Eastern Mediterranean area. It is for these reasons – the national security interests of the United States – that we have been providing military assistance to Turkey.

The problem created by these legislative restrictions with respect to our relations with Turkey are not compensated for in any way by benefits to Greece or the Greek Cypriots. Contrary to the intentions of the supporters of these restrictions, this bill can only hinder progress toward a settlement of the Cypriot dispute which is so much in the interest of both Greece and the people of Cyprus.

As a result of my vetoes of two earlier versions of this continuing resolution, the Congress has eased the most troublesome of the earlier restrictions. Nevertheless, the risks created by the remaining ones fail to provide compensating benefits. I will, of course, do my best to accomplish the goals which we had set before the Congress took this action. Whatever we can still do to assist in resolving the Cyprus dispute will be done. But if we fail despite our best efforts, those in the Congress who overrode the Congressional leadership must bear the full responsibility for that failure.

As enacted, H.J. Res. 1167, approved October 17, 1974, became Public Law 93-448 (88 Stat. 1363).

Ford resubmitted, 18 November, the nomination of Bert Gallegos for OEO Director.

In November a report issued by the Senate Labor and Public Welfare Committee stated that CAA's mission was to "perform a unique and essential function not only in providing services to the poor, but in reflecting the specific concerns of the communities they serve."

26 November, The House and The Senate approved the Fiscal 1975 Appropriations bill for the Department of Health, Education and Welfare and the Department of Labor.

13 December the Senate approved legislation to extend funding for EOA for three additional years and to retain funding at an 80% level for provisions for Community Action Agencies through Fiscal 1977. It defeated Senator Jesse Helms, (R), North Carolina, amendment, 69-21, which allowed the Federal Government "to get out of the poverty field, period." The Senate, without debate, approved the nomination of Bert Gallegos, Director OEO.

On January 4, Ford said in his *Statement on Signing the Headstart, Economic Opportunity, and Community Partnership Act of 1974* (Ford 1975a):

I SIGNED into law H.R. 14449, the

Headstart, Economic Opportunity, and Community Partnership Act of 1974, a bill which continues the Community Action program under a new agency, the Community Services Administration.

Although I have many reservations about features of this bill, I am signing it because the measure is probably the best compromise we can hope to obtain. The deadlock that has continued for several years between the executive branch and the Congress regarding the future of the Community Action program and the existence of a separate Office of Economic Opportunity had to be broken.

This bill authorizes the transfer of a successor agency into the Department of Health, Education, and Welfare. While I would have preferred to end direct Federal financial assistance to community action agencies, the Congress, in this bill, has taken a significant step in the right direction. It has gradually scaled down the Federal funding for these agencies and included the Community Action program in the transfer to HEW.

I believe strongly that Federal social and economic assistance programs should be developed and operated with great sensitivity to the needs of the poor. But I also feel strongly that those needs will be better served when programs that benefit the disadvantaged are considered and managed together.

To this end, I have ordered the development of a reorganization plan, as authorized by this bill, for my review.

I am also considering sending to the Congress proposals that will eliminate unnecessary organizational impediments contained in this measure. These proposals would assure more orderly and efficient management of Federal programs to aid the poor.

Finally, to avoid waste of effort that might occur, I will not seek funding for duplicate program authorities provided in the enrolled bill.

I applaud the efforts of the Congress in helping bring to an end the stalemate over this legislation. I look forward to making these programs an effective part of our overall effort to serve the real needs of the disadvantaged.

Approved January 4, 1975, as Public Law 93-644 (88 Stat. 2291).

All grants now had to be approved at the headquarters

level.

15 January, Ford gave his *Address Before a Joint Session of the Congress Reporting on the State of the Union* at 1:06 p.m. in the House Chamber at the Capitol, introduced by Carl Albert, Speaker, broadcast live on radio and television, in which he stated, in part (Ford 1975b):

> ". . . state of the Union is not good:
> Millions of Americans are out of work.
> Recession and inflation are eroding the money of millions more.
> Prices are too high, and sales are too slow."

> "This year's Federal deficit will be about $30 billion; next year's probably $45 billion.
> The national debt will rise to over $500 billion.
> Our plant capacity and productivity are not increasing fast enough.
> We depend on others for essential energy."

> "To bolster business and industry and to create new jobs, I propose a 1-year tax reduction of $16 billion. Three-quarters would go to individuals and one-quarter to promote business investment."

> "This cash rebate to individuals amounts to 12 percent of 1974 tax payments – a

total cut of $12 billion, with a maximum of $1,000 per return."

"I call on the Congress to act by April 1. If you do – and I hope you will – the Treasury can send the first check for half of the rebate in May and the second by September."

"The other one-fourth of the cut, about $4 billion, will go to business, including farms, to promote expansion and to create more jobs. The 1-year reduction for businesses would be in the form of a liberalized investment tax credit increasing the rate to 12 percent for all businesses."

"People have been pushed into higher tax brackets by inflation, with consequent reduction in their actual spending power. Business taxes are similarly distorted because inflation exaggerates reported profits, resulting in excessive taxes."

"Accordingly, I propose that future individual income taxes be reduced by $16.5 billion. This will be done by raising the low-income allowance and reducing tax rates. This continuing tax cut will primarily benefit lower- and middle-income taxpayers."

"For example, a typical family of four with a gross income of $5,600 now pays $185 in Federal income taxes. Under this tax cut plan, they would pay nothing. A family of four with a gross income of $12,500 now pays $1,260 in Federal taxes. My proposal reduces that total by $300. Families grossing $20,000 would receive a reduction of $210."

"Those with the very lowest incomes, who can least afford higher costs, must also be compensated. I propose a payment of $80 to every person 18 years of age and older in that very limited category."

"State and local governments will receive $2 billion in additional revenue sharing to offset their increased energy costs."

"To offset inflationary distortions and to generate more economic activity, the corporate tax rate will be reduced from 48 percent to 42 percent."

The problems of the national economy as Ford listed them in the first few lines above, would be a recurring problem throughout Ford's stay in the White House. It would seem that Nixon and his staff did not pay much attention to these problems.

Gallegos, 16 January 1975, rescinded the orders to the Regional Directors to end their grant approval activities bringing them back into the business of managing the grants.

Ford submitted his Fiscal 1976 budget requesting $363 million for Community Services Administration (CSA).

In March Ford signed the continuing resolution to fund programs, Public Law 94-7—March 14, 1975, "appropriations shall remain available until March 25, 1975."

Ford, in his April *Remarks at the White House Conference on Domestic and Economic Affairs in San Diego, California*, said, in part (Ford 1975c):

> "I am deeply concerned, quite frankly, that some elements of the Congress will try to pay for additional spending programs by dangerously stripping billions from the defense budget. At a time like this, nothing could be more shortsighted or devastating to our security."

> "Individually, many of the domestic spending programs proposed in the Congress have most attractive aspects. They provide help for some worthy group. It is hard for Members of Congress to oppose those programs. It will be very, very hard for me to veto them if Congress enacts them. But it is not the individual programs that are unacceptable, but the sum total of them, adding up easily to $30 billion or more to bring the deficit into the

$100 billion area."

"Defense spending on the other hand provides no benefits, except the most precious benefit of all – the freedom of our country and the last hope for peace in the world."

"As President Eisenhower so wisely observed, only the strong are free. Certainly, we have ample reason to believe this truth today. My budget recommendations for national defense are the minimum, I believe, essential for our safety."

"It is now a popular idea that because Americans are not fighting anywhere, because we are seeking to broaden every avenue of peace, that we can expand social benefit programs and pay for them out of defense cutbacks. Simple arithmetic proves otherwise. I have seen careful mathematical projections that show if welfare and other transfer payments continue merely at their present rate of growth, about 9 percent annually for the past 20 years, half of the American people will be living off the other half by the year 2000."

"Except for vastly increasing taxes on

those who work, the only way such payments can be continued indefinitely is to take them away from our national defense. Other super powers, I can assure you, are doing nothing of that kind."

In the same month, April, the House-Senate conferees agreed to a fiscal 1975 appropriation of $492.4 million for CSA.

Ford set a message, 8 May, to *Congress Special Message to the Congress Reporting on Budget Rescissions and Deferrals* and stated (Ford 1975d):

"To the Congress of the United States:"

"I herewith report one new proposed rescission and one new deferral as required by the Congressional Budget and Impoundment Control Act of 1974. In addition, I am transmitting one supplementary report which revises a deferral report made to the Congress in a previous special message. The details of the rescission and deferral reports are attached."

"The proposed rescission would affect two programs of the Community Services Administration that duplicate several programs currently operating at Federal, State and local levels. The two deferrals are routine in nature and do not affect program levels in either case."

"I urge the Congress to act promptly on this rescission and other rescission proposals now pending."

Rescission is the cancellation of budget authority previously provided by Congress. The Impoundment Control Act of 1974 specifies that the president may propose to Congress that funds be rescinded. If both Houses have not approved a rescission proposal (by passing legislation) within 45 days of continuous session, any funds being withheld must be made available for obligation.

Ford in June spoke at 12:40 p.m. in the Rose Garden at the White House where Byron R. White, Associate Justice of the Supreme Court, administered the oath of office to the new Ambassador, on his *Remarks at the Swearing In of Daniel P. Moynihan as United States Representative to the United Nations.* Ford said, in part (1975e):

"Mr. Justice White, distinguished Members of the Congress, ladies and gentlemen:"

"It is a great privilege and pleasure for me to have the opportunity of participating in this wonderful occasion today, the swearing in of Ambassador Moynihan as the Representative of the United States at the United Nations and as the newest member of our Cabinet."

"Ambassador Moynihan has served our Nation, both in and out of government, with a refreshing innovation and intellectual distinction. He served in the White House under the previous administration as a Counselor to the President and, more recently, as our Ambassador in India."

"He has combined over the years other Federal and State government service with an outstanding service as an educator. His numerous writings have earned him a reputation as an outstanding political, economic, and social philosopher."

"Above all, he knows what America is all about and what it actually stands for, and he knows our role in international affairs. The challenges that the United Nations now confronts are of tremendous consequence for our own future and for the entire world."

"Our Representative must be a person of high ideals and steadfast purpose. Ambassador Moynihan is the right man for the job."

Ford announced, 8 July, 12:03 p.m. to reporters assembled in the Oval Office at the White House, and Howard H. Callaway, chairman of the President Ford Committee, Robert C. Moot, treasurer, *Remarks Announcing Candidacy for the 1976*

Republican Presidential Nomination and said, in part (1975f):

> "TODAY, I am officially announcing that I am a candidate for the Republican nomination for President in 1976. I do this with the strong support of my family and my friends.
> My campaign will be conducted by outstanding Americans on whose integrity both my supporters and all others can depend. I have found these leaders in Bo Callaway of Georgia, Dave Packard of California, Dean Burch and Bob Moot, and many others from every State and from every walk of life who have volunteered to help."

> "In all the 13 election campaigns I have undertaken, my basic conviction has been that the best politics is always to do the best job I can for all the people. I see no reason to change that successful philosophy."

> "I expect to work hard, campaign forthrightly, and do the very best I can for America in order to finish the job I have begun."

On 14 July the Legal Services Corporation Board of Directors were sworn into office by Lewis Powell, Supreme Court Justice. The Senate Appropriations Committee set $96.466

, funding for the Corporation.

29 July, the *Special Health Revenue Sharing Act of 1975* .ic Law 94-63) was passed.

The law revised and extended the Comprehensive Public alth Centers, Community Mental Health Centers, Migrant ealth Centers, Community Health Centers, and Family lanning programs. The act established specialized centers focusing on specific needs.

In August, CSA reorganized the agency following a rescission of $10 million coupled with a deferred obligation of $16.5 million.

In September the House-Senate conferees agreed to fund the Legal Services Corporation with $88 million for Fiscal Year 1976.

The National Center for Community action released a report, 15 October, which stated that the majority of the 889 Community Action Agencies are located in urban areas and are private non-profit corporations with a jurisdiction that covers 80% of the countries counties, serving 95% of those counties populations.

Ford stated, 19 December, on his *Veto of the Departments of Labor and Health, Education, and Welfare Appropriation Act, 1976*, in part (Ford 1975g):

> I return without my approval H.R. 8069, the Departments of Labor and Health, Education, and Welfare Appropriation Act, 1976.
>
> As you know, I have just vetoed H.R. 5559, which would have extended for six months the temporary tax cut due to

expire on New Year's Eve, because it was not accompanied by a limit on Federal spending for the next fiscal year. H.R. 8069 is a classic example of the unchecked spending which I referred to in my earlier veto message.

H.R. 8069 would provide nearly $1 billion more in spending authority than I had requested. Not only would the $45 billion total in this bill add significantly to the already burdensome Federal deficits expected this year and next, but the individual increases themselves are unjustified, unnecessary, and unwise. This bill is, therefore, inconsistent with fiscal discipline and with effective restraint on the growth of government.

I am not impressed by the argument that H.R. 8069 is in line with the Congress' second concurrent resolution on the budget and is, therefore, in some sense proper. What this argument does not say is that the resolution, which expresses the Congress' view of appropriate budget restraint, approves a $50 billion, or 15 percent, increase in Federal spending in one year. Such an increase is not appropriate budget restraint.

The House of Representatives, 27 January 1976, voted,

310-113, and the Senate, 28 January 1976, voted, 70-24, to override the President's veto. With the vote in the Senate to override the veto. H.R. 8069 was enacted as Public Law 94-206 (90 Stat. 3).

CSA received an appropriation of $400 million (Clark 2000).

January 1976, Ford requested a funding for Fiscal 1977, $344 million for CSA: Community Action Local Initiative, Community Economic Development, Senior Opportunities.

Ford, 21 January, sent his *Annual Budget Message to the Congress, Fiscal Year 1977*, and said, in part (Ford 1976a):

> "My budget also proposes that we replace 59 grant programs with broad block grants in four important areas:
>
> --A health block grant that will consolidate medicaid and 15 other health programs. States will be able to make their own priority choices for use of these Federal funds to help low-income people with their health needs.
>
> --An education block grant that will consolidate 27 grant programs for education into a single flexible Federal grant to States, primarily for use in helping disadvantaged and handicapped children."
>
> --A block grant for feeding needy children that will consolidate 15 complex and overlapping programs. Under existing programs, 700,000 needy children receive no benefits. Under my program, all needy

children can be fed, but subsidies for the nonpoor will be eliminated."

--A block grant that will support a community's social service programs for the needy. This would be accomplished by removing current requirements unnecessarily restricting the flexibility of States in providing such services."

"These initiatives will result in more equitable distribution of Federal dollars, and provide greater State discretion and responsibility. All requirements that States match Federal funds will be eliminated. Such reforms are urgently needed, but my proposals recognize that they will, in some cases, require a period of transition."

Moynihan, 31 January, sent the following letter to Ford:

Dear Mr. President:
Today is the last of my leave from the University. I must return now, or must give up for good my professorship there and, in effect, give up my profession as well. The effort to persuade myself that this is a kind of personal fate that must be accepted has not succeeded. I have spent almost five of the past eight years in government, nine of the past fifteen, thirteen of the past nineteen. It is time to

return to teaching and such are the conditions of my tenure that I return now or not at all.

It has been, for me, a high honor to serve as your Ambassador to India during the latter part of my stay there, and more recently as your representative at the United Nations. Indeed I was scarcely back from the former post before you asked me to take up the new one. You have been unfailing in your encouragement and support and I have with the fullest commitment sought to carry out your general policies and your specific instructions. For that opportunity I am permanently in your debt, even if I must with a heavy and still divided heart, now depart your service.
Most respectfully,
DANIEL P. MOYNIHAN

Ford, 2 February, in his *Letter Accepting the Resignation of Ambassador Daniel Patrick Moynihan, United States Representative to the United Nations,* said (Ford 1976b):

Dear Pat:

Your letter of January 31, expressing your desire to return to the teaching profession, reached me today. I will, of course, accede to your wishes. with the deepest regret and reluctance.

In your letter you mentioned the years you have devoted to public service in the last two decades. You did not mention the enormous positive impact that those years have had.

In every task you have undertaken you have consistently elevated public discourse by puncturing pretense and by eloquently advocating the cause of reason. Nowhere has this been more evident than in your service at the United Nations, where you have asserted our position forcefully, cogently and honestly. In doing so you have not only reminded Americans that we take that institution seriously but also that we take ourselves and the principles for which we stand seriously.

For this service, which most appropriately you have rendered on the occasion of our 200th year, your fellow citizens owe you a debt that can never adequately be repaid. On their behalf Betty and I offer our profound thanks to you and Elizabeth for your service to the Nation.
With warmest personal regards,
Sincerely,

GERALD R. FORD

In February, after a ten-month investigation, the Manpower and Housing Subcommittee reported that the inability of CSA to efficiently manage its own affairs could be traced back to 1973 when the Nixon administration tried to dismantle the agency. The direct result was a breakdown of the mandate to act as an advocate for the poor caused by low employee morale and the loss of dollars on the part of grantees. David Mathews, Secretary HEW, in a press conference said that he had made no decision on moving CSA to HEW. He said that he would be "reluctant to increase the size and complexity" of HEW.

Ford, 3 January, stated, in part, at 3:55 p.m. to reporters assembled in the Briefing Room at the White House, in his *Remarks at a News Briefing on General Revenue Sharing*, (Ford 1976c):

"Good afternoon."

"I just came from a meeting with the Vice President, representatives of the Domestic Council, the Treasury Department, and others discussing how the administration can affirmatively promote the extension of the existing Revenue Sharing Act, general revenue sharing. This, of course, was enacted in 1972."

"So far the Federal Government has distributed roughly $23S billion to some 38,000 to 39,000 State and local units of government. The money has been spent in a broad range of local and State activities."

"The interesting thing to me was that with the $23S billion that has been expended by the Federal Government to State and local units of government, the overhead cost has been one-twelfth of 1 percent, which shows that you can take Federal money and redistribute it to State and local units of government with a minimum of overhead."

"The net result is the States have and local units of government have gotten back virtually all of the money that was taken from them, and they now and will in the future have this money for the necessary local services that they do perform."

"One other point. The Congress was asked by me last year, I think in July, to immediately undertake the reenactment or the extension of the existing general revenue sharing legislation. Thus far there has been no subcommittee action on this legislation. Time is running out."

"Let me give you a concrete illustration. I met with some mayors last week – three or four of them – from the State of Ohio.

They have to publish their budgets for the 12 months beginning January 1 by the middle of 1976. So, unless this legislation is enacted or extended beyond January 1, any municipality in Ohio will have to show that there will be no general revenue sharing money coming, which means they will either have to show a reduction in services or they will have to show, if they want to extend the services, an additional State or local tax."

"Now, this puts municipalities, this puts States in a very difficult situation unless we get some affirmative action from the Congress."

"I have asked the Vice President, who spearheaded the drive for the enactment in the first instance in 1972 of general revenue sharing, to use his talents to convince the Congress that it must act promptly. I believe that he will work with Governors, with State officials in general, with county officials, and with city officials to convince the Congress that delay or a failure to act would be catastrophic in the meeting of local needs or State needs."

"The Vice President knows how it was done in 1972.. I am sure that he will be successful. But time is rapidly running out, and Congress has an obligation to move now if we are to save cities, counties, and States from a serious financial setback.

So, Mr. Vice President, would you tell them how you are going to do this?"

Ford, 23 February, at 9:30 a.m. in the Presidential Ballroom at the Statler-Hilton Hotel, introduced by Republican Governor Robert D. Ray of Iowa, Conference Chairman, in his *Remarks at the Winter Meeting of the National Governors' Conference*, in discussing block grants stated, in part (Ford 1976d):

"In the campaign for general revenue sharing, I think I have worked longer and harder for that legislation than almost any other. You are well aware of how this $30.2 billion, 5-year program is now administered at the Federal level at a cost of a twelfth of a penny for every dollar spent. You know how our States are now making State decisions on the local use of their Federal taxes. I am now vigorously seeking to extend this excellent program for 5 3/4 years."

"It was last April, almost a year ago, when I asked the Congress to renew revenue sharing so that you could make timely plans and decisions for fiscal year

1977 State budgets. Regrettably, the Congress did not share my sense of urgency. Thus far, it has failed to act, and the deadline is getting closer and closer."

"Now, I frankly am encouraged by the way the States and localities are responding to the challenge of balanced federalism. Behind the block grant concept is the conviction that you can do a far, far better job in many ways than the Federal Government, and your performance in the past gives me renewed faith."

"But we have to do a lot more. The State and localities can lead the way. These block grant programs provide a dramatic and effective way to serve local priorities. Under one such block grant – the Community Development Program, enacted into law in late 1974 after a long and controversial struggle, resulted in the following:"

"Federal regulations which a community must follow have decreased from 2,600 pages – 2,600 pages under the categorical program – to 25 pages for the block grant program."

"Under the community development act,

a community need file only one application consisting of 50 pages, rather than the previous average of five applications consisting of 1,400 pages."

"Under this change from categorical to block grant, the processing and approval of a community development block grant application average 49 days, although under the categorical urban renewal program, processing took over 2 years."

"Due to the success that we have had in simplifying the Community Development Program, as I said a moment ago, I am recommending that we use the same approach in other Federal problems involving social services, health, education, and child nutrition."

"Therefore, I am asking the Congress to approve the community services act, and I am sending the proposal to the Congress today. It will significantly increase the flexibility of States in delivering social services to low-income families, and I refer in this category to such programs as day care, foster care, and homemaker services."

"Many of the responsibilities now placed by law in the hands of Federal bureaucrats will be passed back to locally elected or State-elected officials. The basic responsibility on how best to meet the needs of States' low-income families would be returned to each of your respective States. This determination, as I see it, can best be made through an open process of local planning that directly involves your citizens."

"Later this week, I will transmit proposals consolidating Medicaid and 15 other categorical health programs into a single $10 billion block grant. With it – and I think this is significantly important – is a commitment to each of you that your State will receive more Federal funds from this single program in fiscal year 1977 than your State received in 1976 from 16 existing programs."

The same day, 23 January, Ford sent his *Special Message to the Congress Urging Enactment of Proposed Community Services Legislation*, and said, in part (Ford 1976e):

The proposed Financial Assistance for Community Services Act will:
--Eliminate the requirement that States must match one State dollar for three Federal dollars.
--Eliminate numerous restrictive conditions on how Federal funds may be

used: burdensome Federal requirements for child day care; limitations on social services funding for health and institutional care; and procedures for the imposition of fees and the determination of eligibility.

--Concentrate Federal dollars on people most in need, those under the poverty threshold and those receiving public assistance.

--Assure that no State will receive less money as a result of this legislation – than it received in fiscal year 1976.

--Decrease Federal monitoring and oversight of State plan requirements and expenditures of funds with the States assuming greater responsibility in this area.

--Improve the public planning process by which citizens and local governments participate in identifying needs and establishing priorities.

I ask the Congress to enact this legislation promptly so that States may begin to use Federal and local money more effectively.

Bert Gallegos, 9 March, called his top officials and told them he was leaving CSA.

He had been accused of poor management, abuses of civil service personnel, and other actions that resulted in poor morale (Clark 2002). Ford accepted his resignation, effective 15 April, or until the appointment of a successor. Ford nominated Samuel

R. Martinez, the Regional Director, Depart of Labor, Denver, Colorado.

The Senate Labor and Public Welfare Committee recommended $603 million to fund CSA for Fiscal Year 1977.

Martinez, 5 April, told the Senate during his confirmation hearing that he had reached a "strong agreement" with the White Houses that CSA would not be transferred to HEW until the end of Fiscal 1977. He felt that CSA was to be a catalyst bringing resources to other agencies and departments as part of the battle against poverty and that his first job as Director CSA would be the restructuring "to guarantee that we are doing the most effective job with the limited dollars that are available."

Ford, 15 April, spoke at 2:17 p.m. in the Rose Garden at the White House and. referred to David Mathews, Secretary of Health, Education, and Welfare, and Carla A. Hills, Secretary of Housing and Urban Development, *Remarks at the Swearing In of Samuel R. Martinez as Director of the Community Services Administration*, and said (Ford 1976f):

> "Sam and Mrs. Martinez and your family, Secretary Mathews, Secretary Hills, distinguished guests:"

> "Let me welcome you to the White House today for the swearing in of Sam Martinez as Director of the Community Services Organization and Administration [Community Services Administration]. I spent a good deal of time in Sam Martinez' native State, and I feel the next best thing to visiting Colorado is bringing one of its leading citizens to Washington."

"Sam Martinez brings to Washington more than a decade of experience in dealing with public policy at many, many levels. At a time when the American people are concerned about maintaining the roles of the State and local units of government, his experience at those levels makes him especially valuable to all of us."

"Sam Martinez began his administrative career as a principal at Fort Lupton High School in Colorado where he had been a teacher as well as a coach. His involvement in helping people at the State and local level began in 1964 when he was named assistant director of the Colorado Civil Rights Commission. He served the people of Colorado as a special assistant to the Governor and as a State and regional director of the Colorado Office of Economic Opportunity."

"Since that time, Sam Martinez began his responsibility in managing Federal programs and that role has expanded significantly. In the last few years he has served very constructively as Chairman of the Mountain Plains Federal Regional Council and Regional Director of the United States Department of Labor."

"Sam Martinez and I share a personal commitment to help the poor and disadvantaged Americans served by the Community Services Administration. Its programs demand strong and very effective and very imaginative leadership. I am fully confident, Sam, that you will provide that leadership."

"And now I ask the Executive Clerk, John Ratchford, to please administer the oath. John."

No one mentioned that CSA's role as innovator and change agent on behalf of the poor had been severely curtailed and that the research and demonstration capabilities had been dispersed among the old-line Departments (Clark 2000).

House-Senate conferees appropriated $511.17 million for Fiscal 1977 CSA.

The Democratic National Convention met, 12 July - 15 July 15, at Madison Square Garden, New York City, and nominated former Governor Jimmy Carter of Georgia as Presidential candidate, Senator Walter Mondale of Minnesota, a liberal and a protégé of Hubert Humphrey, for the Vice President slot; John Glenn and Barbara Jordan, the first African-American woman, gave the keynote addresses. Jordan's keynote address made her the first woman to deliver the keynote address at a Democratic National Convention. Carter easily won the nomination on the first ballot.

Ford, 29 July, sent his *Special Message to the Congress Reporting on a Budget Rescission* and said (Ford 1976g):

To the Congress of the United States:

In accordance with the Impoundment Control Act of 1974, I herewith propose rescission of $45 million in budget authority appropriated for payment to the Legal Services Corporation.

Approval of this rescission proposal will reduce Federal spending by $45 million over 1977 and 1978. The proposed rescission would prevent unneeded expansion of Legal Services Corporation activities and delay greater geographic coverage until program evaluations are completed.
The details of the proposed rescission are contained in the attached report.

The Republican National Convention, 16 August - 19 August, held in Kemper Arena, Kansas City, Missouri, nominated President Gerald Ford only after narrowly defeating a strong challenge from former California Governor Ronald Reagan. The convention nominated Senator Robert J. Dole of Kansas for Vice President, instead of Vice President Nelson Rockefeller. The keynote address was delivered by Tennessee Senator Howard Baker. Other notable speakers included: Minnesota Representative Al Quie; retired Lieutenant Colonel and former Vietnam prisoner of war Raymond Schrump; former Texas Governor John Connally; Providence, Rhode Island, mayor Vincent Cianci; and, Michigan Senator Robert P. Griffin.

Ford, 29 September, in his message to the *House of Representatives, Veto of the Appropriations Bill for the Departments of Labor and Health, Education, and Welfare*, stated, in part (Ford 1976h):

> Just before adjourning for the final weeks of the election campaign, the Congress has sent me H.R. 14232, the Departments of Labor, and Health, Education, and Welfare appropriations for fiscal year 1977 which begins October 1. This last and second largest of the major Federal appropriation bills to be considered by this Congress is a perfect example of the triumph of election-year politics over fiscal restraint and responsibility to the hard-pressed American taxpayers.
>
> The Congress says it cares about cutting inflation and controlling Federal spending.
> The Congress says it wants to stop fraud and abuse in Federal programs.
> The Congress says it wants to end duplication and overlap in Federal activities.
>
> But when you examine this bill carefully you discover that what the Congress says has very little to do with what the Congress does.

If the Congress really cared about cutting inflation and controlling Federal spending, would it send me a bill that is $4 billion over my $52.5 billion request?

If the Congress really wanted to stop fraud and abuse in Federal programs like Medicaid, would it appropriate more money this year than it did last year without any reform?

If the Congress really wanted to end duplication and overlap in Federal activities, would it continue all of these narrow programs this year – at higher funding levels than last year?

If the Congress really wanted to cut the deficit and ease the burden on the taxpayer, would it ignore serious reform proposals?
The resounding answer to all of these questions is no.

I cannot ask American taxpayers to accept unwarranted spending increases without a commitment to serious reform. I do not believe the people want more bureaucratic business as usual. I believe the people want the reforms I have proposed which would target the dollars on those in real need while reducing

Federal interference in our daily lives and returning more decision-making freedom to State and local levels where it belongs.

I therefore return without my approval H.R. 14323 [14232], and urge the Congress to enact immediately my budget proposals and to adopt my program reforms.

Votes in both the House and Senate, 30 September, overrode the Presidents veto. H.R. 14232 was enacted as Public Law 94-439 (90 Stat. 1418).

On Tuesday, 2 November, Jimmy Carter, (D), Georgia, defeated Gerald Ford, (R), Michigan.

Carter and The Unwilling Congress

"It was obvious to me and my advisors that many Americans were deeply concerned about the competence and integrity of our government. Still fresh in memory were the assassinations of John Kennedy, Robert Kennedy, and Marin Luther King, Jr.; the disgrace of Watergate; the failure in Vietnam and the misleading statements about the war from top civilian and military leaders; and the revelation that emerged from the Frank Church Senate committee that our government's intelligence services had condoned assassination plots against foreign leaders" (Carter 2010).

20 January, at 12:05 p.m., from a platform erected at the East Front of the Capitol, Chief Justice of the United States Warren E. Burger administered the oath of office to Jimmy Carter, then Carter in his *Inaugural Address*, said, in part (Carter 1977a):

> "The American dream endures. We must once again have full faith in our country – and in one another. I believe America can be better. We can be even stronger than before."

> "Let our recent mistakes bring a resurgent

commitment to the basic principles of our Nation, for we know that if we despise our own government, we have no future. We recall in special times when we have stood briefly, but magnificently, united. In those times no prize was beyond our grasp."

"But we cannot dwell upon remembered glory. We cannot afford to drift. We reject the prospect of failure or mediocrity or an inferior quality of life for any person. Our Government must at the same time be both competent and compassionate."

"We have already found a high degree of personal liberty, and we are now struggling to enhance equality of opportunity. Our commitment to human rights must be absolute, our laws fair, our national beauty preserved; the powerful must not persecute the weak, and human dignity must be enhanced."

"We have learned that more is not necessarily better, that even our great Nation has its recognized limits, and that we can neither answer all questions nor solve all problems. We cannot afford to do everything, nor can we afford to lack boldness as we meet the future. So, together, in a spirit of individual sacrifice for the common good, we must simply do our best."

During Carter's administration, the Community Services Administration kept a low profile (Clark 2000).

"I found out quickly that the animosities and distrust that had been prevalent during the eight years of the Republican administration between the White House and Congress was still present . . . " (Carter 2010).

25 January, Joseph Califano was sworn in as Secretary, HEW.

"I was determined to have a complete separation of church and state, compatible with my personal beliefs. This included a departure from custom of some other presidents, who invited Billy Graham and other Christian leaders to hold services in the East Room of the White House" (Carter 2010).

28 January, CSA Director Martinez resigned after a law suit was filed on 18 January over his shifting funds back and forth to impede the rural development fund from being utilized.

29 January, Carter named Joe Aragon, Special Assistant to the President, as Acting Director CSA.

Carter, 31 January, is his *Economic Recovery Program - Message to the Congress*, said, in part (Carter 1977b):

"To the Congress of the United States:"

"I am proposing to you today a two year $31.2 billion economic recovery package, whose budgetary costs will be divided almost equally between fiscal years 1977 and 1978 (Table 1). The main components of the program are:

--an increase of $4 billion in authorizations for local public works;

--an expansion of public service employment by 415,000 jobs;

--an expansion of training and youth programs under the Comprehensive Employment and Training Act (CETA) by 346,000 positions;

--an increase in the countercyclical revenue sharing program designed to pay out an additional $1 billion a year at current rates of unemployment;

--a $4 billion program of tax reform and simplification for individuals, through an increase in the standard deduction;

--individual tax rebates, and payments to Social Security, Supplemental Security Income (SSI) and Railroad Retirement beneficiaries, which will total $11.4 billion;

--an optional credit against income taxes equal to 4 percent of payroll taxes or an additional 2 percent investment tax credit for businesses."

"While a healthy housing industry is also critical to economic recovery, this area requires long-term commitments, rather than a short-range program. The Secretary of Housing and Urban Development is now developing a long-term housing program for low and middle income families, which will contribute to sustained economic growth."

"The economy I found when I took office had 7.5 million Americans out of work, 1.4 million full-time workers forced to take part-time jobs, and still another 1 million workers who had dropped out of the labor force because jobs are so hard to find."

"Employment and Training Programs. The economic stimulus package is designed to cope with both cyclical unemployment, which is caused by the economic recession, and structural unemployment, which affects those who lack the necessary training and skills to find work even in good times. The first group can largely be helped by general economic stimulus. The second group requires special training and placement programs."

"I propose the following programs to help these groups:
a. Public Service Employment. It is time to take our people off welfare and put them to work, with maximum emphasis on creating jobs in the private sector. But it will take time for an expanding private

economy to provide a large number of jobs for the unemployed. In the meantime we must expand temporary public service jobs for those who would find it difficult to obtain work in private industry.

I propose an increase in the number of federally-funded public service jobs under the Comprehensive Employment and Training Act (CETA) from 310,000 now to 600,000 by the end of fiscal year 1977 and to 725,000 for fiscal year 1978. This program would cost $0.7 billion in fiscal year 1977 and $3.4 billion in fiscal year 1978.

This public service program will enable the unemployed to use their talents to serve their fellow citizens in hospitals, in mental institutions, in improving our national parks, in recreation programs, in rehabilitating those parts of our cities where crime is high and hope is scarce, and in energy-saving activities. We will target our public service employment programs to areas of national need – such as the improvement of our national parks, and the insulation of homes and public buildings as well as other energy-saving activities.

b. Youth Training and Employment Programs. Unemployment among our young people is far higher than the national average for workers of all ages, so we must target specific programs to our unemployed youth. I am proposing to expand the youth-oriented programs in CETA, Titles III and V, by 176,000 slots from 422,000 to 598,000.

The basic youth programs will be conducted by the State and local governments which are prime sponsors under CETA. An additional program will be established to take rural and urban young people aged 16 to 21 off of the streets and put them to useful work helping to conserve, develop and maintain our natural resources and recreation areas. This, like the Civilian Conservation Corps of 40 years ago, would be a way to let young people serve their Nation while expanding their own horizons.

For Vietnam-era veterans between the ages of 20 and 24, the unemployment rate is 18%, compared to 12.5% for non-veterans of the same age, with disabled and black veterans hit even harder. More than 20% of young black Vietnam-era veterans are now unemployed."

"I am therefore proposing the creation of 92,000 jobs under Title III of CETA by the end of fiscal year 1978 in a new program called Help Through Industrial Retraining and Employment (HIRE), which will emphasize employment opportunities for Vietnam-era veterans."

". . . I am proposing an increase of 58,000 slots in the Skill Training Improvement Program and a doubling of outlays for apprenticeship programs under Title III of CETA (Table 3). In order to better match our training programs to industry needs, I will instruct the Department of Labor to establish a skill training improvement program authorized under Title III of CETA, to be administered by CETA prime sponsors with full involvement of the private sector."

"Under the expanded apprenticeship program which I have requested, apprentices will be allowed to continue developing their skills even during periods of unemployment. A similar program will be extended to workers at the journeyman level."

"Migrants and Indians require special attention because of their high levels of unemployment. I am therefore proposing an addition of 20,000 slots, largely for migrants and Indians, under Title III of CETA."

2 February, Deputy Director CSA, Robert Chase was called an "interim" director with no permanent Director to be named until the study being made by Aragon on evaluating the "mission and structure" of CSA was completed. "Interim Director" was to avoid the problem that had been created by the illegal appointment of Howard Philips in 1973. The report was to be referred to the President's Domestic Council to make specific policy recommendations by 10 March.

Carter asked for $442.5 million for CSA in Fiscal Year 1978.

"Many people who want to see the budget balanced before I go out of office don't want to have their own personal projects removed. I'm determined to go to the public with these issues if necessary in order to prevail" (Carter 2010).

1 March, Carter appointed Graciela (Grace) Olivarez, a lawyer who advocated for civil rights and for the poor, a New Mexico State Planing Director, to be Director CSA.

2 March, Carter selected Sam Brown to be Head, ACTION Department. Brown, a New Left ideologue and antiwar activist, had been active with Carter's presidential campaign (Clark 2002). Brown had published, 1972, *Storefront Organizing: A Mornin' Glories' Manual*, which contained the nuts and bolts of grassroots organizing including discussion of such topics as establishing a storefront, finding support in your community, planning programs, getting out crowds, handling the press, fund raising, planning rallies, and canvasing and getting out the vote. Brown stated: "Despite our best intentions, the government programs we have supported have unwittingly made the poor dependent and consolidated a new bureaucratic and expert elite that too often denies poor people the opportunities to help themselves" (Clark 2002).

10 March, Olivarez appointed William Allison, Deputy

Director CSA.

11 March, Carter appointed Mary King to be Deputy Director, ACTION.

"It's been difficult for the Democratic Congress to learn to work with a Democratic president. First of all they expect too much, and secondly they still have a combative attitude carried over from the Nixon-Ford years . . . "(Carter 2010).

Cater, 21 March, in his *Memorandum to the Heads of Certain Departments on Urban and Regional Development Policies*, said, in part (Carter 1977c):

> Memorandum for the Secretary of Treasury, the Secretary of Commerce, the Secretary of Labor, the Secretary of Health, Education and Welfare, the Secretary of Housing and Urban Development, the Secretary of Transportation.
>
> I would like you to form a working policy group on urban and regional development. The purpose of the group will be to conduct a comprehensive review of all federal programs which impact on urban and regional areas; to seek perspectives of state and local officials concerning the role of the federal government in urban and regional development; and to submit appropriate administrative and legislative recommendations.

Under Executive Order 11297, Pat Harris
has the responsibility to convene such a
group and will do so shortly.

"I'm beginning to get concerned about the coordination
of a balanced budget, the cost of welfare reform, the cost of tax
reform, and the energy policy consequences" (Carter 2010).

29 April, Graciela Olivarez was sworn in as Director,
CSA. She, in May, shelved the previous reorganization plan,
created under Director Martinez, and drafted what she felt was
best.

"The congressional leadership breakfast was devoted
almost entirely to expressions on the part of the liberal members
(Tip O'Neal, Shirley Chisholm, and John Brademas) that we
neglecting social programs in order to balance the budget in four
years... In my opinion there's no way to have available financial
resources in two or three years for better health care or welfare
reform if we don't put some tight constraints on unnecessary
spending quite early" (Carter 2010).

On 3 June, Carter nominated William Whitaker Allison,
Georgia, Deputy Director, CSA after Robert C. Chase had
resigned. Whitaker had been at Economic Opportunity Atlanta,
were he managed its $20 million budget and provided funds to
programs that helped alleviate poverty in Atlanta. His success
at this organization was why Carter selected him. Allison was
confirmed 24 June.

Haynes Johnson wrote, 30 June, in *The Washington Post*
about Brown's appointment and said, in part (Johnson, Haynes
1977):

ACTION, one of those stirring sounding
names that political hacks dream up and

then foist upon the public, was hardly what its name implied. It was, in fact, the opposite: an "umbrella agency," that familiar governmentese term, to house what was left of the most liberal, idealistic and, yes, naive governmental impulses of the '60s. There, the bones of the Peace Corps, VISTA and the war on poverty rested. In the Nixon years, ACTION became probably the most politicized, dispirited agency in town. Name notwithstanding, its real mission was to slow down and eventually dismantle the program over which it presided.

Jimmy Carter wanted Sam Brown to take over as director. Give the place a rebirth of idealism.

Now he's got people out in the country looking at the programs he administers. Not in-house bureaucrats with a place to protect, nor hotshots newly come to town with reputations to be won. He's commissioned outsiders who live in the communities affected by those programs. His charge: tell him "what the hell this agency does that matters."

And if he finds out that none of it works, or matters? At the age of 33, he's heretical enough to say he'll tell the President and the Congress his programs ought to be broken up, or eliminated. That, of course, would place him in default on the big territorial game. "I'm not a very good imperialist,' he explains.

He's already learning new lessons about the other, bigger Washington game.

"There was a picture of the President and me standing together on page 3 of The Post about a month ago," he recalls. "The next day I got telephone calls returned that hadn't been returned for days and days before."

Brown was disturbed. It was a perceived relationship that wasn't real at all. It makes you wonder how quickly you become like your symbols.

"Now, that's nonsense," Sam says.

No, it's not, Sam. That's Washington.

In July, Carter appointed Carolyn Payton, an African American who was a pioneer in black women's leadership within the American Psychological Association and psychology, Director, The Peace Corps (part of ACTION).

On 15 July, CARTER created three new Assistant Director positions in CSA and nominated to these positions: John B. Gabusi, Arizona; Robert Stern Landmann, New Mexico; and,

Robert Nathaniel Smith, Michigan.

Gabusi had been Director, Office of Survey Associates, Tucson, Arizona, then Special Assistant to Congressman Morris K. Udall, then Staff Director, Subcommittee on the Postal Service, then served on the national Presidential campaign of Udall.

Landmann had been the former State New Mexico planning officer responsible for monitoring major contracts and grants and assisting in budget planning, policy analysis, finance and coordination with other state agencies.

Smith had been the Director of Youth Affairs program of the Democratic National Committee and had managed the DNC's voter registration drive in the previous Presidential election.

July 21, the Senate Committee on Human Resources heard the three nominations.

Gabusi would assume the responsibilities in the budget and management area of CSA; Robert Landmann would assume the responsibilities in the policy and planning area of CSA; Robert Smith would assume the responsibilities relating to local and regional community service programs of CSA (U.S. Senate 1977).

25 July, $596.4 million was provided to CSA for Fiscal 1978.

The House Government Operations Committee released its 2nd report in August and stated that CSA had failed in virtually every one of its responsibilities representing the poor, but that enough of CSA's grantees had been successful enough to demonstrate that Community Action can work. The White House said it would request that all Federal weatherization activities be moved to the newly created, 4 August, Department of Energy, Dr. James Schlesinger, Secretary, and that it would not support CSA funding for energy conservation for Fiscal 1979.

"This last week in the Congress has been like a madhouse with everybody threatening filibusters and constant squabbles within conference committees – almost like the last week of the Georgia legislature" (Carter 2010).

Carter, 5 August, at 2 p.m. in the Rose Garden at the White House, in his *Secretary of Energy Remarks at the Swearing In of James R. Schlesinger*, said, in part (Carter 1977d):

> "I had known Dr. Schlesinger just a few months. He came down to Plains to talk to me late last summer, after returning to our country from a trip to the Far East, including China. And I think it's accurate to say that he and I liked each other immediately and began to confer on many subjects concerning defense, atomic energy, foreign affairs, budget matters, and then, finally, the most important subject of all – energy."

> "He has been the one that the Congress and I and the American people have trusted. He's put together, with the help of an extremely able staff, working sacrificially, a comprehensive energy proposal that the Congress is now addressing in a very effective way."

Schlesinger was educated at the Horace Mann School and Harvard University, B.A. (1950), M.A. (1952), and Ph.D. (1956)

in economics. He taught economics at the University of Virginia, 1955-1963, and published *The Political Economy of National Security*, 1960, moved to the Rand Corporation, 1963-1969, later as Director of Strategic Studies. In 1969, in the Nixon administration, Assistant Director, the Bureau of the Budget, focused on Defense, then, 1971, Member and Chairman of the Atomic Energy Commission (AEC), focusing on extensive organizational and management changes in an effort to improve the AECs regulatory performance. On February 2, 1973, he became Director of Central Intelligence, then Secretary of Defense, 2 July 1973. on other matters. Ford fired Schlesinger for insubordination, 19 November 1975.

Carter, 6 August, in his *Welfare Reform Message to the Congress* said, in part (Carter 1977e):

> As I pledged during my campaign for the Presidency I am asking the Congress to abolish our existing welfare system, and replace it with a job-oriented program for those able to work and a simplified, uniform, equitable cash assistance program for those in need who are unable to work by virtue of disability, age or family circumstance. The Program for Better Jobs and Income I am proposing will transform the manner in which the Federal government deals with the income needs of the poor, and begin to break the welfare cycle.
>
> In May, after almost four months of study, I said that the welfare system was

worse than I expected. I stand by that conclusion. Each program has a high purpose and serves many needy people; but taken as a whole the system is neither rational nor fair. The welfare system is antiwork, anti-family, inequitable in its treatment of the poor and wasteful of taxpayers' dollars.

In my May 2, 1977 statement I established as a goal that the new reformed system involve no higher initial cost than the present system. It was my belief that fundamental reform was possible within the confines of current expenditures if the system were made more rational and efficient. That belief has been borne out in our planning. Thereafter, Secretary Califano outlined a tentative no cost plan which embodied the major reform we have been seeking:
--Consolidation of programs.
--Incentives to work.
--Provision of jobs.
--Establishment of a national minimum payment.
--Streamlined administration.
--Incentives to keep families together.
--Some fiscal relief for State and local governments.

The Program For Better Jobs and Income

will replace $26.3 billion in current programs which provide income assistance to low-income people. In addition, the program will produce savings in other programs amounting to $1.6 billion. The total amount available from replaced programs and savings is $27.9 billion.

A central element of this proposal is a new effort to match low-income persons with available work in the private and public sector. It will be the responsibility of State and local officials to assure an unbroken sequence of employment and training services, including job search, training, and placement. Prime sponsors under the Comprehensive Employment and Training Act, state employment service agencies, and community-based organizations will play major roles in this effort.

A major component of the program is a national effort to secure jobs for the principal wage earners in low income families with children. The majority of poor families – including many who are on welfare for brief periods of time – depend upon earnings from work for most of their income. People want to support themselves and we should help them do so. I propose that the Federal government assist workers from low income families to find regular employment in the private and public sectors. When such employment cannot be found I propose to provide up to 1.4 million public service jobs (including part-time jobs and training) paying at the minimum wage, or slightly above where states supplement the basic Federal program.

I propose to scrap and completely overhaul the current public assistance programs, combining them into a simplified, uniform, integrated system of cash assistance. AFDC, SSI and Food Stamps will be abolished. In their place will be a new program providing: (1) a Work Benefit for two-parent families, single people, childless couples and single parents with no child under 14, all of whom are expected to work full-time and required to accept available work; and (2) Income Support for those who are aged, blind or disabled, and for single parents of children under age 14. Single parents with children aged 7 to 14 will be required to accept part-time work which does not interfere with caring for the children, and will be expected to accept full-time work where appropriate day care is available.

Because of the complexity of integrating the different welfare systems of the 50 states and the District of Columbia into a more unified national system, we estimate that this program will be effective in Fiscal Year 1981. Moreover, we recognize that the National Health Insurance plan which will be submitted next year must contain fundamental reform and rationalization of the Medicaid program, carefully coordinated with the structure of this proposal. However, we are anxious to achieve the swiftest implementation possible and will work with the Congress and State and local governments to accelerate this timetable if at all possible.

I hope the Congress will move expeditiously and pass this program early next year.

Carter, 11 August, in his *Memorandum for the Heads of Executive Departments and Agencies on Government Reorganization*, released 12 August, wrote, in part (Carter 1977f):

Memorandum for the Heads of Executive Departments and Agencies
Subject: Government Reorganization

Government reorganization for better

Government performance is one of my main goals, and I am encouraged by the progress made so far. How we handle the personnel aspects will be important to our ultimate success. I am committed to accomplishing the reorganization with a minimum of hardship to employees.

The reorganization will unquestionably require consolidation of functions and, in some cases, the closing of certain activities. In the event employees of your agency cannot be transferred with the same functions, you should do everything you can to place them in other suitable positions, including filling vacancies within your agency with qualified employees scheduled to be displaced, working through the Civil Service Commission's Displaced Employee Program to facilitate placements in other agencies, and providing opportunities for retraining.

I am counting on your cooperation and resourcefulness to help us carry out the transition to greater governmental effectiveness as smoothly as we can.

Carter, 22 August, said in his *Memorandum for the Heads of Executive Departments and Agencies on Advisory Committee Review*, announced by the White House Press Office, 24 August, in part (Carter 1977g):

> Memorandum for the Heads of
> Executive Departments and Agencies
> Subject: Advisory Committee Review
>
> I am pleased that, as a result of the actions recommended, the 1,189 advisory committees reviewed will be reduced by 480 or forty percent of the total. I commend you for your part in this effort to make the government more effective and efficient.

In Executive Order 12007, Carter terminated: The Citizens' Advisory Council on the Status of Women; The Citizens' Advisory Committee on Environmental Quality; and, The President's Advisory Board on International Investment.

On 25 August, Carter directed the Reorganization Project staff at the Office of Management and Budget to begin a review of the economic policy and analysis machinery of the Federal Government outside the Executive Office of the President and to focus on 33 agencies employing approximately 5,000 economists.

Carter had campaigned as a Washington "outsider" being critical of President Gerald Ford and the Democratic Congress. After the election, Carter demanded the power to reorganize the executive branch. During Nixon's tenure Congress had passed a series of reforms that removed power from the president. Most members of Congress were unwilling to restore that power. Unreturned phone calls, verbal insults, and an unwillingness to trade political favors soured many on Capitol Hill which deeply affected Carter's ability to enact his agenda (Jensson 1977).

CSA Director Olivarez, 1 September, send a letter to Congressional leaders stating that the weatherization authority was unnecessary and should be removed from the Economic Opportunity Act, and said: "While it is obviously difficult for an Federal agency to 'give up' one of its programs, I believe that consolidation represents the fulfillment of one of our agency's basic missions – the development of innovative ways to assist the poor."

Carter, 13 September, signed an Executive Order 12009 to activate the new Department of Energy on October 1.

"Had lunch with Senator Ted Kennedy, who has a 100 percent voting record as far as our program is concerned. He's the only member of Congress that does, as far as I know" (Carter 2010).

Olivarez, 14 September, is a letter sent to all Community Action Agency Directors and Board Chairman stated the CSA funds going to the National Community Action Agency Executive Directors Association and the National Association for Community Development would be in a moritorium.

"A the cabinet meeting we discussed a wide range of issues, including the fact that Canada with its public health program had 7 percent of its GDP spent on health – our figure is 10 percent" (Carter 2010).

On 1 October all agencies covered by the Labor-HEW funding bill ran out of funds due to the House and Senate deadlock over anti-abortion language in the funding bill. Carter signed an 18-day continuing resolution to carry the agencies to the end of the month. The House and Senate passed continuing resolutions to fund the agencies until 30 November.

The Senate accepted a House compromise on the funding bill. This freed up $596.4 million for CSA in Fiscal Year 1978.

11 October, Carolyn Payton became Director, Peace Corps.

"The biggest congressional action today [4 November] is the Senate consideration of Social Security. The Congress is almost spineless when considering extra benefits for special interest groups, in this case retired people. They are on the verge of putting the Social Security fund back into bankruptcy by eliminating restrictions on earnings levels for SS recipients, which would cost $3 or $4 billion a year. We spent all day working to get these amendments eliminated, and finally succeeded" (Carter 2010).

"Jim Schlesinger reported [3 December] progress on the energy package – They've been in a virtual stalemate since September on Social Security, natural gas, crude oil, conservation measures, and rate reform" (Carter 2010).

Carter, 6 December, in his statement, *Labor-HEW Continuing Appropriations Bill Statement on Signing H.J. Res. 662 Into Law*, as enacted, H.J. Res. 662 became Public Law 95-205, approved December 9, said, in part (Carter 1977h):

> "I am pleased to sign into law H.J. Res. 662, which incorporates the FY 1978 appropriations for the Department of Labor, the Department of Health, Education, and Welfare, the Community Services Administration, and other agencies."

> "H.J. Res. 662 reflects some of the efforts which this administration undertook last February in its FY 1978 budget revisions, for it incorporates provisions which:

--expand the Job Corps by 14,000 positions;

--increase by 400,000 the number of college students receiving Basic Educational Opportunity Grants and raise the maximum award to $1,600 a year;

--provide funds to begin to ensure that every child in America is immunized against dangerous communicable diseases;

--provide additional funds to help residents of rural and inner-city areas get high-quality medical care through the National Health Service Corps."

"I had budget appeals this afternoon [15 December] from HEW, a very difficult session. It's always hard to know where to draw the line at different levels of aid to poor people, when the additional costs are enormous but the need is evident" (Carter 2010).

"I signed [20 December] the Social Security Act, which I hope and expect will put the system on a sound basis for the next forty years. It's a substantial tax increase for those above twenty-thousand-dollar income levels" (Carter 2010).

Pine, 24 January 1978, wrote in *'Lean and Tight' Carter Budget Seeks $500.2 Billion* and said, in part (Pine 1978):

> President Carter sent Congress yesterday a "lean and tight" $500.2 billion budget for fiscal 1979 that would increase spending barely more than is needed to offset inflation and would shrink the

impact of government on the economy.

The spending plan contains virtually no major new initiatives. Carter asked for a small increase in job-creation programs and promised to propose a new urban-aid plan sometime this spring. He recommended a sizable increase in defense spending.

Despite the absence of major new programs, the budget would produce a deficit of $60.6 billion, essentially unchanged from this year's $61.8 billion red-ink total. The President pointed out that part of the deficit would stem from the $24.5 billion net tax cut he is proposing.

Reaction to the President's proposal predictably was mixed, with Democrats generally complaining the president had been too tight-fisted, and Republicans chiding the administration for overspending. Most observers expect that Congress will increase spending beyond what Carter proposed.

In 1978, Brown asked Carolyn Payton for her resignation. She first agreed to resign, then withdrew her resignation, issued a statement that implied she would not leave unless asked directly by president Carter. He asked shortly thereafter. She stated that Brown had wanted to 'send volunteers for short periods to developing countries and then bring back the skills they had learned to fight poverty in the United States," and that such policy went against the original goals of the Peace Corps and that Brown was "trying to turn the corps into an arrogant, elitist political organization intended to meddle in the affairs of foreign governments." After her resignation, Carter took the Peace Corps out from under ACTION, by executive order, and made it a fully autonomous agency.

Later, in 2001, in hearings on Brown's suitability to serve as a Head of Delegation to the Conference on Security and Cooperation in Europe, members stated: "Sam Brown's gross mismanagement and politicization of the ACTION Agency when he directed that agency, his total lack of experience in security issues, and his questionable loyalty to basic American principles all make him a poor choice for any position in the Federal Government. . . . Now is not the time for amateur hour . . . Our first objection to Sam Brown is that we think he is unqualified for any management position. An investigation by the House Appropriations Committee of the Action Agency under Sam Browns stewardship found that improper procurement practices were the norm, including practices that were in clear violation of the law, such as failing to obtain a Certificate of Current Cost on each contractual action exceeding $100,000. The investigation also found excessive financial mismanagement, including the obligation of $417,000 that had not been approved by Congress. Another problem uncovered was that VISTA grants were being award noncompetitively, with a number of those grants going to friends and former associates of the VISTA Director. The House Appropriations Committee staff also discovered that ACTION regularly violated personnel and salary requirements with improper hiring practices and excessive pay. Given this record of sloppy management, we are not surprised, though we are outraged, that Sam Brown also tried to eliminate ACTION's Inspector General office." *Peace Corps Online Magazine*, 14 July 2001.

By the end of Carter's term public opinion of both VISTA and The Peace Corps had become problematic, at best (Clark 2002).

"I had a heated meeting [6 April], surprisingly, with Ted Kennedy, Doug Fraser, George Meany, and others concerning national health insurance. Apparently Kennedy and Califano had a real run-in about it. I told them to work it out between now and May, and I would present principles that I would be responsible for and no one else in the ad ministration. I believe Kennedy was posturing in front of the labor leaders" (Carter 2010).

"I spent a good bit of time studying the background on national health programs, which is going to be a very difficult political decision – contrasting the need to bring order out of chaos and avoid future waste of money by proposing any increase in health expenditures. There's an intense interest [as of 1 June] in this matter by a good many of the cabinet officers, most of whom don't want to see us make any moves on national health" (Carter 2010).

Carter, 26 June 19768, at his thirty-fourth news conference began at 4 p.m. in Room 450 of the Old Executive Office Building, broadcast live on radio and television, said, in part, at the beginning of *The President's News Conference:*

>"At the beginning of this year, I proposed to Congress substantial tax relief for almost every taxpayer in our country. I also asked that some important and

long-overdue reforms be made in our unfair and very complicated tax laws."

"Last week it became clear that the Congress is seriously considering a tax bill that contains no major reforms at all. That's bad enough, but this new congressional proposal is even worse. It actually attempts to take a step backward through some version of the so-called Steiger capital gains amendment. This proposal would add more than $2 billion to the Federal budget deficit. Eighty percent of its tax benefits would go to one-half of 1 percent of the American taxpayers, who make more than $100,000 a year. Three thousand millionaires would get tax reductions averaging $214,000. The other 99 1/2 percent of our taxpayers would not do quite so well."

"For instance, a middle-income family making between $20,000 and $30,000 a year would get a tax reduction from this proposal of less than $1. And the working man or woman who makes $20,000 or less a year would get no more than 25 cents."

"The American people want some tax relief from the heavy burden of taxation on their shoulders, but neither they nor I will tolerate a plan that provides huge tax windfalls for millionaires and two bits for the average American. That underestimates the intelligence of the American people."

"After my regular news conference I met with Ted Kennedy. Told him that we were interested ultimately in a comprehensive health program, but because of constraints of inflation and the budget it would be years before we could impose it. I'll make a speech on prevention of illness, and perhaps Kennedy could have some hearings on this, along with cost containment later this year" (Carter 2010).

27 July. "Kennedy is upset because of the time schedule and some other factors involving the national health system . . . I talked to Kennedy at length this afternoon, and he insists we send up legislation before the election. I insist it will not be sent up because the Congress members couldn't stand up under pressure from the AMA, Hospital Association, Chamber of Commerce, NAM (National Association of Manufacturers), and others and it would take months to marshal support for the plan. I'll see how much of it we can send to Kennedy's consideration late this fall" (Carter 2010).

28 July. "Kennedy had a press conference to blast us on the health care system" (Carter 2010).

Carter, 25 January 1979, *Annual Message to the Congress: The Economic Report of the President*, said, in part (Carter 1979d):

"My 1980 budget provides important building blocks for the future in many areas:
• Health programs, which I have expanded substantially during my first 2

years in office, will be maintained at those levels and in some cases increased. In addition, consistent with the development of a National Health Plan, new resources have been provided for the Child Health Assessment Program, which will extend Medicaid benefits to over 2 million low-income children. Funds have also been provided for extending Medicaid coverage to 100,000 low-income pregnant women not now eligible.

• Publicly assisted housing will be provided through subsidies for 325,000 new units for families with low or moderate incomes.

• Job-related programs will include funds that will support an average of 546,000 public service jobs, phasing down to 467,003 jobs by the end of 1980. These jobs have been targeted more tightly to serve the structurally unemployed. Another 424,000 training opportunities also will be provided for the structurally unemployed. Programs to provide employment and training opportunities for youths remain a high priority. More private sector job opportunities will be made available through the new private sector initiative and the targeted employment tax credit.

• A welfare reform program, to take effect in 1982, will expand aid to families with dependent children, increase the earned income tax credit for low-wage workers, substantially improve employment opportunities for the Nation's neediest citizens, and provide fiscal relief to State and local governments with severe welfare burdens. Important reforms in the administration of the program will make America's welfare system easier to operate.

• Aid to our cities and counties will continue to be provided through revenue sharing, community development block grants, urban mass transit assistance, and urban development action grants. My budget provides new resources for the National Development Bank and requests funding in fiscal 1979 and 1980 for a new program of special fiscal assistance to cities and counties with severe unemployment problems."

23 February 1979. "I told Joe Califano to announce that we will propose a comprehensive health plan to the public and the Congress, but we'd only move this year on the first part. He will continue consultations with liberal members of the Congress, convincing them that Kennedy's proposals would be excessively expensive and impossible to pass" (Carter 2010).

Carter, 16 March1979, stated in his *Peace Corps Memorandum From the President*, in part (Carter 1979b):

Memorandum for the Director of

ACTION, the Director of Peace Corps, the Director of the Office of Management and Budget
Subject: Establishment of the Peace Corps as an Autonomous Agency within

ACTION.

I have today signed the attached Executive order to establish the Peace Corps as an autonomous agency within ACTION. The purpose of this order is to strengthen the vitality, visibility, and independence of the Peace Corps while preserving its position as a joint venture with our domestic volunteer service programs within the framework of ACTION.

This Executive order supersedes Executive Order 11603, issued in 1971. Executive Order 11603 assigned to the ACTION Director the authority to direct the Peace Corps. The attached order delegates that authority to the Peace Corps Director.

• ACTION shall continue to be the principal agency within the Federal Government for administering volunteer service programs. The Director of ACTION shall be responsible for the coordination of programs under the Domestic Volunteer Service Act of 1973, the Peace Corps Act, and other Federal acts authorizing volunteer service programs.

• The Director of the Peace Corps shall have budgetary authority for the Peace Corps, to include responsibility for establishing and controlling a separate Peace Corps budget, subject only to ACTION policy guidance regarding coordination with domestic programs.

• The Director of Peace Corps shall direct and control the operations of the Peace Corps and such support functions as are necessary to carry out the responsibilities delegated by the Executive order. The Director of ACTION shall direct and control support functions which continue jointly to serve ACTION domestic volunteer components and Peace Corps. Decisions concerning the allocation of support functions are to be made jointly by the Peace Corps and ACTION Directors.

23 March. "Kennedy was disappointed that Califano announced our health policy without Kennedy knowing the details. He's emotional about this issue and also knowledgeable. But he's come a long way and has been more flexible than some

labor leaders and aged groups, with whom he works" (Carter 2010).

Beginning at noon on 15 May 1969, about 3,000 people appeared in Sproul Plaza at nearby UC Berkeley for a rally, the original purpose of which was to discuss the Arab–Israeli conflict. The crowd responded spontaneously, moving down Telegraph Avenue toward People's Park chanting, "We want the park!"

Governor Ronald Reagan had been publicly critical of university administrators for tolerating student demonstrations at the Berkeley campus and had received popular support for his 1966 gubernatorial campaign with a promise to crack down on what the public perceived as a generally lax attitude at California's public universities. Reagan called the Berkeley campus "a haven for communist sympathizers, protesters, and sex deviants."

At 4:30 a.m., Governor Reagan sent California Highway Patrol and Berkeley police officers into People's Park, overriding Chancellor Heyns' May 6 promise that nothing would be done without warning. Edwin Meese III, former district attorney from Alameda County, Reagan's Chief of Staff, with a reputation for firm opposition to those protesting the Vietnam War at the Oakland Induction Center and other places, assumed responsibility for the governmental response to protest, called in the Alameda County Sheriffs deputies, which brought the total police presence to 791 officers from various jurisdictions who were told to use whatever methods they chose against the crowd, approximately 6,000 people.

The deputies fired shotguns at people sitting on the roof at the Telegraph Repertory Cinema. James Rector, a student, was killed when shot by police. The buckshot was the same size as a .38 caliber bullet. Reagan conceded that Rector was probably shot by police and said, "It's very naive to assume that you should send anyone into that kind of conflict with a flyswatter."

That evening, Reagan declared a state of emergency in Berkeley and sent in 2,700 National Guard troops.

On May 20, 1969, National Guard helicopters flew over the Berkeley campus, dispensing airborne tear gas. The winds dispersed over the entire city, sending school children miles away to hospitals. This was one of the largest deployments of tear gas during the Vietnam era protests. Reagan would concede that this might have been a "tactical mistake."

In an address before the California Council of Growers, 7 April 1970, almost a year after "Bloody Thursday" he defended his decision to use the California National Guard to quell Berkeley protests: "If it takes a bloodbath, let's get it over with. No more appeasement."

Reagan's actions were used as one of the supports for his presidential bid in 1980 (Rose 2008).

12 June. "I announced a new health insurance program with Jim Corman, Charlie Rangel, Harley Staggers, Russell Long, Abe Ribicoff, Gaylord Nelson, all of whom vowed to support the proposal. Kennedy continueing his irresponsible and abusive attitude, immediately condemned our health plan. He couldn't get five votes for his, and I told Stu and Joe Califano to fight it out with him through the public news media. It's really time to do something about health care, catastrophic illness, the problem with the very poor not having health care at all, also prevention for children, prenatal to the one-year level. This kind of coverage is lacking in our country, and it's needed. We want to implement this by 1983" (Carter 2010).

12 June, Carter proposed a National Health Plan to Congress. It eventually fell through when Ted Kennedy pulled

his support from it.

On 21 June Walsh wrote, in part, in *Carter Proposes $100 Million Solar Energy Bank* (Walsh 1979):

> From the roof of the West Wing of the White House, President Carter called yesterday for creation of a $100 million solar energy bank to help move the country toward a goal of getting 20 percent of its power from the sun and other renewable sources of energy by the year 2000.
>
> "There is no longer any question that solar energy is feasible and cost effective," the president said.
>
> In his rooftop talk and in a lengthy message to Congress, Carter called for a quadrupling of energy supplied by solar power and other renewable sources of energy by the year 2000. Currently, these sources account for about 5 percent of the energy consumed in the United States, the bulk of it in the form of hydroelectric power.
>
> According to administration officials, about one-third of the 20 percent goal would come from direct solar power, with the rest coming from hydroelectric power, the conversion of waste products

into energy, the use of wind to generate power and other renewable sources of energy.

19 July 1979, Califano resigned as Secretary of HEW.

20 July 1979, Carter replaced Schlesinger as part of a broader Cabinet shakeup. According to journalist Paul Glastris, correspondent for *U.S. News & World Report*, "Carter fired Schlesinger in 1979 in part for the same reason Gerald Ford had—he was unbearably arrogant and impatient with lesser minds who disagreed with him, and hence inept at dealing with Congress."

Patricia Roberts Harris, the first African American woman to enter the Presidential line of succession, served 1977-1979, Secretary of Housing and Urban Development (HUD), then in 1979, Secretary of Health, Education, and Welfare, the largest Cabinet agency, replacing Schlesinger.

Carter, 25 July, in his fifty-first news conference, 9 p.m., the East Room at the White House, broadcast live on radio, *The President's News Conference* said about Harris (Carter 1979a):

> Q. Mr. President, does Mrs. Harris have your full approval and encouragement to continue such HEW programs as the desegregation of the North Carolina college system, the desegregation of public schools in Chicago and other cities, and the antismoking campaign? And if the answer to that question is yes, why did you fire Secretary Califano?
>
> THE PRESIDENT. The answer is yes.

I think the reasons for my replacement of the Cabinet are something that I don't care to discuss publicly. I have nothing but gratitude and admiration for the people that have served in my administration and left.

I expect Mrs. Harris to carry out the provisions of the laws of this country, to represent our Nation in the courts when suits are brought concerning equal opportunity in all its phases, and to be responsible for the health of Americans. And she will have my support just as the previous Secretary had.

I have no doubt that she will do an excellent job both in the administration of that very complicated bureaucracy-Health, Education, and Welfare—and I have no doubt that she has a basic commitment to the service of the constituent groups that are uniquely dependent upon government, particularly HEW. And I have no doubt that she will be a superb teamplayer, able to work with me, to work with the White House staff, to work with the Congress, and to work with other Cabinet members to carry out the policies of my administration, once those policies have been established by me.

Carter, 3 August, 1:17 p.m. at the ceremony in the East Room at the White House, Associate Justice of the Supreme Court Thurgood Marshall administered the oath of office, in his *Department of Health, Education, and Welfare Remarks at the Swearing In of Patricia Roberts Harris as Secretary*, said, in part (Carter 1979c):

> "When I formed my Cabinet almost 3 years ago, there was one major department in Government that had not adequately performed its function. It had been far short of its potential after 8 years of Republican administration. The Department of Housing and Urban Development was one that was formed with a clear recognition of a great need—poor were homeless, cities were destitute. They reached toward Washington with disappointment and frustration. The Department was poorly organized, and its effectiveness was severely in doubt."

> "Pat Harris came as Secretary of HUD, and with her superb management capabilities, she transformed this weak department into one of the most strong and able and effective and sensitive in government."

> "Her's has been a sterling performance as

a manager with a heart. All who know her realize that she is bold, strong, outspoken. Anyone who looks to Pat Harris as a "yes woman" would be both foolish and ill-advised. [Laughter] I have never been that foolish, and I have never been advised." [Laughter]

"She fights for her beliefs, and her beliefs are sound and she wins her fights. She has a big heart. With her background and with her experience, with her innate sensitivity and compassion, she has brought to that agency a superb record of performance. And if there's one area where my own political fortunes have been enhanced tremendously by the actions of a Cabinet officer, you could certainly not overlook the new confidence that local and State officials have in our Government, who have to deal with housing, urban development, the reconstitution, the rebuilding of our communities, and the provision of housing for those who often suffer by the lack of it."

Cutter wrote in *The Battle of the Budget* and said, in part (Cutter 1981):

President Carter's 1980 budget was tougher than that of any other Democratic president in modern history. In January 1979, he announced a budget for fiscal year 1980 of $532 billion in spending and $503 billion in receipts. The deficit of $29 billion hit the mark he had set publicly the previous November. The domestic budget fell in real terms; grants to state and local governments fell in real terms. Reductions of $600 million in Medicare and Social Security were recommended. Defense spending was proposed to grow 3 percent in real terms.

In December [1978] the Democratic party's second midterm convention was held in Memphis, Tennessee.

. . . the convention made clear that if President Carter continued to pursue his stated budget policies, he was risking major problems with an important part of the Democratic party. The party was not ready to embrace budget restraint.

12 November 1979. "I worked on the hospital cost containment [bill] in the afternoon, calling the members of Congress, many of whom have been bribed by the hospital industry. This is the worst example of a powerful special interest that I've ever seen in office" (Carter 2010).

Carter, 28 January 1980, 9:31 a.m. in the Cabinet Room at the White House, in his *Budget Message Remarks at the Signing Ceremony*, said, in part (Carter 1980a):

"We've come together this morning to have the official signing of the budget for our Nation for fiscal year 1981. I will send this document to the Congress at noon today."

". . . we have a strong commitment to energy. A major portion of the funds to be allocated for energy purposes will come from the windfall profits tax, now in the final stages of deliberation by the Congress. This money will go for increased production of energy in our country; for the alleviation of the fiscal burden on the shoulders of poor people by increasing energy costs; for research and development in the energy field; for increased transportation; and of course, in addition to that, for the conservation effort, which is greater than any this country or the world, indeed, has ever seen."

"This is a fairly stringent budget. There is no waste in it that we could possibly eliminate. It has, as one of its prime characteristics, a marked reduction in the Federal deficit. We have cut the Federal deficit since 1976 by $50 billion, and this is a budget which has the lowest deficit in 7 years. As a matter of fact, in 1976 the

percentage of our GNP covered by the
Federal deficit was 4.6 percent. This
budget encompasses a deficit of six-tenths
of 1 percent, a major reduction."

The Republican Party Convention, 14-17 July, held in The
Joe Louis Arena in Detroit, Michigan, nominated former
Governor Ronald W. Reagan of California for President and
former congressman George H. W. Bush of Texas for Vice
President. Reagan, ran on the theme "Let's Make America Great
Again."

31 July. "In preparing my own acceptance speech notes,
it's become more and more obvious that Reagan and I have
perhaps the sharpest divisions between us of any two
presidential candidates in my lifetime. Also, his policies are a
radical departure from those of Ford and Nixon" (Carter 2010).

One of Carter's assistants said: "We don't think Ted
Kennedy can win the nomination, but he can cost us the election.
He could so divide the party that it would be impossible to win
against any legitimate candidate" (Light 1983).

Democratic Party Convention, 11-14 August, held in
Madison Square Garden in New York City, nominated President
Jimmy Carter and Vice President Walter Mondale for reelection.

Carter, 14 August, 10:28 p.m., remarks were broadcast
live on radio and television, in his *Remarks Accepting the
Presidential Nomination at the 1980 Democratic National Convention
in New York* said, in part (Carter 1980b):

" . . . I have learned that the Presidency is
a place of compassion. My own heart is
burdened for the troubled Americans.
The poor and the jobless and the afflicted

– they've become part of me. My thoughts and my prayers for our hostages in Iran are as though they were my own sons and daughters."

"The life of every human being on Earth can depend on the experience and judgment and vigilance of the person in the Oval Office. The President's power for building and his power for destruction are awesome. And the power's greatest exactly where the stakes are highest— in matters of war and peace."

"And I've learned something else, something that I have come to see with extraordinary clarity: Above all, I must look ahead, because the President of the United States is the steward of the Nation's destiny. He must protect our children and the children they will have and the children of generations to follow. He must speak and act for them. That is his burden and his glory."

"And that is why a President cannot yield to the shortsighted demands, no matter how rich or powerful the special interests might be that make those demands. And that's why the President cannot bend to the passions of the moment, however popular they might be. That's why the

President must sometimes ask for sacrifice when his listeners would rather hear the promise of comfort."

"The only way to build a better future is to start with the realities of the present. But while we Democrats grapple with the real challenges of a real world, others talk about a world of tinsel and make-believe."

"Let's look for a moment at their make-believe world."

"In their fantasy America, inner-city people and farm workers and laborers do not exist. Women, like children, are to be seen but not heard. The problems of working women are simply ignored. The elderly do not need Medicare. The young do not need more help in getting a better education. Workers do not require the guarantee of a healthy and a safe place to work. In their fantasy world, all the complex global changes of the world since World War II have never happened. In their fantasy America, all problems have simple solutions — simple and wrong."

"It's a make-believe world, a world of good guys and bad guys, where some politicians shoot first and ask questions later. No hard choices, no sacrifice, no tough decisions — it sounds too good to be true, and it is."

"The path of fantasy leads to irresponsibility. The path of reality leads to hope and peace. The two paths could not be more different, nor could the futures to which they lead. Let's take a hard look at the consequences of our choice."

1 October, the Congress passed a continuing resolution, Public Law 96-369, for 1981.

Carter, 10 October, 4:55 p.m., was asked a question as he departed from the South Portico of the White House, in his *Ronald Reagan Informal Exchange With a Reporter on Departure for Camp David,* said (Carter 1980c):

Q. Mr. President, did you mean to suggest that Reagan is untrustworthy in your interview?

THE PRESIDENT. Very trustworthy.

Reagan campaigned with the slogan on his campaign poster, "Let's Make America Great Again."

4 November, Ronald Reagan, with a large majority of the electoral vote and 50.7% of the popular vote, defeated Jimmy Carter. Due to the rise of conservativism following Reagan's victory, some historians consider the election to be a realigning

election that marked the start of the "Reagan Era".

Brinkley wrote, in part (Brinkley 1988):

> It seemed impossible for Carter's team to believe that Americans would really elect a president who blamed trees for smog, who expressed doubts about evolution and favored teaching "creationism" in the public schools.

Reagan – The End of Government Oversight

Reagan, 20 January, 1981, at 12 noon from a platform erected at the West Front of the Capitol, broadcast live on radio and television, said in his *Inaugural Address*, in part (Reagan 1981a):

> "The business of our nation goes forward. These United States are confronted with an economic affliction of great proportions. We suffer from the longest and one of the worst sustained inflations in our national history. It distorts our economic decisions, penalizes thrift, and crushes the struggling young and the fixed-income elderly alike. It threatens to shatter the lives of millions of our people."

> "Idle industries have cast workers into unemployment, human misery, and personal indignity. Those who do work are denied a fair return for their labor by a tax system which penalizes successful

achievement and keeps us from maintaining full productivity."

"But great as our tax burden is, it has not kept pace with public spending. For decades we have piled deficit upon deficit, mortgaging our future and our children's future for the temporary convenience of the present. To continue this long trend is to guarantee tremendous social, cultural, political, and economic upheavals."

"It is my intention to curb the size and influence of the Federal establishment and to demand recognition of the distinction between the powers granted to the Federal Government and those reserved to the States or to the people. All of us need to be reminded that the Federal Government did not create the States; the States created the Federal Government."

"It is no coincidence that our present troubles parallel and are proportionate to the intervention and intrusion in our lives that result from unnecessary and excessive growth of government."

"In the days ahead I will propose removing the roadblocks that have slowed our economy and reduced productivity. Steps will be taken aimed at restoring the balance between the various levels of government."

Immediately after Reagan's address, he was sworn into office by Chief Justice Warren Burger.

21 January, Reagan appointed David Stockman, B.A. in History from Michigan State University (1968), graduate student studying theology at Harvard University (1968–1970), Director, The President's Office of Management and Budget.

Greider, in his article wrote, in part (Greider 1981):

> In private, Stockman agreed that his former congressional mentor, John Anderson, running as an independent candidate for President in 1980, had asked the right question: How is it possible to raise defense spending, cut income taxes, and balance the budget, all at the same time?
>
> "We've got to figure out a way to make John Anderson's question fit into a plausible policy path over the next three years," Stockman said. "Actually, it isn't all that hard to do."
>
> "The whole thing is premised on faith," Stockman explained. "On a belief about how the world works."

But liberal politics in its later stages had lost the ability to judge claims, and so yielded to all of them, Stockman thought, creating what he describes as "constituency-based choice-making," which could no longer address larger national interests, including fiscal control.

An OMB computer, programmed as a model of the nation's economic behavior, was instructed to estimate the impact of Reagan's program on the federal budget. It predicted that if the new President went ahead with his promised three-year tax reduction and his increase in defense spending, the Reagan Administration would be faced with a series of federal deficits without precedent in peacetime — ranging from $82 billion in 1982 to $116 billion in 1984. Even Stockman blinked. If those were the numbers included in President Reagan's first budget message, the following month, the financial markets that Stockman sought to reassure would instead be panicked. Interest rates, already high, would go higher; the expectation of long-term inflation would be confirmed.

Stockman saw opportunity in these shocking projections. "All the conventional estimates just wind up as mud," he said. "As absurdities. What they basically say, to boil it down, is that the world doesn't work."

Stockman set about doing two things. First, he changed the OMB computer. Assisted by like-minded supply-side economists, the new team discarded orthodox premises of how the economy would behave. Instead of a continuing double-digit inflation, the new computer model assumed a swift decline in prices and interest rates. Instead of the continuing pattern of slow economic growth, the new model was based on a dramatic surge in the nation's productivity.

The original apostles of supply-side, particularly Representative Jack Kemp, of New York, and the economist Arthur B. Laffer, dismissed budget-cutting as inconsequential to the economic problems, but Stockman was trying to fuse new theory and old. "Laffer sold us a bill of goods," he said, then corrected his words: "Laffer wasn't wrong—he didn't go far enough."

On the first Wednesday in January, Stockman had two hours on the President-elects schedule to describe the "dire shape" of the federal budget; for starters, the new administration would have to go for a budget reduction in the neighborhood of $40 billion. "Do you have any idea what $40 billion means?" he said. "It means I've got to cut the highway program. It means I've got to cut milk-price supports. And Social Security student benefits. And education and student loans. And manpower training and housing. It means I've got to shut down the synfuels program and a lot of other programs. The idea is to show the magnitude of the budget deficit and some suggestion of the political problems."

Consider the budget in simple terms, as a federal dollar representing the entire $700 billion. The most important function of the federal government is mailing checks to citizens — Social Security checks to the elderly, pension checks to retired soldiers and civil servants, reimbursement checks for hospitals and doctors who provide medical care for the aged and the poor, welfare checks for the dependent, veterans checks to pensioners. Such disbursements consume forty-eight cents of the dollar.

Another twenty-five cents goes to the Pentagon, for national defense. Stockman knew that this share would be rising in the next four years, not shrinking, perhaps becoming as high as thirty cents. Another ten cents was consumed by interest payments on the national debt, which was fast approaching a trillion dollars.

That left seventeen cents for everything else that Washington does. The FBI and the national parks, the county agents and the Foreign Service and the Weather Bureau—all the traditional operations of government—consumed only nine cents of the dollar. The remaining eight cents provided all of the grants to state and local governments, for aiding handicapped children or building highways or installing tennis courts next to Al Stockman's farm. One might denounce particular programs as wasteful, as unnecessary and ineffective, even crazy, but David Stockman knew that he could not escape these basic dimensions of federal spending.

As he and his staff went looking for the $40 billion, they found that most of it would have to be taken from the seventeen cents that covered government operations and grants-in-aid. Defense was already off-limits. Next Ronald Reagan laid down another condition for the budget-cutting: the main benefit programs of Social Security, Medicare, veterans' checks, railroad retirement pensions, welfare for the disabled—the so-called "social safety net" that Reagan had promised not to touch — were to be exempt from the budget cuts. In effect, he was declaring that Stockman could not tamper with three fourths of the forty-eight cents devoted to transfer payments.

After the budget working group reached a decision, it would be taken to Reagan in the form of a memorandum, on which he could register his approval by checking a little box. "Once he checks it," Stockman said, "I put that in my safe and I go ahead and I don't let it come back up again."

The check marks were given to changes in twelve major budget entitlements and scores of smaller ones. Eliminate Social Security minimum benefits. Cap the runaway costs of Medicaid. Tighten eligibility for food stamps. Merge the trade adjustment assistance for unemployed industrial workers with standard unemployment compensation and shrink it. Cut education aid by a quarter. Cut grants for the arts and humanities in half. "Zero out" CETA and the Community Services Administration and National Consumer Cooperative Bank.

Greider's article caused a political storm.

Stockman told Moynihan in 1985 that Reagan had acknowledged in 1981 that he wanted a huge deficit in order to force Congress to cut the social spending that Reagan felt was too costly (Jansson1997).

Stockman was quoted as saying about Johnson's Great Society programs, "Substantial parts of it will have to be heaved overboard" (Kleinknecht 2009).

The term "Laffer curve" was reportedly coined by Jude Wanniski (a writer for The Wall Street Journal) after a 1974 dinner meeting at the Two Continents Restaurant in the Washington Hotel with Arthur Laffer, Wanniski, Dick Cheney, Donald Rumsfeld, and his deputy press secretary Grace-Marie Arnett (Laffer 2004).

The Laffer Curve illustrates the basic idea that changes in tax rates have two effects on tax revenues: the arithmetic effect and the economic effect. The arithmetic effect is simply that if tax rates are lowered, tax revenues (per dollar of tax base) will be lowered by the amount of the decrease in the rate. The reverse is true for an increase in tax rates. The economic effect, however, recognizes the positive impact that lower tax rates have on work, output, and employment — and thereby the tax base — by providing incentives to increase these activities (Laffer 2004).

Reaganomics, a term created by Paul Harvey who did twice-daily, 15-minute news commentaries, from Chicago, called "Rest of the Story", referred to Ronald Reagan's ideas and economics.

Supply-side economics was promoted by the Wall St. Journal opinion editor, Robert Bartley, bachelor's degree, journalism, Iowa State University, master's degree, political science, University of Wisconsin–Madison, editor of the editorial page of *The Wall Street Journal* for more than 30 years, and his right-hand man Jude Wanniski, columnist, the *National Observer*, 1965-72, associate editor, *The Wall Street Journal*, 1972-1978. Supply-side economics states that the need is to give tax cuts to the rich, then the rich will be stimulated to work much harder and they are the ones who are most productive and that will make the economy hum again.

Reagan, 18 February, at 9 p.m. in the House Chamber, introduced by Speaker of the House, Thomas P. O'Neill, Jr., in his *Address Before a Joint Session of the Congress on the Program for Economic Recovery* said, in part (Reagan 1981b):

> " . . . I'm asking that you join me in reducing direct Federal spending by $41.4 billion in fiscal year 1982, and this goes along with another $7.7 billion in user fees and off-budget savings for a total of $49.1 billion. And this will still allow an increase of $40.8 billion over 1981 spending."

> "The Food Stamp program will be restored to its original purpose, to assist those without resources to purchase sufficient nutritional food. We will, however, save $1.8 billion in fiscal year 1982 by removing from eligibility those who are not in real need or who are

abusing the program."

"We will tighten welfare and give more attention to outside sources of income when determining the amount of welfare that an individual is allowed. This, plus strong and effective work requirements, will save $520 million in the next year."

"I stated a moment ago our intention to keep the school breakfast and lunch programs for those in true need. But by cutting back on meals for children of families who can afford to pay, the savings will be $1.6 billion in the fiscal year 1982."

". . . the Postal Service has been consistently unable to live within its operating budget. It is still dependent on large Federal subsidies. We propose reducing those subsidies by $632 million in 1982 to press the Postal Service into becoming more effective, and in subsequent years the savings will continue to add up."

"Our proposal is for a 10-percent across the-board cut every year for 3 years in the tax rates for all individual income taxpayers, making a total cut in the tax-cut rates of 30 percent. This 3-year reduction will also apply to the tax on unearned income, leading toward an eventual elimination of the present differential between the tax on earned and unearned income."

"Again, let me remind you that while this 30-percent reduction will leave the taxpayers with $500 billion more in their pockets over the next 5 years, it's actually only a reduction in the tax increase already built into the system. Unlike some past "tax reforms," this is not merely a shift of wealth between different sets of taxpayers. This proposal for an equal reduction in everyone's tax rates will expand our national prosperity, enlarge national incomes, and increase opportunities for all Americans."

Kleinknecht stated that the highest income bracket was lowered from 70 to 50% (Kleinknecht 2009).

27 February, CSA's Acting Director, resigned.

With the resignation, no one had been designated to act in the capacity of Director so the agency was without leadership for several months. Thus the actions taken from this time until September to close CSA and implement a transition to a block grant approach for providing community services were operated by any plan agreed upon by all participating agencies. However, had the Congress provided a more reasonable amount of time for CSA to complete its activities, the closeout might have been done in a more orderly and efficient manner

(GAO 1981).

Reagan felt that governmental programs actually aggravated the problems of the poor, furthering trapping them in a cycle of dependency and poverty. He felt that the poor desired their way of life and no aid could help them. He made large cuts in the budget for food stamps, loans for students, jobs in public service, welfare, lunches for schoolchildren, mas transit in urban centers, and training programs (Aksamit 2014). The official policy eventually emphasized what it could not accomplish and how doing things for the poor could be counterproductive (Danziger 1986).

In the 1960's when Reagan was giving speeches to gain national attention, he declared: the progressive income tax was a Marxist tool creating a socialist state, calling mandatory an unfair restraint on those who could make better provisions for themselves" (Dallek 1984).

The time permitted by the legislation to close out CSA and implement the Community Services Block Grant program was 48 calendar days. CSA identified the following things that would be required for this to be accomplished: 200 tasks involving its headquarters, 10 regional offices, and 1,500 personnel. The interagency team, representatives from the White House's Office of Policy Development, the Office of Management and Budget, and the Department of Energy, said that planning for the closure of CSA could proceed, but that actual termination could not be initiated until the block grant affecting CSA was enacted (GAO 1981).

18 March, the new Director of OMB sent a memorandum to the Director of CSA with instructions to "begin now to plan carefully for the resolution of your agency's activities."

Ronald Smothers, 11 April, in his article in *The New York Times* wrote, in part (Smothers 1981):

It is the public service aspect that the Reagan Administration proposes to cut back this year by $153 million and to eliminate entirely in 1982 by withdrawing $3.1 billion that had been proposed for it by President Carter. The act is administered by the Department of Labor.

This year's cutback meant that many of the 310,000 CETA-paid workers in local government and community organization jobs around the country were laid off last week while others may keep their jobs until Sept. 30. In New York City, 11,500 people hold jobs under this program that could be abolished as early as June 30 unless the city uses its own money to pay them.

A study by the National Association of Counties found that, of 340,261 public service employees who entered that program from October 1979 to June 1980, 142,537, or 42 percent, had moved by last October into jobs in the public or private sector that were not paid for by Federal funds.

Reagan, 27 April, stated, in part, in his *Message to the Congress Reporting Budget Rescissions and Deferrals* (Reagan 1981c):

To the Congress of the United States:

In accordance with the Impoundment Control Act of 1974, I herewith report six revisions to previously transmitted rescission proposals. Three of the revisions decrease the total amount proposed for rescission by $3.7 million. The other revisions to proposed rescissions make technical changes to appropriation language which do not affect the amounts proposed for rescission. In addition, I am reporting two new deferrals totaling $6.4 million and revisions to five previously reported deferrals.

The revisions to rescission proposals affect programs in the Departments of Agriculture and Energy, as well as ACTION and the National Science Foundation. The new deferrals and revisions to existing deferrals involve programs in the Departments of Agriculture, Commerce, Energy, Health and Human Services, and Transportation, as well as the Board for International Broadcasting and the International Communication Agency.

1 May, President Reagan announced his intention to nominate a Director of CSA. The nomination was received by

the Senate, 29 May, with confirmation, 25 June (GAO 1981). The new director, Dwight Albert Ink, was sworn in 30 June, with a charge to close the agency by September 30.

Dwight Albert Ink, a career public servant, an Iowa State alumnus (1947) served a number of federal government agencies under seven presidential administrations and held positions at American University and the Institute for Public Administration as well. Ink also served on government-wide groups such as the Alaskan Reconstruction Committee and the Personnel Management Project (Iowa State University n.d.).

By June 30, there were 657 overdue audits, for grants totaling $363 million, which CSA program managers had not obtained. Earlier in the month, Congress had passed a Continuing Resolution which included funding CSA operations through September 30 with no provisions to permit use of the 1981 appropriations to begin the transition into the Social Services Block Grant program or to fund the closure of CSA (GAO 1981).

James H. Burnley 4th was named Director Volunteers in Service (1981-1982). He was known for being for being strong-willed, aggressive and, at times, stubborn (Williams 1987). He exemplified "the legion of ambitious, inexperienced and idealistic young conservatives who fanned out through the Government spreading Mr. Reagan's message on such issues as deregulation, returning Federal responsibility to the states and turning over Government operations to private industry" (Johnston 1988). His job was to dismantle the agency aided by Mark Levin, and Tom Pauken, both original Reaganites (Shirley and Cannon 1981). Burnley stated "I am working as hard as I can to be the last director of VISTA" (Clark 2002).

Paukin was named Director of the ACTION agency. He reduced the staff from 1,000 to 500 and the budget was reduced

25%, from $160 million to $120 million.

Levin was Chief of Staff for Attorney General Edwin Meese. Meese also served as a liaison to the conservative evangelical community, arranging for meetings between social-conservative leaders and the president.

July 2, 2 days after his swearing in, Ink wrote to OMB concerning the cost of closing out CSA's activities stating that he felt that the total cost would be higher than earlier anticipated (GAO 1981).

August 13, 1981, the Omnibus Budget Reconciliation Act of 1981 (95 Stat. 519) was enacted into law. It created the Community Services Block Grant program, Subtitle B of Title VI, which provided that the Secretary of Health and Human Services (HHS) would administer block grants through the Office of Community Services, a new unit established by the law. This replaced the Community Services Administration whose closure was to be effective 30 September with the block grants to begin 1 October (GAO 1981).

Rather than following the usual policy of allowing Federal employees to transfer into other programs, about 1,000 were fired. The new office, Community Services, had about 30 staff for the transition and regular operations (Masters 2014).

The Omnibus Reconciliation Act of 1981 also amended title XX of the Social Security Act establishing the Social Services Block Grant (SSBG) to allocate funds to States/Territories to support social services for vulnerable children, adults, and families. The recipients have broad discretion in which specific services they support with the funds, funds that may be tailored over time to changes in the needs of their populations.

Social services funded by States/Territories must be linked to one or more of the statutory goals:

Achieve or maintain economic self-support to prevent,

reduce, or eliminate dependency;

Achieve or maintain self-sufficiency, including reduction or prevention of dependency;

Prevent or remedy neglect, abuse, or exploitation of children and adults unable to protect their own interests or preserve, rehabilitate, or reunite families;

Prevent or reduce inappropriate institutional care by providing for community-based care, home-based care, or other forms of less intensive care; and

Secure referral or admission for institutional care when other forms of care are not appropriate, or providing services to individuals in institutions.

Richard S. Schweiker, (R), considered a moderate to liberal Republican, was a member of the House (1960-1968), the Senate (1968-1981), became the Secretary of HHS (1981–1983).

August 14, the HHS Office of Human Development Services was assigned responsibility for administering the implementation of the Community Services Block Grant program with no responsibilities related to the closeout of CSA (GAO 1981).

Hinds wrote, 12 November, *Decision File; Solar Bank Now Open*, in *The New York Times*, and said, in part (Hinds 1982):

> The Solar Bank, originally conceived by the Carter Administration as a $3 billion project to subsidize consumer loans for installation of solar energy systems, has finally opened its doors. But it took a court order to put it in business.
>
> The bank, which is part of the

Department of Housing and Urban Development, has a staff of six, a budget of $21 million and a policy forbidding loans for most mechanical solar heating systems. By early next year, it hopes to be subsidizing loans, primarily for weatherizing homes.

The Reagan Administration, which opposes subsidies for such conservation programs, had wanted nothing to do with Mr. Carter's solar bank and refused to organize it for about 18 months. So a coalition of Government officials and consumer groups, led by the Solar Lobby, took the matter to United States District Court in New York.

The bank was mandated by law, and Congress already had appropriated money to finance it, they argued. The President, they added, was obligated to execute the law.

The court agreed. '"We feel there were better ways of encouraging investment in conservation," said Richard Francis, the comptroller of the new bank. "It would have been much more effective and efficient to distribute the money through tax credits or another existing Federal agency."

August 25, HHS notified the governors of the 50 States about the Community Services Block Grant program and requested that each State notify the appropriate HHS regional office by September 11 as to whether the State wanted to administer the block grant program for fiscal year 1982 (GAO 1981).

September 5, the Director of OMB notified the Secretary of HHS and the Director of CSA that HHS would provide needed services, grantee management and grantee closeout, to CSA grantees until the current grant funds were expended, a task which OMB estimated would take 90 staff years and about a funding of $4.6 million (GAO 1981).

On December 23, 1981, the HUD Appropriation Act was enacted. It provided $23 million for the Bank which would remain available until September 30, 1983. The Office of Management and Budget (OMB) then reduced the appropriation by 5 percent, or $1.15 million, under section 501 of the appropriation act. This left an appropriation of $21.85 million for the Bank (Comptroller General of the United States 1982).

Reagan, 25 January 1983, in his *Address Before a Joint Session of the Congress on the State of the Union,* at 9:03 p.m. in the House Chamber of the Capitol, broadcast live on nationwide radio and televison, said, in part:

> The problems we inherited were far worse than most inside and out of government had expected; the recession was deeper than most inside and out of government had predicted. Curing those problems has taken more time and a higher toll than any of us wanted. Unemployment is far too high. Projected

Federal spending — if government refuses to tighten its own belt – will also be far too high and could weaken and shorten the economic recovery now underway.

The Federal budget is both a symptom and a cause of our economic problems. Unless we reduce the dangerous growth rate in government spending, we could face the prospect of sluggish economic growth into the indefinite future. Failure to cope with this problem now could mean as much as a trillion dollars more in national debt in the next 4 years alone. That would average $4,300 in additional debt for every man, woman, child, and baby in our nation.

To assure a sustained recovery, we must continue getting runaway spending under control to bring those deficits down. If we don't, the recovery will be too short, unemployment will remain too high, and we will leave an unconscionable burden of national debt for our children. That we must not do.

Let's be clear about where the deficit problem comes from. Contrary to the drumbeat we've been hearing for the last few months, the deficits we face are not rooted in defense spending. Taken as a percentage of the gross national product, our defense spending happens to be only about four-fifths of what it was in 1970. Nor is the deficit, as some would have it, rooted in tax cuts. Even with our tax cuts, taxes as a fraction of gross national product remain about the same as they were in 1970. The fact is, our deficits come from the uncontrolled growth of the budget for domestic spending.

I will request that the proposed 6-month freeze in cost-of-living adjustments recommended by the bipartisan Social Security Commission be applied to other government-related retirement programs. I will, also, propose a 1-year freeze on a broad range of domestic spending programs, and for Federal civilian and military pay and pension programs. And let me say right here, I'm sorry, with regard to the military, in asking that of them, because for so many years they have been so far behind and so low in reward for what the men and women in uniform are doing. But I'm sure they will understand that this must be across the board and fair.

Second, I will ask the Congress to adopt specific measures to control the growth of the so-called uncontrollable spending programs. These are the automatic spending programs, such as food stamps, that cannot be simply frozen and that have grown by over 400 percent since 1970. They are the largest single cause of the built-in or structural deficit problem. Our standard here will be fairness, ensuring that the taxpayers' hard-earned dollars go only to the truly needy; that none of them are turned away, but that fraud and waste are stamped out. And I'm sorry to say, there's a lot of it out there. In the food stamp program alone, last year, we identified almost [$]1.1 billion in overpayments. The taxpayers aren't the only victims of this kind of abuse. The truly needy suffer as funds intended for them are taken not by the needy, but by the greedy. For everyone's sake, we must put an end to such waste and corruption.

In 1983 we seek four major education goals: a quality education initiative to encourage a substantial upgrading of math and science instruction through block grants to the States; establishment of education savings accounts that will give middle and lower-income families an incentive to save for their children's college education and, at the same time, encourage a real increase in savings for economic growth; passage of tuition tax credits for parents who want to send their children to private or religiously affiliated schools; a constitutional amendment to permit voluntary school prayer. God should never have been expelled from America's classrooms in the first place.

Over the past year, our Task Force on Private Sector Initiatives has successfully forged a working partnership involving leaders of business, labor, education, and government to address the training needs of American workers. Thanks to the Task Force, private sector initiatives are now underway in all 50 States of the Union, and thousands of working people have been helped in making the shift from dead-end jobs and low-demand skills to the growth areas of high technology and the service economy. Additionally, a major effort will be focused on encouraging the expansion of private community child care. The new advisory council on private sector initiatives will carry on and extend this vital work of encouraging private initiative in 1983.

By 1983, Reagan's White House advisors had given up trying to change his mind on major policy issues. He was focused along with lower social spending on the belief that lower taxes were required to shrunk the size of government while at the same creating greater military strength to face down the Russians was necessary (Dallek 1984). At the same time the evangelical campaign to banish waste, fraud, and abuse from federal program no longer dominated conversations about the economy (Reagan, Donald T. 1983).

15 April, 1989, Louis W. Sullivan, M.D., Secretary HHS, stated "to place greater emphasis and greater focus on the needs of America's children and families" created the Administration for Children and Families, holding Head Start, Job Opportunities and Basic Skills, Aid to Families with Dependent Children, Child Support Enforcement, Adoption Assistance, Foster Care, Social Services Black Grant, Child Care and Development Block Grant, and the child abuse programs, with Jo Anne B. Barnhart, Assistant Secretary.

> And here is the end of our story. There are still many programs throughout the United States that are direct offspring of the many attempts to provides services to the poor and other populations requiring help. But the stated purpose of all these pages has been met, i.e., the history of the War on Poverty, from its beginning to its ignoble end.

Final Comments

Throughout this history, from start to where it ended, one of the things that recurs over and over, is this: mythological thinking.

It began with "maximum feasible participation," the idea that is some manner, undefined, and not really thought about, that by placing such a term inside program operations that "the poor" would automatically gain a place at the table. That the term would automatically give the poor a voice in planning and implementing the programs affecting them, giving them a real voice in their institutions (as Ted Kennedy stated in 1964).

There was "Revenue Sharing" which would, somehow, make local officials respond to local conditions and local constituencies who will decide what should happen, that Revenue Sharing would close the gap between promise and performance (a Nixon scheme with as much lack of oversight in the operation of the proposed program as was given to "Maximum feasible participation").

David Stockman (Reagan's Director of OMB) who felt that economic policy was "premised on faith, on a belief about how the world works."

And, as a final illustration, "We propose reducing these subsidies by $632 million in 1981 to press the Postal Service into becoming more effective, and in subsequent years the saving will continue to add up" (Reagan 1982).

I would submit that mythological thinking occurs on the part of governmental policy makers and politicians at all levels, city, towns, counties, States, National Government, as well as most of the citizens of this county or any where else, it is alive and well and very active indeed. Of course this is so. It is always easier to "believe" than to "think."

Well, end of the editorial! The unhappy folk can always send an e_mail :)

Rose (2008) summarized the history of the War On Poverty this way:

> Although the War on Poverty had minimal economic success, the poverty programs did reach people. Even in 2008, programs like Head Start continue to make a difference in the lives of the urban and rural poor. Free lunch programs for children in schools still exist. Financial aid for college students is still in effect, as are various volunteer programs. The War on Poverty helped the poor to realize that they were no longer an invisible entity within the nation but could make a difference in . . .politics . . . and the lives of their families, a legacy that lives on today.

Tom Paine wrote in *The Rights of Man* (1791-1792) that:

> When it shall be said in any country in the world, my poor are happy;

neither ignorance nor distress is to be found among them; my jails are empty of prisoners, my streets of beggars; the aged are not in want, the taxes are not oppressive . . . when these things can be said, then may that country boast its constitution and its government.

Tyranny, like hell, is not easily conquered; yet we have this consolation with us, that the harder the conflict, the more glorious the triumph. What we obtain too cheap, we esteem too lightly; it is dearness only that gives everything its value (quoted in Lapham 2017).

References

Aaron, Henry J.

    1973   *Why Is Welfare So Hard to Reform?* The Brookings Institution: Washington, D.C.

Abransky, Sasha

    2014   "The Battle Hymn of the War on Poverty." In, *The Nation*, January 15, 2014.

Adler, George

    1994   "Community Action and Maximum Feasible Participation: An Opportunity Lost But Not Forgotten for Expanding Democracy at Home." In, *Notre Dame Journal of Law, Ethics & Public Policy*, Vol. 8, Article 6, Issue 2, *Symposium on Voice in Government*.

Ahart, Gregory J.

    1969   "GAO Review of the Economic Opportunity." In, *The GAO Review. Summer.* U.S. General Accounting Office: Washington, D.C.

Aksamit, Daniel Victor

    2014   *"Absolutely Sort of Normal": The Common Origins of the War on Poverty At Home and Abroad, 1961-1965.* A Dissertation submitted in partial fulfillment for the requirements for the degree Doctor of Philosophy, Department of History, College of

Arts and Sciences. Kansas State University: Manhattan, Kansas.

Anon
    1965   "Poverty War Out of Hand?" In, *U.S. News and World Report* (August 23, 1965).
    1968   "Nixon Gives Moynihan Urban Affairs Position." In, *The Harvard Crimson*, December 11, 1968.

Arizona Republic
    1970   *Fired Officials Charge OEO "Run By Bigots."* Sunday, 22 November 1970. Phoenix, Arizona.

Arnstein, Sherry R.
    1969   "A Ladder of Citizen Participation." In, *Journal of the American Institute of Planners,* Vol. 35, No. 4, pp. 216-224.

ASPE
    2000   Reasons for Measuring Poverty in the United States in the Context of Public Policy–A Historical Review, 1916-1995. The Period Leading Up to the War on Poverty. 06/01/2000. Office of the Assistant Secretary of Planning And Evaluation. Http://apse.gov/report.

Augenbraun, Eric
    2009   "Protest To Preparation: The Very Different Histories of Community Action and the Opportunities Industrial Centers in Philadelphia's War on Poverty." In, *Penn History Review*, Vol. 17,

Issue 1, Fall 2009, Article 5.

Bae, Lena
  2011 "Why You've Never Heard of Community Action: Civic Participation and Poverty." In, *Harvard Political Review*, harvardpolitics.com

Bailey, Martha J, and Nicolas J. Duquette
  2014 "How John Fought the War on Poverty: The Economics and Politics of Funding at the Office of Economic Opportunity." In, *J Econ Hist*. 2014 June 74(2): 351-388.

Baum, Dan
  2016 "Legalize It All. How to win the war on drugs." In, *Harper's Magazine*, 2016 April.

Bennett, Michael, and Cruz Reynoso
  1972 "California Rural Legal Assistance (CRLA): Survival of a Poverty Law Practice." In, *Chicano Law Review*, Vol. 1 No. 1

Bonamo, Mark J.
  2006 "Hudson County's culture of corruption its local roots and prospects for change." In, *Hudson Reporter.com*, October 25, 2006.

Bookbinder, Hyman
  1957 "It's Official." In, *The New Republic, A Journal of Opinion*, Correspondence, Vol. 156, No. 15, Issue 2733, April 15, 1967.

Brinkley, Douglas

    1988   *The Unfinished Presidency.* Viking Adult: New York.

Britten, Thomas A.

    2017   "Urban American Indian Centers in the late 1960s-1970s: An Examination of their Function and Purpose Indigenous Policy." In, *Indigenous Policy Journal* Vol. XXVII, No. 3 (Winter 2017)

Brisbon, Lauren D.

    2015   *The Social Activism and Theology of Adam Clayton Powell, Jr.* Ph.D. Dissertation, Humanities Doctoral Program and Department of African American Studies, Africana Women's Studies, and History. Clark Atlanta University. Atlanta, Georgia.

Cahn, Edgar S., and Jean C. Cahn

    1964   "The War on Poverty: A Civilian Perspective." In, *The Yale Law Journal*, Vol. 73, No. 8 (Jul., 1964), pp. 1317-1352

Cannon, William B.

    1985   "Enlightened Localism: A Narrative Account of Poverty and Education in the Great Society." In, *Yale Law & Policy Review*, Vol. 4, Issue 1, Article 3.

Carter, Jimmy

    1977a "Inaugural Address." January 20, 1977. Online by Gerhard Peters and John T. Woolley, The American Presidency Project.

http://www.presidency.ucsb.edu/ws/?pid=6575.

1977b "Economic Recovery Program - Message to the Congress." January 31, 1977. Online by Gerhard Peters and John T. Woolley, The American Presidency Project.
http://www.presidency.ucsb.edu/ws/?pid=7344.

1977c "Memorandum to the Heads of Certain Departments on Urban and Regional Development Policies." March 21, 1977. Online by Gerhard Peters and John T. Woolley, The American Presidency Project.
http://www.presidency.ucsb.edu/ws/?pid=7219.

1977d "Secretary of Energy Remarks at the Swearing In of James R. Schlesinger." August 5, 1977. Online by Gerhard Peters and John T. Woolley, The American Presidency Project.
http://www.presidency.ucsb.edu/ws/?pid=7940.

1977e "Welfare Reform Message to the Congress." August 6, 1977. Online by Gerhard Peters and John T. Woolley, The American Presidency Project.
http://www.presidency.ucsb.edu/ws/?pid=7942.

1977f "Memorandum for the Heads of Executive Departments and Agencies on Government Reorganization." August 11, 1977. Online by Gerhard Peters and John T. Woolley, The American Presidency Project.
http://www.presidency.ucsb.edu/ws/?pid=7950.

1977g "Memorandum for the Heads of Executive Departments and Agencies on Advisory Committee Review." August 22, 1977. Online by Gerhard Peters and John T. Woolley, The

American Presidency Project.
http://www.presidency.ucsb.edu/ws/?pid=7990.

1977h "Labor-HEW Continuing Appropriations Bill
Statement on Signing H.J. Res. 662 Into Law."
December 9, 1977. Online by Gerhard Peters and
John T. Woolley, The American Presidency
Project.
http://www.presidency.ucsb.edu/ws/?pid=7000.

1978a "The President's News Conference." June 26,
1978. Online by Gerhard Peters and John T.
Woolley, The American Presidency Project.
http://www.presidency.ucsb.edu/ws/?pid=30999.

1979a "The President's News Conference." July 25,
1979. Online by Gerhard Peters and John T.
Woolley, The American Presidency Project.
http://www.presidency.ucsb.edu/ws/?pid=32653.

1979b "Peace Corps Memorandum From the
President." May 16, 1979. Online by Gerhard
Peters and John T. Woolley, The American
Presidency Project.
http://www.presidency.ucsb.edu/ws/?pid=32353.

1979c "Department of Health, Education, and Welfare
Remarks at the Swearing In of Patricia Roberts
Harris as Secretary." August 3, 1979. Online by
Gerhard Peters and John T. Woolley, The
American Presidency Project.
http://www.presidency.ucsb.edu/ws/?pid=32699.

1979d "Annual Message to the Congress: The
Economic Report of the President." January 25,
1979. Online by Gerhard Peters and John T.
Woolley, The American Presidency Project.
http://www.presidency.ucsb.edu/ws/?pid=32712.

1980a "Budget Message Remarks at the Signing Ceremony." January 28, 1980. Online by Gerhard Peters and John T. Woolley, The American Presidency Project. http://www.presidency.ucsb.edu/ws/?pid=32850.

1980b "Remarks Accepting the Presidential Nomination at the 1980 Democratic National Convention in New York." August 14, 1980. Online by Gerhard Peters and John T. Woolley, The American Presidency Project. http://www.presidency.ucsb.edu/ws/?pid=44909.

1980c "Ronald Reagan Informal Exchange With a Reporter on Departure for Camp David." October 10, 1980. Online by Gerhard Peters and John T. Woolley, The American Presidency Project. http://www.presidency.ucsb.edu/ws/?pid=45255.

2010 White House Diary. Farrar, Straus and Giroux: New York.

Cazenave, Noel A.
2007 *Impossible Democracy: The Unlikely Success of the War on Poverty Community Action Programs*. State University of New York Press: Albany, New York.

Clark, Robert F.
2000 *Maximum Feasible Success. A History of the Community Action Program*. National Association of Community Action Agencies: Washington, D.C.

2002 *The War on Poverty. History, Selected Programs and*

Ongoing Impact. University Press of America, Inc. New York.

Comptroller General of the United States
1982   Letter to The Honorable Richard L. Ottinger Chairman, Subcommittee on Energy, Conservation and Power, Committee on Energy and Commerce, House of Representatives, May 1, 1982.

Conference On Economic Progress
1962   "Poverty and Deprivation." In, *The U.S. The Plight of Two-fifths Of A Nation.* Study directed by Leon H. Keyserling, with assistance of Mary Dublin Keyserling, Lawrence A. Leonard, Philip M. Ritz, and Nettie S. Shapiro. Conference On Economic Progress: Washington, D.C.

Congressional Quarterly
1974   President Ford: The Man and his Record. August, 1974. In, *Congressional Quarterly, Inc.*: Washington, D.C.

Congressional Record
1967(a)   Senate, Wednesday, August 16, 1967.
1967(b)   House, Congressional Record, November 13, 1967

Coontz, Stephanie
1997   *The Way We Really Are. Coming To Terms With America's Changing Families.* Basic Books: New York.

Cordes, Sam M.

    1989   "The Changing Rural Environment and the Relationship between Health Services and Rural Development." In, *Health Services Research*, 23:6 (February 1989).

Cohen, Nathan E.

    1965   "A National Program for the Improvement of Welfare Services and the Reduction of Welfare Dependency." In, *Poverty In America* (1965). Margaret S. Gordon, Editor. Pp. 278-298.

CQ Almanac

    1969a "Congress Extends Anti-poverty Program for Two Years." In, *CQ Almanac 1969*, 25th ed., pp 485-98. Congressional Quarterly, 1970: Washington, D.C.

    1969b "OEO Legal Services." In, *CQ Almanac 1970*, 26th ed., 10-774. Washington, DC: Congressional Quarterly, 1971.

    1971   "Major Senate and House Votes During 1971 session." In, *CQ Almanac 1971*, 27th ed., 05-64-05-74. Washington, DC: Congressional Quarterly, 1972. http://library.cqpress.com/cqalmanac/cqal71-1252558.

    1974   "Congress Wins Restrictions on AID to Turkey." In, *CQ Almanac 1974*, 30th ed., 547-53. Washington, DC: Congressional Quarterly, 1975. http://library.cqpress.com/cqalmanac/cqal74-1221392.

(CSA) Community Services Administration

    1966   Organizational Manual, dated July 16, 1976.

    [1969] The Office of Economic Opportunity During the
        Administration of President Lyndon B. Johnson.
        November 1963 - January 1969. Vol. I -
        Administrative History. Part I. Acting Deputy
        Director Robert Perrin - supervision, Herbert
        Kramer - direction, Bennet Schiff - General
        Editor, Bennet Schiff and Stephen Goodell -
        writers, James F. Donnelly and Mary Jo Kelly -
        Research Assistants, Pamela Hebson and
        Florence Johnston - Secretaries. Community
        Services Administration: Washington, D.C. LBJ
        Library, The University of Texas at Austin,
        Texas.

Cutter, W. Bowman

    1981   "The Battle of the Budget." In, *The Atlantic
        Monthly*, March 1981.

Dallek, Robert

    1984   *Ronald Reagan: The Politics of Symbolism.* Harvard
        University Press: Cambridge, Massachusetts.

Danziger, Sheldon H., and, Daniel H. Weinberg

    1986   "Introduction," In, *Fighting Poverty. What Works
        and What Doesn't.* Harvard University Press:
        Cambridge, Massachusetts.

Davidson, Robert H.

    1969   "The War on Poverty: Experiment in
        Federalism." In, *Evaluating the War of Poverty,*

*The Annals of the American Academy of Political
and Social Science,* Vol. 385, September, pp. 1-13.

Duncan, Ottis Dudley
    1969   *Inheritance of Poverty or Inheritance of Race? In,
           Perspectives on Poverty I. On Understanding
           Poverty. Perspectives From the Social Sciences.*
           Daniel P. Moynihan, Editor.

Duncan, Otis Dudley, and, David L. Featherman, Beverly
Duncan
    1968   Socioeconomic Background and Occupational
           Achievement: Extensions Of A Basic Model.
           Final Report. Project No. 5-0074 (EO-191)
           Contract No. OE-5-85-072. Office of Education.
           Bureau of Research. U.S. Department of Health,
           Education, and Welfare.

Economic Opportunity Act of 1964, As Amend.(P.L. 88-452).
           U.S. Government Printing Office, 12-1-65.
Economic Opportunity Amendments of 1967 (P.L. 90-222).
           U.S. Government Printing Office, O - 67.

Ford Foundation
    1966   To Advance Human Welfare. *Annual Report.*
           October 1, 1965 to September 30, 1966.
    1973   *Community Development Corporation: A Strategy
           for Depressed Urban and Rural Areas.*

Ford, Gerald R.
    1974a "Memorandums on the Transition of the
           Presidency." August 10, 1974. Online by

Gerhard Peters and John T. Woolley, The American Presidency Project. http://www.presidency.ucsb.edu/ws/?pid=4631.

1974b "Proclamation 4311—Granting Pardon to Richard Nixon." September 8, 1974. Online by Gerhard Peters and John T. Woolley, The American Presidency Project. http://www.presidency.ucsb.edu/ws/?pid=4696.

1974c "Remarks on Intention To Nominate Nelson A. Rockefeller To Be Vice President of the United States.," August 20, 1974. Online by Gerhard Peters and John T. Woolley, The American Presidency Project. http://www.presidency.ucsb.edu/ws/?pid=4487.

1974d "The President's News Conference." August 28, 1974. Online by Gerhard Peters and John T. Woolley, The American Presidency Project. http://www.presidency.ucsb.edu/ws/?pid=4671.

1974e "Statement on House Action To Suspend United States Military Assistance to Turkey." October 8, 1974. Online by Gerhard Peters and John T. Woolley, The American Presidency Project. http://www.presidency.ucsb.edu/ws/?pid=4433.

1974f "The President's News Conference. October 9, 1974. Online by Gerhard Peters and John T. Woolley, The American Presidency Project. http://www.presidency.ucsb.edu/ws/?pid=4440.

1974g "Memorandum on Fiscal Year 1975 Budget Cuts." October 10, 1974. Online by Gerhard Peters and John T. Woolley, The American Presidency Project. http://www.presidency.ucsb.edu/ws/?pid=4446.

1974h "Remarks on Signing Veto of Continuing Appropriations Resolution Containing an Amendment Suspending Military Aid to Turkey." October 14, 1974. Online by Gerhard Peters and John T. Woolley, The American Presidency Project. http://www.presidency.ucsb.edu/ws/?pid=4459.

1974i Veto of Second Continuing Appropriations Resolution Providing for Suspension of Military Aid to Turkey." October 17, 1974. Online by Gerhard Peters and John T. Woolley, The American Presidency Project. http://www.presidency.ucsb.edu/ws/?pid=4472.

1974j Statement on Signing the Continuing Appropriations Resolution." October 18, 1974. Online by Gerhard Peters and John T. Woolley, The American Presidency Project. http://www.presidency.ucsb.edu/ws/?pid=4481

1974k "Address to a Joint Session of the Congress." August 12, 1974. Online by Gerhard Peters and John T. Woolley, The American Presidency Project. http://www.presidency.ucsb.edu/ws/?pid=4694.

1975a "Statement on Signing the Headstart, Economic Opportunity, and Community Partnership Act of 1974.." January 4, 1975. Online by Gerhard Peters and John T. Woolley, The American Presidency Project. http://www.presidency.ucsb.edu/ws/?pid=4761.

1975b "Address Before a Joint Session of the Congress Reporting on the State of the Union." January 15, 1975. Online by Gerhard Peters and John T.

Woolley, The American Presidency Project.
http://www.presidency.ucsb.edu/ws/?pid=4938.

1975c "Remarks at the White House Conference on
Domestic and Economic Affairs in San Diego,
California." April 3, 1975. Online by Gerhard
Peters and John T. Woolley, The American
Presidency Project.
http://www.presidency.ucsb.edu/ws/?pid=4813.

1975d "Special Message to the Congress Reporting on
Budget Rescissions and Deferrals." May 8, 1975.
Online by Gerhard Peters and John T. Woolley,
The American Presidency Project.
http://www.presidency.ucsb.edu/ws/?pid=4903.

1975e "Remarks at the Swearing In of Daniel P.
Moynihan as United States Representative to the
United Nations." June 30, 1975. Online by
Gerhard Peters and John T. Woolley, The
American Presidency Project.
http://www.presidency.ucsb.edu/ws/?pid=5033.

1975f "Remarks Announcing Candidacy for the 1976
Republican Presidential Nomination." July 8,
1975. Online by Gerhard Peters and John T.
Woolley, The American Presidency Project.
http://www.presidency.ucsb.edu/ws/?pid=5056.

1975g "Veto of the Departments of Labor and Health,
Education, and Welfare Appropriation Act,
1976." December 19, 1975. Online by Gerhard
Peters and John T. Woolley, The American
Presidency Project.
http://www.presidency.ucsb.edu/ws/?pid=5446.

1976a "Annual Budget Message to the Congress,
Fiscal Year 1977." January 21, 1976. Online by

Gerhard Peters and John T. Woolley, The
American Presidency Project.
http://www.presidency.ucsb.edu/ws/?pid=5711.

1976b "Letter Accepting the Resignation of
Ambassador Daniel Patrick Moynihan, United
States Representative to the United Nations."
February 2, 1976. Online by Gerhard Peters and
John T. Woolley, The American Presidency
Project.
http://www.presidency.ucsb.edu/ws/?pid=6066.

1976c "Remarks at a News Briefing on General
Revenue Sharing." February 3, 1976. Online by
Gerhard Peters and John T. Woolley, The
American Presidency Project.
http://www.presidency.ucsb.edu/ws/?pid=6099.

1976d "Remarks at the Winter Meeting of the National
Governors' Conference." February 23, 1976.
Online by Gerhard Peters and John T. Woolley,
The American Presidency Project.
http://www.presidency.ucsb.edu/ws/?pid=5607.

1976e "Special Message to the Congress Urging
Enactment of Proposed Community Services
Legislation." February 23, 1976. Online by
Gerhard Peters and John T. Woolley, The
American Presidency Project.
http://www.presidency.ucsb.edu/ws/?pid=5608.

1976f "Remarks at the Swearing In of Samuel R.
Martinez as Director of the Community Services
Administration." April 15, 1976. Online by
Gerhard Peters and John T. Woolley, The
American Presidency Project.
http://www.presidency.ucsb.edu/ws/?pid=5848.

1976g   "Special Message to the Congress Reporting on a Budget Rescission." July 29, 1976. Online by Gerhard Peters and John T. Woolley, The American Presidency Project. http://www.presidency.ucsb.edu/ws/?pid=6242.

1976h   "Veto of the Appropriations Bill for the Departments of Labor and Health, Education, and Welfare." September 29, 1976. Online by Gerhard Peters and John T. Woolley, The American Presidency Project. http://www.presidency.ucsb.edu/ws/?pid=6388.

Frank, Thomas

    2008   *The Wrecking Crew: How Conservatives Rule.* Metropolitan Books: New York.

Gans, Herbert J

    1964   "The Poverty Problem." In, *Commentary Magazine,* July 1, 1964.

GAO

    1972   Charges of Improper Practices Regarding Two Contracts Between The Office of Economic Opportunity and Booz, Allen and Hamilton, Inc. Office of Economic Opportunity. By The Controller General of The United States. United States General Accounting Office: Washington, D.C.

    1981   Statement of Morton E. Henig, Associate Director, Human Resources Division Before the House Subcommittee On Manpower and Housing On the Closure Of the Community Services

Administration and Implementation Of the Community Services Block Grant Program. United States General Accounting Office: Washington, D.C.

1982   Statement of Morton E. Henig, Associate Director, Human Resources Division Before the House Subcommittee on Manpower and Housing On the Closure of the Community Services Administration and Implementation of the Community. United States General Accounting Office: Washington, D.C.

Garza, Lorenzo

1969   *The Local Administration Of the War On Poverty With the Maximum Feasible Participation of the Poor; Its Problems and Prospects: Community Action Program.* Thesis. Presented to the Graduate Council of the North Texas State University in Partial Fulfillment of the Requirements for the Degree of Master of Arts. Denton, Texas. May, 1969.

Gillette, Michael L.

2010   *Launching the War on Poverty. An Oral History*, 2nd Edition. Oxford University Press, Inc.: New York.

Glazer, Nathan

1965   "Paradoxes of American Poverty." In, *The Public Interest*, No. 1, Fall 1965.

Goldstein, Alyosha

    2012   *Poverty in Common. The Politics of Community Action during the American Century.* Duke University Press: Durham and London.

Gordon, Margaret S. (Editor)

    1961   *Poverty in American.* Proceedings of a national conference held at the University of California, Berkeley, February 26-28, 1965. Chandler Publishing Company: San Francisco.

Greider, William December

    1981   "The Education of David Stockman." In, *The Atlantic*, December Issue

Gruson, Lindsey

    1987   "End of Federal Revenue Sharing Creating Financial Crises in Many Cities." In, *The New York Times*, January 31, 1987.

Hanson, Hilary

    2016   "Nixon Aides Suggest Colleague Was Kidding About Drug War Being Designed To Target Black People. Former officials are disavowing decades-old comments attributed to adviser John Ehrlichman saying the war on drugs was racially motivated." In, *Huffpost, Politics* 03/25/2016 05:32 pm ET.

Harward, Jennifer Sue

    2016   *Utah's War On Poverty: Local Programs Of And Reactions To the Economic Opportunity Act.* A dissertation submitted to the Faculty of The University of Utah in partial fulfillment of the requirements for the degree of Doctor of Philosophy. Department of History. The University of Utah. May 2016.

Himmelman, Harold
    1973   *The Rise and Fall of the Office of Economic Opportunity.* Washington, D.C.: Lawyer's Committee for Civil Rights Law.

Hinds, Michael deCourcy
    1982   "Decision File; Solar Bank Now Open." In, *The New York Times*, November 12, 1982.

Humphrey, Senator Hubert H.
    1964   *War on Poverty.* McGraw-Hill Book Company: New York.

Ille, Majorie M.
    1976   *Social Problems and Collaborative Planning: Toward A Theory and Model of Social Planning.* A dissertation submitted to the Faculty of Urban Studies in partial fulfillment of the requirements for the degree of Doctor of Philosophy. Portland State University: Portland, Oregon.

Iowa State University
    n.d.   Special Collections Department. RS 21/7/241. Dwight Ink (1922-). Papers, 1915-2012, undated. Ames, Iowa

Jansson, Bruce S.

    1977   *The Reluctant Welfare State. American Social Welfare Policies: Past, Present, And Future.* 3rd Edition. Brooks/Cole Publishing Company: Pacific Grover, CA.

Johnson, Haynes

    1977   "Sam Brown's Call to ACTION: An Outsider Who Came Inside." In, *The Washington Post,* June 30, 1977.

Johnson, Lydon B.

    1964a Annual Message to the Congress on the State of the Union, 4 January 1964. Online by Gerhard Peters and John T. Woolley, *The American Presidency Project.* http//www.presidency.ucsb.edu.

    1964b Economic Report of the President. Together with The Annual Report of the Economic Advisors. 20 January 1964 Washington, D.C.: United States Government Printing Office.

    1964c Special Message to the Congress Proposing a Nationwide War on the Sources of Poverty. 16 March 1964. Online by Gerhard Peters and John T. Woolley, *The American Presidency Project.* http//www.presidency.ucsb.edu.

    1964d The Great Society. 22 May 1964, Ann Arbor, MI. Text transcription directly from audio by Michael E. Eidenmuller. AmericanRhetoric.com 2008

    1964e "Commencement Address at Howard University. 'To Fulfill These Right' " June 4,

1964. In, *Public Papers of the President of the United States; Lyndon B. Johnson, 1965,* Vol. 2. Government Printing Office: Washington, D.C. 1966.

1965a   Annual Message to the Congress on the State of the Union, January 4, 1965. In, *Public Papers of the President of the United States; Lyndon B. Johnson, 1965,* Vol. 1, entry 2, pp 1-9. Government Printing Office: Washington, D.C. 1966.

1965b   The President's Inaugural Address, January 20, 1965. In, *Public Papers of the President of the United States; Lyndon B. Johnson, 1965,* Vol. 1, entry 27, pp 71-74. Government Printing Office: Washington, D.C. 1966.

1966   Annual Message to the Congress on the State of the Union, January 12, 1966. In, *Public Papers of the President of the United States; Lyndon B. Johnson, 1966,* Vol. 1, entry 6, pp 3-12. Government Printing Office: Washington, D.C. 1967.

1967a   Economic Report of the President. Transmitted to the Congress January 1967. Together with The Annual Report of the Council of Economic Advisors. January 10 1967. Washington, D.C.: United States Government Printing Office.

1967b   "Annual Message to the Congress on the State of the Union," January 10, 1967. Online by Gerhard Peters and John T. Woolley, The American Presidency Project. http//www.presidency.ucsb.edu.

1967c   "Special Message to the Congress: America's Unfinished Business, Urban and Rural Poverty."

14 March 1967. Online by Gerhard Peters and John T. Woolley, The American Presidency Project. http//www.presidency.ucsb.edu.

1968a Annual Message to the Congress on the State of the Union, January 17, 1968. In, *Public Papers of the President of the United States; Lyndon B. Johnson, 1968-1969,* Vol. I, entry 14, pp 25-33. Government Printing Office: Washington, D.C. 1970.

1968b "President's Address to the Nation." 31 March 1968. Online by Gerhard Peters and John T. Woolley, The American Presidency Project. http//www.presidency.ucsb.edu.

1968c "Executive Order 11399—Establishing the National Council on Indian Opportunity." March 6, 1968. Online by Gerhard Peters and John T. Woolley, The American Presidency Project. http://www.presidency.ucsb.edu/ws/?pid=76359.

1969 Annual Message to the Congress on the State of the Union, January 14, 1969. In, *Public Papers of the President of the United States; Lyndon B. Johnson, 1968-1969,* Vol. II, entry 676, pp 1263-1270. Government Printing Office: Washington, D.C. 1970.

Johnston, David

1988 "Working Profile: Jim Burnley; Transportation Chief Plots Course for Short Haul." Special to *The New York Times,* March 23, 1988

Joint Committee on the Economic Report
> 1950 Joint Economic Report. Report of the Joint
> Committee on the Economic Report on the
> January 1950 Economic Report of the President
> Together With the Minority Reports. 81st
> Congress, 2nd Session, Report No. 1843.
> Washington, D.C.: United States Government
> Printing Office.
>
> 1955 Joint Economic Report. Report of the Joint
> Committee on the Economic Report on the
> January 1955 Economic Report of the President
> Together With the Minority Reports. 84th
> Congress, 1st Session, Report No. 60.
> Washington, D.C.: United States Government
> Printing Office.

Joseph, Robert T.
> 2015 *Spiritualizing The Political Without Politicizing
> Religion: R. Sargent Shriver's Leadership Of The
> "War On Poverty."* A Thesis submitted to the
> Faculty of The School of Continuing Studies and
> of The Graduate School of Arts and Sciences in
> partial fulfillment of the requirements for the
> degree of Master of Arts in Liberal Studies.
> March 6, 2015. Georgetown University:
> Washington, D.C.

Keyserling, Leon H.
> 1964 *Progress Or Poverty. The U.S. At The Crossroads.*
> Conference On Economic Progress: Washington,
> D.C.

Kilpatrick, Carol (Washington Post Staff Writer)
    1974   "Nixon Resigns." In, *The Washington Post*,
           Friday, August 9, 1974; Page A01

Kleinknecht, William
    2009   *The Man Who Sold The World*. Ronald Reagan and
           the Betrayal of Main Street America. Nation
           Books: Philadelphia, PA.

Kravitz, Sanford
    1969   "The Community Action Program–Past, Present,
           and Its Future?" In, *Perspectives on Poverty. II. On
           Fighting Poverty: Perspectives From Experience.*
           (1969). James L. Sundquist, editor.

Kravitz, Sanford, and Ferne K. Kolodner
    1969   "Community Action: Where Has It Been? Where
           Will It Go?" In, *Evaluating the War of Poverty, The
           Annals of the American Academy of Political and
           Social Science*, Vol. 385, September, pp. 30-40.

Laffer, Arthur B.
    2004   *The Laffer Curve: Past, Present, and Future.*
           Executive Summary Backgrounder, No. 1765,
           June I, 2004. The Heritage Foundation:
           Washington, D.C.

Langer, Emily
    2013   "Howard J. Phillips, conservative activist and
           three-time presidential candidate, dies at 72." In,
           The Washington Post. Obituaries. April 24, 2013.

Lapham, Lewis H.
    2017   *Age Of Folly. American Abandons Its Democracy.*
           Verso: London.

Levitan, Sar A.
    1968   "Is OEO Here To Stay?" In, *Poverty and Human
           Resources Abstracts*, Vol. III, No. 2, March April
           1968. Ann Arbor, Michigan.
    1969   *The Great Society's Poor Law: A New Approach to
           Poverty.* Baltimore: The John Hopkins Press.

Lewis, Neil A.
    1000   "Adam Yarmolinsky Dies at 77; Led Revamping
           of Government." In, *The New York Times,* Jan. 7,
           2000.

Light, Paul Charles
    1983   *The President's Agenda: domestic policy choice from
           Kennedy to Carter (with notes on Ronald Reagan).*
           The John Hopkins University Press: Baltimore.

Los Angeles Times
    1995   *Douglass Cater; Journalist, Presidential Aid.*
           September 20, 1995.

Lydon, Christopher
    1973   "4 Democratic Governors Assail Nixon's
           Revenue Sharing Policy." In, *The New York
           Times,* February 28, 1973.

McKee, Guian A.
  2010 Lyndon B. Johnson and the War on Poverty:
        Introduction to the Digital Edition.
  2014 "Lyndon Johnson and the War on Poverty." In,
        Presidential Recordings Digital Edition.
        University of Virginia.

MacDonald, Dwight
  1963 Our Invisible Poor. *The New Yorker* (January 19,
        1963)

Mar, Hattie, and Lea Heine
  1969 Me. From the Children of the Deep South comes
        a cry for help that cannot be ignored. OEO
        Pamphlet 4100-7, June 1969. Volunteers In
        Service To America: Washington, D.C.

Masters, Jim
  [2014] A History of Community Action. Community
        Action Partnership: Washington, D.C.

Meter, Linda Van
  2017 "Mingo County." e-WV: The West Virginia
        Encyclopedia. 03 June 2013. Web 02 December
        2017.

Moynihan, Daniel P.
  1965 "The Professionalization of Reform." In, *The
        Public Interest*, No. 1, Fall 1965.
  1966 "What Is 'Community Action'?" In, *The Public
        Interest*, No. 5, Fall 1966.
  1967 "A Crisis of Confidence?" In, *The Public Interest*,

No. 7, Spring 1967.

1968 "The Professors and the Poor." In, *Commentary*,
       August 1, 1968.

1969a *Maximum Feasible Misunderstanding.* New York:
       The Free Press.

1969b *Perspectives On Poverty I. On Understanding
       Poverty. Perspectives From the Social Sciences.*
       Daniel P. Moynihan (Editor) with the assistance
       of Corinne Saposs Schelling. Basic Books, Inc.,
       Publisher: New York

Nathan, Richard P.

2011 Anniversary of President Nixon's National
      Televison Address on the "New Federalism."
      Prepared for the Richard M. Nixon Library.
      Yorba Linda, California. August 8, 2011.

National Demonstration Water Project

1977 Rural Community Action: Status and
      Recommendations.

National Center for Community Action

n.d. OEO-1969: An Interpretive History of the 1969
      Economic Opportunity Act Amendments.

1978 Why Not the Best – For America's Poor? Finally,
      the Truth about Community Action.

Nelson, Gaylord

1964 "Conservation Address to Farm and Home
      Week, University of Wisconsin, - Thursday,
      April 2, 1964."

New Haven Register

> 2000   Editorial. *Anti-Poverty pioneer dies*. Thursday, October 26, 2000.

New Republic

> 1967a "No Staying Power?" In, *The New Republic, A Journal of Opinion*, Vol. 156, No. 3, Issue 2721, pp. 7-8, January 21, 1967.

> 1967b "T.R.B. from Washington." In, *The New Republic, A Journal of Opinion*, Vol. 156, No. 12, Issue 2730, March 27, 1967.

New York Times

> 1966   8 February
> 28 April story.
> 5 November front page editorial.

> 1973   "PRESIDENT SIGNS MANPOWER BILL." Special to the New York Times, DEC. 29, 1973

Newsweek

> 1965   "The War on Poverty." pp. 22-29 (September 13, 1965).

Nixon, Richard

> 1969a "Inaugural Address," January 20, 1969. Online by Gerhard Peters and John T. Woolley, The American Presidency Project. http://www.presidency.ucsb.edu/ws/?pid=1941.

> 1969b "Executive Order 11452—Establishing the Council for Urban Affairs," January 23, 1969. Online by Gerhard Peters and John T. Woolley, The American Presidency Project.

http://www.presidency.ucsb.edu/ws/?pid=105995

1969c "Executive Order 11453—Establishing the
Cabinet Committee on Economic Policy,"
January 24, 1969. Online by Gerhard Peters and
John T. Woolley, The American Presidency
Project.
http://www.presidency.ucsb.edu/ws/?pid=105996.

1969d "Special Message to the Congress on the
Nation's Anti-poverty Programs," February 19,
1969. Online by Gerhard Peters and John T.
Woolley, The American Presidency Project.
http://www.presidency.ucsb.edu/ws/?pid=2397.

1969e "Address to the Nation on Domestic
Programs.," August 8, 1969. Online by Gerhard
Peters and John T. Woolley, The American
Presidency Project.
http://www.presidency.ucsb.edu/ws/?pid=2191.

1969f "Statement on the Office of Economic
Opportunity." August 11, 1969. Online by
Gerhard Peters and John T. Woolley, The
American Presidency Project.
http://www.presidency.ucsb.edu/ws/?pid=2195.

1970   "Special Message to the Congress on Indian
Affairs." July 8, 1970. Online by Gerhard Peters
and John T. Woolley, The American Presidency
Project.
http://www.presidency.ucsb.edu/ws/?pid=2573.

1971a "Veto of the Economic Opportunity
Amendments of 1971." December 9, 1971.
Online by Gerhard Peters and John T. Woolley,

The American Presidency Project. http://www.presidency.ucsb.edu/ws/?pid=3251. Dated December 9, 1971, was transmitted to the Senate on December 10

1971b "Statement on Signing Bill Extending Special Assistance to Depressed Rural Areas." August 5, 1971. Online by Gerhard Peters and John T. Woolley, The American Presidency Project. http://www.presidency.ucsb.edu/ws/?pid=3103.

1971c "Annual Message to the Congress on the State of the Union." January 22, 1971. Online by Gerhard Peters and John T. Woolley, The American Presidency Project. http://www.presidency.ucsb.edu/ws/?pid=3110.

1971d "Message to the Congress Transmitting Reorganization Plan 1 of 1971 To Establish ACTION." March 24, 1971. Online by Gerhard Peters and John T. Woolley, The American Presidency Project. http://www.presidency.ucsb.edu/ws/?pid=2947.

1971e "Executive Order 11603 — Assigning Additional Functions to the Director of ACTION." June 30, 1971. Online by Gerhard Peters and John T. Woolley, The American Presidency Project. http://www.presidency.ucsb.edu/ws/?pid=106653.

1971f "Special Message to the Congress on Drug Abuse Prevention and Control." June 17, 1971. Online by Gerhard Peters and John T. Woolley, The American Presidency Project. http://www.presidency.ucsb.edu/ws/?pid=3048.

1971g "Remarks About an Intensified Program for

Drug Abuse Prevention and Control." June 17, 1971. Online by Gerhard Peters and John T. Woolley, The American Presidency Project. http://www.presidency.ucsb.edu/ws/?pid=3047.

1972a "The President's News Conference." June 22, 1972. Online by Gerhard Peters and John T. Woolley, The American Presidency Project. http://www.presidency.ucsb.edu/ws/?pid=3472.

1972b "The President's News Conference." October 5, 1972. Online by Gerhard Peters and John T. Woolley, The American Presidency Project. http://www.presidency.ucsb.edu/ws/?pid=3617.

1972c "Address on the State of the Union Delivered Before a Joint Session of the Congress." January 20, 1972. Online by Gerhard Peters and John T. Woolley, The American Presidency Project. http://www.presidency.ucsb.edu/ws/?pid=3396.

1972d "Statement About the General Revenue Sharing Bill." October 20, 1972. Online by Gerhard Peters and John T. Woolley, The American Presidency Project. http://www.presidency.ucsb.edu/ws/?pid=3636.

1972e "Oath of Office and Second Inaugural Address." January 20, 1973. Online by Gerhard Peters and John T. Woolley, The American Presidency Project. http://www.presidency.ucsb.edu/ws/?pid=4141.

1973a "The President's News Conference." March 2, 1973. Online by Gerhard Peters and John T. Woolley, The American Presidency Project. http://www.presidency.ucsb.edu/ws/?pid=4123.

1973b "The President's News Conference." March 15,

1973. Online by Gerhard Peters and John T. Woolley, The American Presidency Project. http://www.presidency.ucsb.edu/ws/?pid=4142.

Oakland Wiki
2013   John C. Houlihan.

Office of Economic Opportunity
n.d.   The Tide of Progress: 3rd Annual Report.

Orshansky, Mollie
1963   "Children of the Poor."*Social Security Bulletin*, Vol. 26, No. 7, July, pp. 3-13.
1965   "Counting the Poor: Another Look at the Poverty Profile." *Social Security Bulletin*, Vol. 28, No. 1, January, pp. 3-29.
1966   "The Shape of Poverty in 1966." In, *Social Security Bulletin*, Vol. 31, No. 3 March, pp. 3-32.

Patterson, James T.
2015   "Moynihan and the Single-Parent Family." In, *EducationNext*, Vol. 15, No. 2. (Spring 2015).

Perlstein, Rick
2001   *Before The Storm. Barry Goldwater And the Unmaking of The American Consensus.* Nation Books: New York.
2014   *The Invisible Bridge. The Fall of Nixon and the Rise of Reagan.* Simon & Schuster: New York.

Perry, Huey, and, Jeff Biggers
2010   *"They'll Cut Off Your Project." A Mingo County*

Chronicle. (Second Edition). West Virginia University Press. Morgantown. First Edition (1972). Praeger Publishers, Inc.: New York.

Pine, Art
    1978   " 'Lean and Tight' Carter Budget Seeks $500.2 Billion." In, *The Washington Post*, January 24, 1978.

Raab, Earl
    1966   "What War and Which Poverty?" In, *The Public Interest*, No. 3, Spring 1966.

Rainwater, Lee, and William L. Yancey
    1967   The Moynihan Report and the Politics of Controversy. Including the full text of *The Negro Family: The Case for National Action* by Daniel Patrick Moynihan. The M.I.T. Press: Cambridge, Massachusetts.

Raskin, A. H.
    1964   "Generalissimo." In, *The New York Times*, Nov. 22, 1964.

Reagan, Donald T.
    1983   *For The Record: From Wall Street To Washington.* Harcourt Brace Jovanovich, Publishers: New York.

Reagan, Ronald
    1981a "Inaugural Address." January 20, 1981. Online by Gerhard Peters and John T. Woolley, The

American Presidency Project.
http://www.presidency.ucsb.edu/ws/?pid=43130.

1981b "Address Before a Joint Session of the Congress on the Program for Economic Recovery." February 18, 1981. Online by Gerhard Peters and John T. Woolley, The American Presidency Project.
http://www.presidency.ucsb.edu/ws/?pid=43425.

1981c "Message to the Congress Reporting Budget Rescissions and Deferrals." April 27, 1981. Online by Gerhard Peters and John T. Woolley, The American Presidency Project.
http://www.presidency.ucsb.edu/ws/?pid=43750.

1983 "Address Before a Joint Session of the Congress on the State of the Union." January 25, 1983. Online by Gerhard Peters and John T. Woolley, The American Presidency Project.
http://www.presidency.ucsb.edu/ws/?pid=41698.

Reichley, A. James
1981 *Conservatives in the Age of Change. The Nixon and Ford Administrations.* The Brookings Institution: Washington, D.C.

Ripley, Anthony
1973 "Poverty Chief Scored at House Hearing." In, *The New York Times*, February 28, 1973.

Rose, Harriett DeAnn
2008 *Dallas, Poverty, and Race: Community Action Programs In The War on Poverty.* Thesis Prepared for the Degree of Master of Arts. University of

North Texas. Denton, Texas.

Rosenthal, Jack
 1970 "LEGAL AID CHANGE PUT OFF BY O.E.O".
   In, *The New York Times*, December 11, 1970.

Rubin, Lillian B.
 1969 "Maximum Feasible Participation: The Origins,
   Implications, and Present Status." In,
   Evaluating the War of Poverty, *The Annals of the
   American Academy of Political and Social Science*,
   Vol. 385, September, pp. 14-29.

Rumsfeld, Donald
 2011 *Known and Unknown. A Memoir.* Sentinal. New
   York.

Selover, William C.
 1969 "The View from Capitol Hill: Harassment and
   Survival." In, *Perspectives on Poverty. II. On
   Fighting Poverty: Perspectives From Experience.*
   (1969). James L. Sundquist, editor.

Semple, Jr., Robert B.
 1972 "THE 1972 CAMPAIGN." In, *The New York
   Times*, October 26, 1972.

Shirley, Craig, and Lou Cannon
 1981 *Last Act: The Final Years and Emerging Legacy of
   Ronald Reagan.* Thomas Nelson, HarperCollins
   Publishers: New York.

Small, Melvin
> 1999   *The Presidency of Richard Nixon.* University of
> Kansas Press: Lawrence, Kansas.

Smothers, Ronald
> 1981   "CETA CUTBACKS LEAVING THOUSANDS
> UNEMPLOYED; The Budget Targets Last of
> eight articles on key pro- grams the President
> wants to cut." In, *The New York Times*, April 11,
> 1981.

Spangler, Stephanie
> 2012   "President Nixon and Childcare." Comment
> posted on *The Center for the Study of the
> Presidency & Congress – Presidential Fellows Blog.*
> March 20, 2012

Stone, Gene
> 1988   "Almost Heaven? This Corrupt Corner of West
> Virginia Was More Like the Other Place."
> people.com/archive/almost-heaven-this-corrupt-
> corner-of west-virginia-was-more-like-the other-
> place-vol-30-no-20/

Stout, David
> 1998   *Terry Sanford, Pace-Setting Governor in 60's, Dies
> at 80.* In, *The New York Times*, April 19, 1998.

Stubbendeck, Megan
> 2013   *"The Wrongs Done to My People": Street Gangs,
> Historical Agency, and Crime Politics in Postwar
> America.* A Dissertation presented to the

Graduate Faculty of the University of Virginia in
Candidacy for the Degree of Doctor of
Philosophy. Department of History.

Sundquist, James L.
1969   *Perspective On Poverty. II. On Fighting Poverty:*
        Perspectives From Experience. Edited by James L.
        Sundquist with the assistance of Corinne Saposs
        Schelling. Basic Books, Inc., Publishers: New
        York.

Susskind, Lawrence
1974   "Revenue Sharing and the Lessons of the New
        Federalism." In, *Urban Law Annual ; Journal of*
        Urban and Contemporary Law, Vol. 8, January
        1974.

Thomas, Jr., Robert McG.
1995   *Douglass Cater Is Dead at 72; Educator and*
        Presidential Aide. In, *The New York Times.*
        Obituaries. September 16, 1995.

Trattner, Walter T.
1994   *From Poor Law To Welfare State,* 5th Edition. New
        York: The Free Press.

U.S. House of Representatives
n.d.   Green, Edith Starrett. In, *History, Art & Archives.*
        Http://history.house.gov/People/Detail/14080.

U.S. Senate
1977   Hearings before the Committee on Human

Resources United States Senate, Ninety-Fifth
Congress, First Session, July 21, 1977. U.S.
Government Printing Office: Washington, D.C.

Vecsey, George
  1971   "Hill People Support Poverty Program." In, *The
          New York Times*, June 7, 1971.

Walsh, Edward
  1979   "Carter Proposes $100 Million Solar Energy
          Bank." In, *The Washington Post*, June 21, 1979.

Weeks, Christopher
  1967   *Job Corps. Dollars and Dropouts*. Little, Brown and
          Company: Boston.

Williams, Lena
  1987   "MAN IN THE NEWS: James Horace Burnley
          4th; TOUGH CABINET NOMINEE." Special to
          The New York Times, October 10, 1987

Wofford, John G.
  1969   "The Politics of Local Responsibility:
          Administration of the Community Action
          Program–1964-1966." In, *Perspectives on Poverty.
          II. On Fighting Poverty: Perspectives From
          Experience*. (1969). James L. Sundquist, editor.

Wright, Amy Nathan
  2007   *Civil Rights "Unfinished Business": Poverty, Race,
          and the 1968 Poor People's Campaign*. Dissertation.
          Presented to the Faculty of the Graduate School

of The University of Texas at Austin in Partial
Fulfillment of the Requirements for the Degree
of Doctor of Philosophy. The University of Texas
at Austin, August, 2007.

Yamolinsky, Adam
　　1969　"The Beginnings of OEO." In, *Perspectives on
　　　　　Poverty. II. On Fighting Poverty: Perspectives From
　　　　　Experience.* (1969). James L. Sundquist, editor.

Zarefsky, David
　　1986　*President Johnson's War on Poverty. Rhetoric and
　　　　　History.* The University of Alabama Press:
　　　　　Alabama.

Zielbauer, Paul Von
　　2003　"Richard C. Lee, 86, Mayor Who Revitalized
　　　　　New Haven." In, *The New York Times*, Feb. 4,
　　　　　2003.

About the Author

George R. Mead began to study anthropology in 1962 after being discharged (honorably) from the U. S. Army, Combat Engineers. He eventually received a B.A., M.A., and Ph.D. in his chosen field, before that an A.A. in Engineering. And many years later an M.S.W. in Clinical Social Work. He has worked in aerospace, taught at the college and university levels, worked in a community action agency, ran a restaurant, been unemployed, and worked for the U. S. Forest Service. He is now retired from the work-a-day world but does a certain amount of consulting, writing, and research. He lives seven miles outside of the small town of La Grande, Oregon, with his wife, one cat, and one dog named Jettz (all Lab).

Made in the USA
Middletown, DE
14 January 2021